Anastasia Dukova holds a PhD in crime and policing history from the University of Dublin, Trinity College. She is a member of the Irish Association of Professional Historians and the Professional Historians Association (Queensland). Her research on nineteenth-century Irish and Australian policing history and historical criminology has been published widely, and her doctoral and postdoctoral findings were published in 2016 as *A History of the Dublin Metropolitan Police and its Colonial Legacy* in Palgrave Macmillan's World Histories of Crime, Culture and Violence series. She has held fellowships with the State Library of Queensland, Harry Gentle Resource Centre and Griffith Criminology Institute, as well as a postdoctoral fellowship at the University of Toronto and a postgraduate scholarship with the Irish Research Council. Anastasia is a partner investigator on an Australian Research Council Discovery Project that investigates the policing of migrant communities in Britain and Australia throughout the twentieth century (DP180102200). She also lends her historical crime and policing expertise to public and professional lectures, as well as popular history projects such as *Century Ireland*, RTÉ and *Who Do You Think You Are?*

TO PRESERVE AND PROTECT

POLICING COLONIAL BRISBANE

ANASTASIA DUKOVA

First published 2020 by University of Queensland Press
PO Box 6042, St Lucia, Queensland 4067 Australia

uqp.com.au
uqp@uqp.uq.edu.au

Copyright © Anastasia Dukova 2020
The moral rights of the author have been asserted.

This book is copyright. Except for private study, research, criticism or reviews, as permitted under the *Copyright Act*, no part of this book may be reproduced, stored in a retrieval system, or transmitted in any form or by any means without prior written permission. Enquiries should be made to the publisher.

Cover design by Christa Moffitt
Author photograph by Nicole Lapierre Photography
Typeset in 12/16pt Adobe Garamond Pro Regular by Post Pre-press Group, Brisbane
Printed in Australia by McPherson's Printing Group

The University of Queensland Press is assisted by the Australian Government through the Australia Council, its arts funding and advisory body.

A catalogue record for this book is available from the National Library of Australia

ISBN 978 0 7022 6014 8 (pbk)
ISBN 978 0 7022 6228 9 (epdf)
ISBN 978 0 7022 6229 6 (epub)
ISBN 978 0 7022 6230 2 (kindle)

University of Queensland Press uses papers that are natural, renewable and recyclable products made from wood grown in well-managed forests and other controlled sources. The logging and manufacturing processes conform to the environmental regulations of the country of origin.

Contents

Foreword by Queensland Police Commissioner Katarina Carroll, APM vii
Introduction 1

1 Ex-Convict to Policeman: Peter 'Duff' Murphy 13
2 A Career Policeman: Samuel Sneyd 33
3 Queensland's First Detective: Samuel Lloyd 56
4 Beat Policing: Thomas Tyrrell 80
5 Policing Female Criminality: Susan McGowan 102
6 Policemen as Prosecutors: James Nethercote 119
7 Habitual Offending and Punishment: Charles 'Dubious' Durant 143

Conclusion 167
Acknowledgements 172
Appendix A: Queensland Police Officers – 1828 to 1863 174
Appendix B: Queensland Police Officers – 1864 to 1900 178
Appendix C: Brisbane Night Duty Beats 199
Notes 202
Index 227

Foreword

by Queensland Police Commissioner Katarina Carroll, APM

Brisbane had its own police well before the Queensland Police Force was centrally organised in 1863 with the first constables taking to the streets on 1 January 1864. Some of the founding fathers of Brisbane's early police were originally convicts who, through their model behaviour, were charged with the role of protecting the community.

The individuals who embodied the colonial police institution are at the forefront of this book, but the narrative would not be complete without the life stories of the community, the policed. The pages of *To Preserve and Protect* provide a rare opportunity to showcase the progress of our organisation and the transition from convict police to the professional, centrally organised institution.

These colonial stories are vitally important for our organisation to remember and celebrate as they map our heritage and journey over the past two centuries.

This book also illustrates the crucial changes and developments that have shaped our organisation over the past 155 years. I am proud to reflect on the unique Brisbane policing history and acknowledge our journey.

Today, the Queensland Police Service has grown into one of the largest police services in the world and witnessed a great deal of change since the colonial days, but the principles of community safety, crime prevention, preservation of peace, and protection of life and property remain at our core.

Introduction

OATH – I do swear that I will well and truly serve our Sovereign Lady the Queen in the office of constable, without favor or affection, malice or ill-will, for the period of one year from this date, and until I am legally discharged; that I will see and cause Her Majesty's peace to be kept and preserved, and that I will prevent, to the best of my power, all offences against the same; and that while I shall continue to hold the said office I will, to the best of my skill and knowledge, discharge all the duties thereof faithfully, according to law – So help me God.

'Oath', *Rules for the General Government and Discipline of Members of the Police Force of Queensland*[1]

THE FIRST CHIEF constable of the 'Edenglassie' police, John McIntosh, arrived in Moreton Bay in 1828.[2] McIntosh, a 24-year-old from Glasgow, Scotland, had been transported to New South Wales in 1814 after being sentenced to penal servitude for life. In 1826, following an unsuccessful term as a superintendent of convicts in Liverpool, McIntosh was investigated and found guilty of gross irregularities, and lost his ticket of leave (a form of parole).[3] Two years later, he earned another ticket of leave and was appointed chief constable of the local police. McIntosh's story is surprising but not unusual within the early Australian colonial context. In 1789, the first Sydney police, a form of night watch, were organised in response to the theft of stores by several marines. This initial force in Sydney was staffed and headed by the local convicts, and the first chief constable of Sydney, Henry Kable, was a transportee from England who was convicted of burglary and initially sentenced to death by hanging.

This book is a study of the police of Brisbane from 1828 to the early 1900s. It examines the individuals and the institution, and traces the transition from convict police to the professional, centrally organised Queensland Police Force. As twentieth-century sociologist C Wright Mills shows, individuals and society, biography and history are inextricably linked: an individual 'lives out a biography, and lives it out within some historical sequence. By the fact of this living, [the individual] contributes, however minutely, to the shaping of this society and to the course of history, even as [they are] made by society and by its historical push and shove.'[4] This book explores the inner life and external career of a variety of individuals, including colonial police officers Peter 'Duff' Murphy, Samuel Sneyd, Samuel Lloyd, Thomas Tyrrell and James Nethercote, as well as the criminals they policed, such as Susan McGowan and Charles Durant. By recreating the biographies of these individuals and placing them within the wider setting of the police organisation and the society it served, this book reveals how the colonial society both formed and was formed by the individuals within it.[5]

In its essence, this book is a history of interactions between the police and the policed. By drawing on police court witness statements and expert testimonies, internal departmental correspondence, newspaper editorials and memoirs, *To Preserve and Protect* offers a glimpse into the daily lives of nineteenth-century Brisbanites, their experience of the city's bustling street life and their all too frequent run-ins with the law.

Prior to the organisation of the civilian convict police, enforcement of law and order in the convict settlement of Moreton Bay was the duty of the military commandants. The Military Mounted Police were organised by Sir Thomas Brisbane, the governor of New South Wales, in 1825 and consisted of soldiers from colonial garrisons armed with sabres, pistols and carbines. The penal settlement was established in 1824 'to provide a place of security and subsistence for runaways from Port Macquarie'.[6] By April 1825, Moreton Bay had received 36 prisoners, 26 of whom had moved to the settlement voluntarily.[7] Initially, explorer John Oxley and Military Commandant Lieutenant Henry Miller chose 'Red Cliff Point' for the site of the new settlement, but, in May 1825, it was moved to the river mouth at Breakfast Creek. An early Brisbanite described the river banks as 'lined with foliage whose beauty it were almost impossible to describe', but this 'veritable garden of Eden' was the site of a brutal convict system.[8] The iconic Australian folk ballad *Moreton Bay* evokes a bleak image of the settlement.[9] The words convey the isolation and terrible fate prisoners suffered, and compares the conditions of sentences served at Port Macquarie, Norfolk Island, Emu Plains, Castle Hill and 'cursed Toongabbie'. It singles out Moreton Bay as the worst of them:

> At all those settlements I've worked in chains
> But of all places of condemnation,
> And penal stations of New South Wales,
> To Moreton Bay I have found no equal:
> Excessive tyranny each day prevails.
>
> For three long years I was beastly treated,
> And heavy irons on my legs I wore;
> My back with flogging is lacerated,
> And often painted with crimson gore.
> And many a man from downright starvation
> Lies mouldering now underneath the clay,
> And Captain Logan he had us mangled
> At the triangles of Moreton Bay.[10]

Captain Patrick Logan, a veteran soldier from Scotland, was appointed to command the convict settlement in 1826. Logan was reputedly a harsh disciplinarian who freely imposed corporal punishment, and he was despised by the convicts he controlled. The severity of the sentences he pronounced increased over his years commanding the settlement, and, in 1828, he sentenced several men to 200 lashes each.[11] Logan's successor, James Oliphant Clunie (commander from 1830 to 1835), another Scotsman with extensive experience on the battlefield, surpassed him in brutality by once sentencing a convict to 300 lashes for stealing a horse. Chief Constable John McIntosh, whose term partially coincided with Clunie's appointment as the settlement's commandant, remained in Brisbane until 1833 when he received permission to return to Sydney.[12]

In 1833, Richard Bottington (also Bettingen or Bellington) took over the command of the Brisbane Police. Like McIntosh, Bottington had been a convict transported from Surrey in 1818 on the *John Berry (1)*, and he was re-convicted in Sydney in 1827 for bigamy. He in turn was succeeded by William Whyte in 1836. Whyte was a free man, an officer of the 57th Regiment, who became overseer at Moreton Bay 'after he suffered financial ruin on his farm in Van Diemen's Land'.[13] Prior to his appointment with the police, Whyte was the commandant's clerk and postmaster, as regulations at the time prohibited convicts from serving in the former capacity.

The town's *Police Act of 1838* (2 Vic., no. 2) officially codified a variety of common behaviours as criminal and regulated the police response to them. Following the promulgation of the Act, the majority of daily activities in the settlement were regulated; these ranged from damaging a public building to extinguishing a street lamp, and from bathing near or within view of a public wharf to allowing animals to stray.[14] At this time, the settlement had 'no streets, and nothing that could by any stretch of the imagination, be tortured into a town'.[15] The *Police Act of 1838* also provided for the appointment of police magistrates and justices to suppress riots, tumults and affrays. However, the Act lacked provisions for custodial sentencing as a form of punishment, as there was no local jail.

The Moreton Bay penal settlement closed in 1842 and the area was thrown open to free settlement. By this stage, the convict police were living out their last days as the general perception was that there was 'too much of a fellow-feeling' between the police and the policed.[16] As free immigrants started to arrive in large numbers, there was opposition to appointing convicts and ex-convicts to the police force. Despite the anti-convict attitudes, as late as the 1860s, transportees still made up over 10 per cent of the general male population in Queensland.[17] In 1843, the convict police were reorganised and Chief Constable William Fitzpatrick and four ordinary constables (Martin Higgins, Jeremiah Scanlon, James Ramsay/Ramsey and John McGrath) were appointed and equipped with muskets, pistols and ammunition.[18] Before his appointment as chief constable of the Brisbane force, Fitzpatrick had been assistant superintendent of the Sydney Police. He was favoured for the Brisbane position over Port Macquarie District Constable, and ex-convict, Peter 'Duff' Murphy.

Prior to the establishment of *An Act to Consolidate and Amend the Laws Relating to the Police Force* (1863), also known as the *Queensland Police Act*, the territory outside of the Brisbane police district, also known as the Northern Districts of New South Wales, was patrolled by a variety of organised volunteer paramilitary groups, both cavalry and infantry. The men in these groups were identifiable by their uniforms: the 'Brisbane Volunteers' cavalry wore grey uniforms with black facings and the infantry wore green uniforms with red facings.[19] As the colonial population grew and expanded further outside the Brisbane district, the policing network also expanded and specialised forces were formed. These included the Water Police Force (1840–53), which controlled the river traffic, ships and boats moored at Moreton Bay; the Native Police or Mounted Aboriginal Police (1848–59), which operated primarily in northern New South Wales (now Queensland); and the Border Police (1839–46), which was responsible for policing land regulations in the remote districts.[20] None of these forces performed a preventative policing role by using police presence to deter crime; instead, these paramilitary groups carried out reactionary and retaliatory actions against Aboriginal Australians and bushrangers.[21] In his study of the Native Police, *The Secret War: A true history of Queensland's Native Police*, Jonathan Richards narrates a detailed history of the atrocities committed by the Native Police and the critical role they played in the dispossession of the Indigenous peoples in Australia. Richards argues that the Native Police were a key part of a 'divide and rule' colonising tactic.[22]

Indigenous historian Ray Kerkhove shows that Aboriginal camps were still occupied well into the 1870s and even 1900s. He maintains the sites are still present within the 'layout of modern "town camps"' and shows how these sites underpin the development of most Australian urban settlements. He also explains how many present-day urban roads follow Aboriginal pathways, and suburban placenames are drawn from ancient living areas. In southern Queensland, vital communal areas such as 'water reserves and green spaces' are often found to be 'relics of camping grounds'. Further, many central business districts have grown 'from colonial interactions with important Aboriginal base camps.'[23]

The centralised Queensland Police Force was formally organised four years after the colony separated from New South Wales when the *Queensland Police Act* came into effect in 1863.[24] At this time, the settled area of the colony was divided into 17 districts, each with its own police force under a chief constable who took orders from the local magistrate. The magistrates performed a dual role as prosecutors and adjudicators, which left ample room for corruption and abuse of power. This corruption continued to be part of the local state and police governance for decades to come until it was exposed by the Fitzgerald Inquiry in 1988. Mark Finnane's *Policing in Australia: Historical perspectives* and *Police and Government: Histories of policing in Australia* offer a wide-lens history of policing in Australia from its inception in the mid-nineteenth century to the peak in corruption scandals during the 1980s and 1990s.[25] His works deliver a new perspective on policing as a fundamental responsibility of government and break down the police–government relationship into three aspects: police and the executive, police and the public, and police self-governance. Prior to the reforms recommended by the Fitzgerald Report in 1989, police organisations were an extension of the government and vice versa, which led to abuse of power on both executive and community levels despite the progressive principles of reciprocal obligations both social organisations were founded on.

In the first quarter of the nineteenth century, there was general resistance to the idea of a police force as this type of organisation continued to be equated with military control. As police historian David Taylor describes, 'even when the principle won more general support there was considerable debate about the precise form and nature of the new police'.[26] The structure of policing that finally came into being 'was a product of compromise' and can be analysed through three theoretical perspectives proposed by Taylor: orthodox, revisionist and synthetic. The orthodox theory views the new police as a response to the collapse of law and order, and as responsible for enforcing the law and maintaining appropriate societal discipline. The revisionist approach examines the social and economic context of historical developments where the new police were seen as agents of social control whose responsibilities transcended the scope limited by the basic definition of criminality. The synthetic theory argues that the police had succeeded in finding its niche within the social structure and secured a degree of legitimacy.[27] The new organised police thus received discretionary powers to exercise their authority 'to detect and prevent crime' as well as to regulate social norms and behaviours by maintaining 'a constant unceasing pressure of surveillance upon all facets of life in working-class communities'.[28] This surveillance included monitoring and reporting on the activities of trade unions and public political opinions, as well as recreational activities undertaken by citizens in public places.

The nineteenth century saw the formation and transformation of policing and legal systems in the British Isles and across the Empire. The line of duty of the colonial city-beat policeman was as extensive and diverse as that of a Dublin or London bobby.[29] It included an array of responsibilities, which ranged from enforcing trading hours to traffic control, and from carrying out arrests to recovering missing children. In his detailed study of the Melbourne Police, *The Beat: Policing a Victorian city*, Dean Wilson successfully relates the intricacies of police service in the city, the difficulties of beat duty and, more often than not, the precarious nature of the police–public relationship, especially within an urban environment.[30] The colonial capitals were bustling centres of trade and business, with rapidly expanding populations policed by the metropolitan units of the colonial forces. Contrary to the paramilitary squads that patrolled the frontier, the city constable was 'little more than a citizen in uniform', or a bobby on a beat.[31]

Chapter One of this book chronicles Peter 'Duff' Murphy's journey from a juvenile recidivist thief sentenced to transportation for life to a district constable in Brisbane. Murphy was among a handful of men who formed the first convict police forces across New South Wales. This chapter also traces the development of organised policing from 1780s Ireland to post-convict colonial settlement in Brisbane, as well as the impact of transportation on the changing community.

Chapter Two follows the long-running career of public servant Samuel Sneyd, who emigrated from England as a guard on a convict ship bound for Sydney in 1832. By the time he took command of the Brisbane Police in the 1850s, Brisbane town was a rapidly expanding settlement with its own police comprised of free men. Fears of growing power abuse by the local magistrates during this time led to the reorganisation of the colony's police administrative structure, which effectively ended the domination of the police force by the magistracy. Sneyd resigned after three decades of colonial police service and took up the appointment of jailer at the new Brisbane Gaol on Petrie Terrace. His career change coincided with Queensland's separation from New South Wales and marked a new chapter in Brisbane's policing history.

Chapter Three traces the life and service of Brisbane's first detective, Samuel Lloyd, a gentleman's son from Cork who immigrated to Victoria in the early 1850s and joined the local police. In 1859, Queensland gained political independence, but it inherited a policing system in need of reform and weary of power abuse propagated by the local magistracy. Having debated the police systems across the British dominions, the Queensland Parliament settled on emulating Irish or Victorian policing organisations. Detective Constable Lloyd was 'headhunted' by the Queensland force to take charge of the Queensland Police Detective Office in 1864, an early example of routine personnel exchange between the Australian colonial forces and overseas organisations.

Chapter Four follows Constable Thomas Tyrrell, who immigrated to Brisbane from Ireland, where he had been a policeman. He applied to join the local force in 1864, and was sworn in early the following year when he was 28 years old. Recruitment and training at the time took place in Brisbane at the Police Depot. Candidates for the Queensland force had to be single men under the age of 30 (or 35 if they had previous service experience). They had to be 'of good character for honesty fidelity and activity', not been convicted of any felony, nor be a hired servant, and they could not have kept 'a house for the sale of beer wine or spirituous liquors by retail'.[32] This chapter also examines how police regulations were constructed to instil obedience and order. Foot constables' duty was to ensure the town laws were enforced by continuous, and often arduous, presence on the streets on day and night beats, with each beat committed to the care of a constable. Police court reports from the time show charges for assault and 'drunk and disorderlies' of both men and women ensured policemen's hands were full.

Chapter Five focuses on the life of Susan McGowan, a young woman of 'negotiable affections'. Between 1880 and 1890, she made 29 appearances in the police court and prison records. She was regularly arrested for using obscene language or for drunk and disorderly behaviour. In addition to crime prevention, the role of police organisations in the Victorian era was morality policing. A female offender, or 'immoral' woman, was perceived as offending against the law as well as against her nature of being a caregiver and moral guardian. As a result, women committing offences that were deemed an affront to femininity were judged differently, and more harshly, than men.

Chapter Six explores the standardisation of the judiciary and prosecutions, as well as the professionalisation of the police, in response to the eighteenth-century 'new science' of policing. In the late 1800s, following a series of reforms influenced by the concepts of prevention, utilitarianism, humanism and morality popularised by the English and Scottish enlightenments, victims of crimes could turn to the organised police for detection, apprehension and prosecution of the offender at no charge, with the financial burden carried by local taxpayers.[33] A century before, such avenues for retribution did not exist. This chapter traces the development of the judicial system, its growth in complexity and the role of the police as prosecutors under the Common Law representation system. James Nethercote, formerly of the Bradford Borough Police Force in Yorkshire, was sworn in in 1876 and, for the next three decades, he made consistent and numerous appearances in the city police court by supporting, and later prosecuting, a range of offences, which exemplifies the change in public prosecution practices.

Chapter Seven examines the history of crime and punishment, as well as penal reforms and the medicalisation of deviancy. Throughout the 1830s, the rise in popularity of phrenology and other (pseudo-)scientific concepts aided the change of perception of criminality as a choice to a moral deficiency or natural deviancy. The life of Charles 'Dubious' Durant, one of Queensland's hardened recidivists who spent the better part of his life behind bars, reflects the changing attitudes to criminality and criminal experience during this period. He experienced all of the major penal establishments, police jails and lock-ups of the colony as they changed and adapted to suit the changes in prosecution practices, including panopticon-styled buildings, solitary confinement cells and public works.

The Conclusion reviews the changes in approach to urban policing in colonial Brisbane over the course of the nineteenth century. It also charts the early-twentieth-century technological and scientific innovations, such as the emergence of forensics and wireless communication, that influenced policing practices and transformed policing into a professional scientific enterprise. Further, this chapter connects the principles of modern policing with the philosophers of the Age of Enlightenment.

The historical material in this book draws from a wide variety of repositories that tell the stories of individuals, such as birth, death, marriage and immigration records, as well as sources that re-create institutional histories, such as police and penal departmental records, personnel files, colonial statistical tables, government correspondence and reports, almanacs, diaries, memoirs and newspapers. Appendix A and Appendix B list all police officers who served in the Moreton Bay Penal Colony, Brisbane and Ipswich from 1828 to 1900. Combined, this material creates a personal history of policing in colonial Brisbane. Most people see social issues through biography; that is, our personal point of view. However, we also must understand how history and social structures, such as family, education and religion, as well as economic, political and legal systems, affect the individual. By taking both micro and macro approaches to the history of policing colonial Brisbane, *To Preserve and Protect* reveals a clearer picture of the police institution and its place within colonial society. Through these lenses, the book also explores the differences between metropolitan aspirations and colonial reality. The case studies presented in this book highlight how, despite the reforms in the 1800s, issues such as political power abuse, professional burnout, mistreatment of patrol constables, moralising and gendered justice, corruption, and mismanagement of prisons persisted in an organisation tasked to preserve and protect.

1

Ex-Convict to Policeman

Peter 'Duff' Murphy

He looked at me, and said: 'Go with you sir? I will go to ___ with you!' I said I did not intend to go there at present, but was well pleased to have him go out with me on my little expedition. We had a pack-horse and a sheep-dog with us, and carried biscuit and bacon, tea and sugar, trusting our guns for fresh meat, and lines and hooks for fish, and we lived exceedingly well. We had a spare shirt and pair trousers each, and a single blanket.

'Patrick Leslie's Diary'[1]

SCOTTISH PIONEER AND grazier Patrick Leslie and his convict man, Peter 'Duff' Murphy, embarked on what Leslie believed to be a pioneer expedition of the Darling Downs district in 1840. Their intended destination was Brisbane town, which Murphy finally reached just over half a decade later as a free man. When Murphy arrived in Brisbane in 1846, he became the first district constable for the newly established township of Kangaroo Point, an area of housing and workshop allotments, which eventually included Murphy's cottage and a police lock-up.[2] The township population was highly transient and the daily policing routine consisted of dealing with drunkards, catching thieves and apprehending 'leavers' without permits, with an occasional ghastly murder.

Peter 'Duff' Murphy, Noted Mud Islander[3]

Peter Murphy was born into a working-class Protestant family in Dublin in 1806, only a few years after a failed uprising shook the capital in 1803.[4] This rebellion sought to restore the rights and liberties lost in the aftermath of the dissolution of the Irish Parliament under the *Act for the Union of Great Britain and Ireland* (1801) after the unsuccessful 1798 uprising. As the Anglo-Irish Protestant Ascendancy departed the capital in the first decades of the nineteenth century, the Dublin trades and industries experienced a marked decline. Amid the overall economic distress, and with Catholics excluded from holding land or professional posts (until the *Act for the Relief of His Majesty's Roman Catholic Subjects* in 1829), the local Roman Catholic population particularly struggled.[5] The deindustrialisation of the city contributed to a discernible rise of pauperism in thousands of the once-prosperous inhabitants.[6] Murphy lived in an impoverished area of the city called Spring Gardens, which was colloquially known as Mud Island. The name of this insalubrious neighbourhood derived from the mudflats across the Tolka River in the north of Dublin.[7] Murphy, a plasterer by trade and a Catholic, turned to crime to survive in the time of hardship, as did many men before and after him.

At the turn of the nineteenth century, Dublin was a relatively heavily policed city, with roughly 1 policeman per 320 persons (a ratio of 1 policeman per 400 to 450 persons was considered the benchmark at the time).[8] In the 1780s, exacerbated by the economic downturn, extremely cold winters and a succession of poor harvests, Dublin witnessed a series of demonstrations and protests, which culminated in an occupation of Parliament House in College Green in 1784. The following year, Ireland's attorney-general proposed a bill outlining an armed and uniformed force of 440 Protestant men. This proposed force was closely modelled on plans for a London force that were rejected by Westminster a year earlier. In their opposition to the idea of a police force, Englishmen cited their historic liberties and abhorrence of despotism and centralisation.

Ireland, on the other hand, was viewed as a 'social laboratory' where individual rights and liberties were not equally prioritised with those of the English, and so it became the setting for organisational experimentation.[9]

In 1786, the *Act for Improving the Police of the City of Dublin* established the Metropolitan Police within the new Dublin Metropolitan District. The new police force was mostly greeted with suspicion, and it was farewelled with resentment when it was disbanded a few years later. Following a series of reorganisations throughout the early decades of the 1800s, Dublin saw its peace and property preserved by the police during the daylight hours and the watchmen after sundown – two parallel but vastly different organisations. Various contemporary accounts depict the night watchmen as old, infirm and completely unfit for the job, and they were renowned for being 'always prepared to allow a prisoner to escape on the production of half-a-crown'.[10]

Despite the substandard policing of Dublin, Peter Murphy first found himself apprehended for the theft of clothes at the age of 15.[11] Murphy, in the company of a man named Jonathan Brennan, was witnessed fencing a military plaid coat, a cotton dressing gown, a pair of leather breeches, a pair of pantaloons and two handkerchiefs. According to the 'Police Intelligence' section of *The Irish Times*, which published police court proceedings regularly, Murphy and Brennan were held over for examination. As the majority of Dublin court records were destroyed in the fire at the Public Records Office, Four Courts in 1922, the outcome of this police inquiry is unknown. Murphy reappears in the police records in 1825 when he found himself awaiting trial for burglary and felony at the Newgate Prison.[12] The result of this trial is not known, but Murphy appears in the records again a year later with a new accomplice, a 13-year-old boy named Christopher Monks, when they were indicted for having 'barbarously and feloniously entered the house of Pat. Barnewall, Spring-gardens, Newcomen-bridge and taken therefrom certain articles, the property of Mr Barnewall (Barnwell), and also some clothes the property of Miss Anne Frued'.[13] The Newcomen Bridge ran over the canal extending to Ballybough Road (from *Baile Bocth* or *Bog* meaning 'Poor Town') and was a haunt of robbers and rogues. John Daly, one of the residents of the house, was alarmed by a noise at the back of the property around 3 am on Saturday 3 June 1826. Daly got out of bed and found the door open and two persons at it, one holding a bundle of clothes in his hands. According to Daly's witness testimony, published by *The Morning Register* (Dublin), 'There were some bricks taken out of the wall of the house, and a hole made sufficient to admit a boy.'[14] Barnewall was roused by Mr McKane (who shared lodgings with him) and immediately engaged in pursuit, and Murphy and Monks abandoned their loot during the chase. At the trial, McKane testified that he knew Murphy, as both he and Murphy lived in the area. The sworn statement of John Graham, one of the watchmen on duty at the time, sealed the unlucky robbers' fate:

> John Graham sworn and examined […] remembers that Barnewall was robbed; saw two prisoners running across a field from the gardens; witness took a short cut through a lane; and at the corner of it met Duff, alias Murphy; Duff immediately pulled a pistol from under his coat, presented it at witness, and told him to stand back or he would blow the contents of it through him. The witness here identified Duff.[15]

Further cross-examination did not elicit any new facts, so the judge recapitulated the evidence, and the jury brought the verdict against both prisoners as guilty of felony robbery, and not guilty of burglary. Their sentence was to be transported for life.

'Sentence – to be transported for life'

The first attempts at transporting persistent offenders from England date back to the early seventeenth century and the American colonies. Those perceived 'incorrigible in their persistence in roguery' were the primary candidates for the scheme.[16] In the early nineteenth century, transportation for life was substituted as the maximum punishment for several offences that had previously been punishable by death. Murphy's transportation record shows he was indicted and convicted of street robbery in the Dublin City Court and sentenced for transportation to Australia for the period of his natural life. Robbery, along with over 150 felonies, was a transportable offence. Between 1787 and 1868, more than 160,000 persons from Great Britain were transported to Australia.[17] In 1827, eight convict ships left Dublin for New South Wales, carrying 1,257 males and 192 females; some, like Murphy and his young accomplice, Christopher, were sentenced to transportation for life, while others were sentenced to three to seven years.[18] Due to the length of the journey (the quickest passage lasted 107 days), and the cost of the voyage back, many transportees were forced to make Australia their permanent home. Murphy made his passage over on the convict ship *Countess of Harcourt (4)*. The vessel sailed from Dublin on 14 February 1827 and, following a journey of 134 days, arrived in Sydney on 28 June 1827.[19]

Countess of Harcourt was built in India in 1811, but only made her maiden voyage as a convict ship in 1821. She was an impressive 517-tonne two-decker. There were no major incidents during the voyage to New South Wales, apart from digestive complaints among the convicts. The ship's surgeon, Robert Armstrong, attributed this to the prisoners' drastic dietary change from potatoes and oatmeal 'to a diet to which they had never before been accustomed'.[20] The majority of transportees were semiskilled and single. Given the deplorable economic conditions and rigid social structure in nineteenth-century Ireland, the life of an emancipated convict in the colonies was, if not happier, often a better one. Thomas Reid, another convict ship surgeon, visited *Countess of Harcourt* in Cork and remarked, 'the condition of a convict in New South Wales is ten thousand times more comfortable than that of a peasant in Ireland, – in fact, there can be no comparison between them'.[21]

In *Botany Bay: The story of convicts transported from Ireland to Australia, 1791–1853*, historian Con Costello also states that 'it was rumoured in Ireland that men and women deliberately committed crimes in hopes of being transported, and thus being able to enjoy a better life in Australia.'[22] It is difficult to support or disprove this claim, as well as Dr Reid's comments, as sources such as the convict ballad *Moreton Bay* depict the penal settlement as a place of excessive tyranny and starvation.[23]

A year after his conviction, nearly to the day on 28 June 1827, Murphy arrived in Sydney along with 22 transported countrymen (eight of them lifers).[24] Murphy was a common Irish surname, so Peter's name was supplemented by 'Duff', which derives from the Gaelic *dubh*, meaning dark or black, because of his complexion. According to Murphy's transportation record, he had brown hair and brown eyes with a distinct scar across the centre of his forehead.[25] Initially, he was assigned to the engineers department, but his convict records show that he did not stay there long. Following an escape attempt, Murphy was recommitted to the iron gang and sentenced to hard labour in chains in Parramatta, with an additional three months added to his term.[26] There is no record of Murphy reoffending. Instead, in 1838, he was assigned as a servant man to Patrick Leslie, a pioneer and a grazier who had arrived in Sydney from Scotland four years previously.[27] As a settler, Leslie 'was entitled to request the services of one convict for every hundred acres of land received'.[28]

A number of studies have explored the rate of reconviction among offenders transported to Australia's penal colonies and found differences between reconviction in colonial Australia and post-revolutionary United States. As H Maxwell-Stewart and R Kippen argue, 'convict transportation was notable for its success in reducing crime rates in colonial Australia, whereas in the post-revolutionary United States a reliance on the penitentiary had the opposite effect'.[29] A marked difference between the penal regimes in Australia and America was the emphasis that the former placed on the effective utilisation of convicts' skills. Apart from material support in both the state and private sector, convict labour had a long-term positive effect in helping to resocialise former offenders. The practices of rewarding good behaviour and providing a chance to resocialise combined amounted to a system of 'restorative justice', or the rehabilitation of criminals.[30]

'So meritorious an officer'

In 1840, Patrick Leslie, his assigned servant, Peter 'Duff' Murphy, and two other graziers embarked on an expedition first to the Great Dividing Range and then to the Darling Downs. *The Transportation Act for Removal to England Under Conditional Pardons of Colonial Offenders* (1824) provided men like Leslie with a legal right to hire out or sell their assigned servants, and limited the governor's right to recall or pardon servants before the termination of their sentence. In essence, this equated assigned servants to land or other holdings. Patrick Leslie's expedition stock consisted of several thousand breeding sheep and cattle, a team of horses and dray, 10 saddle horses, and 22 convicts. According to Leslie, these men, 'all ticket-of-leave, or convicts', were 'as good and game a lot of men as ever existed […] worth any forty men', and they did not cause the expedition a moment's trouble.[31]

Murphy distinguished himself during the Darling Downs expedition on a number of occasions by repelling attacks by local Aboriginal people. On one morning in particular, the expedition party woke to find themselves surrounded. As recorded in excerpts of Leslie's diary in *The Queenslander*, Murphy and Leslie 'stood back-to-back with their guns loaded. Leslie took aim but his hand was so unsteady that Murphy said, "Here, I'll fire", which he did, and after a few warning shots the blacks decamped.'[32] In his diary, Leslie described Murphy as 'the best plucked fellow' and, when Leslie returned to Sydney, he asked the governor, Sir George Gipps, to grant Murphy a ticket of leave in gratitude for his services before the expiration of his sentence, which, of course, was life. Murphy was subsequently granted his ticket of leave on 13 June 1842, with the conditions of his parole allowing him to stay within the Moreton Bay district. In the year prior to receiving his ticket, Murphy resided in Port Macquarie where he performed the duties of district constable. A fortnight before his parole, Murphy successfully prosecuted Patrick Gowan, who was free by servitude, for the theft of two pairs of boots from Mrs Georgiana Kinnear's shop. The coincidence of Murphy being an expert prosecution witness in a case similar to the one that saw him convicted and transported to New South Wales 14 years previously is not surprising given that larceny of clothes was one of the most common offences at the time. Murphy's evidence and testimony were reported in *The Australian*:

> From the evidence of Peter Murphy District Constable, it appeared, that, being informed of Mrs Kinnear's loss and suspicions; he searched after the prisoner, whom he found; but at that time had nothing on him. He watched him narrowly for a considerable time; and saw him come from the house of John Hilton. Witness went and asked Hilton's wife 'how many pairs of boots Gowan had left?' she answered, 'Only two.' They were produced to him, and identified by Mrs Kinnear as her property. Witness apprehended the prisoner, who stated he had bought the boots.[33]

Initially, the case was heard at the court of petty sessions, or the lower court, which disposed misdemeanours summarily without a jury. However, Gowan's claim to have purchased the boots was viewed as an aggravating factor, and he was committed to stand trial at the quarter sessions. The courts of general or quarter sessions were established by the *Act for the Better Administration of Justice in New South Wales* in 1823. These courts administered an intermediary level of justice and had the same powers as the courts of general or quarter sessions in England. The main role of the courts was to try criminal matters committed in the colony, or on the voyage to New South Wales, other than capital offences or those punishable by the death penalty. As the name suggests, quarter sessions were held quarterly. In July 1842, Gowan was found guilty of larceny (felony) and sentenced to 'one year ironed gang'.[34] A note in the summary trial transcript hinted at Murphy's promotion to the chief constableship in Moreton Bay, and described the promotion as 'a situation which will yield full scope for the exercise of his zeal and ability'. The note also praised Murphy's character by stating, 'All who know him feel pleased at his advancement of so meritorious an officer.'[35] It would be some years before Murphy received the honour, but he demonstrated his 'zeal and ability' soon after the trial by apprehending three bushranger runaways from a 'road party' hard-labour gang.[36]

Following his professional successes, Murphy's personal life took a happy turn. On 29 November 1842, in the presence of Mary Anne and William Tyrell, Peter Murphy married Catherine Thompson at St Mary's Roman Catholic Church in Sydney.[37] Unlike Murphy, who was able to read and write, Catherine signed the marriage certificate with a mark, as did her witness. In the county of Macquarie (present-day Port Macquarie) at the time, for every three men there was one woman over 21 years of age who could read and write.[38] Literacy rates in Brisbane were even lower at four men to one woman.[39] Peter and Catherine went on to have five living children and five sons and one daughter who died in infancy. Margaret (1844), Elizabeth (1846), Peter (1848), John (1850) and Edward Joseph (1853) were born and baptised in Moreton Bay.[40]

Free Settlement

During the years of the Moreton Bay penal settlement, a total of 2,062 men and 150 women (half of them Irish) served sentences in the Brisbane area. Of these convicts, over 200 died and 700 fled, 98 of whom were never recaptured. In May 1842, Moreton Bay was opened for free settlement and all convicts except for 39 men were removed. Simultaneously, the New South Wales Border Police unit was established to police Moreton Bay, and Captain John

Clements Wickham was appointed as police magistrate. It is around this time that Murphy and his family reached the free settlement of Brisbane and Murphy took up his position as a policeman. The police force of Brisbane town that he joined consisted of Chief Constable William Whyte, Bush Constable George Brown (a free man), and four convicts employed as assistant constables: Francis Black (arrived on *Hadlow*), Robert Giles (*Exmouth*), WH Sketland or 'Thompson' (*Sophia*) and John Egan.[41] That same year, Constable Brown was dismissed due to 'insolent and disrespectful' behaviour, but Sketland and Giles had their sentences commuted and were granted tickets of leave.[42] Murphy, along with the convict constables Black, Giles and Thompson (later district constable), was a living example that restorative justice, or rehabilitation via resocialisation of transported convicts, not only worked but also provided the means to turn one's fortunes around.

As the free settlement expanded, demands for free constables who were not connected to the penal settlement escalated as the public believed there was 'too much of a fellow-feeling' between the police and the policed. This was exemplified by the burglary from 'the stores of Mr Le Breton', which were 'broken open on the night of the 2nd inst [December], and property to the value of £30 abstracted therefrom'. When the stolen articles were traced, they were found to be 'in the possession of two men attached to the Survey Department'.[43] Due to the public demand for experienced and professional constables, William Fitzpatrick, who had previously served with the Sydney Police, succeeded Chief Constable Whyte in 1843.[44] Fitzpatrick and four ordinary constables – Martin Higgins, Jeremiah Scanlon, James Ramsay and John McGrath – were appointed into the local police at a salary of £4 (Fitzpatrick) and £2 10s (the constables) per week, and equipped with muskets and pistols, including 80 musket balls and 80 pistol balls for ammunition.[45]

By March 1846, Brisbane's population was 936 males and 470 females, with 595 and 201 aged between 21 and 45 respectively.

The second most numerous age bracket was two to seven years old, which demonstrated natural population growth.[46] The demographics were further broken down into 218 married to 718 single men and 217 married women to 253 single.[47] Out of almost 1,000 men, 488 were free men born in the colony or arrived free, 278 other free persons, 153 'leavers', one government employee and 16 on private assignment. The majority of women were free, with 467 free women, two holding tickets of leave and one on private assignment.[48] Denominationally, the population was largely representative of 'the mother country', with Church of England outnumbering Roman Catholics roughly two to one, followed by a variety of Anglican doctrinal strands and Methodists, one Jewish person, and two people labelled as 'Mahaommedans and Pagans'.[49]

One of the 488 free men was Peter 'Duff' Murphy. On 31 December 1846, following the petition of Patrick Leslie, Murphy received a conditional pardon three years after he was granted a ticket of leave. The pardon's conditions allowed Murphy freedom of movement in all parts of the world, except the United Kingdom of Great Britain and Ireland. If he returned to the United Kingdom, his pardon would 'thenceforth be and become wholly void, as by Her Majesty's Commands expressly limited and directed' (Figure 1.1).[50] Murphy's pardon was published in *The Australian* as pardon lists were regularly advertised in the local newspapers at the time.

Constable Murphy of the Brisbane Police

As the settlement continued expanding, its administrative systems also grew in complexity, which led to the courts of petty sessions being established in 1846. Between 1846 and 1850, Brisbane's population more than tripled from just under 1,000 to 3,150 inhabitants.[51] The town landscape also expanded and, in the mid-1840s, a third township emerged – Kangaroo Point (Figure 1.2) – where land sold for £5 per acre. This price was 20 times lower than the building allotments in North and South Brisbane.[52] Due to the township's position on the river and the downstream

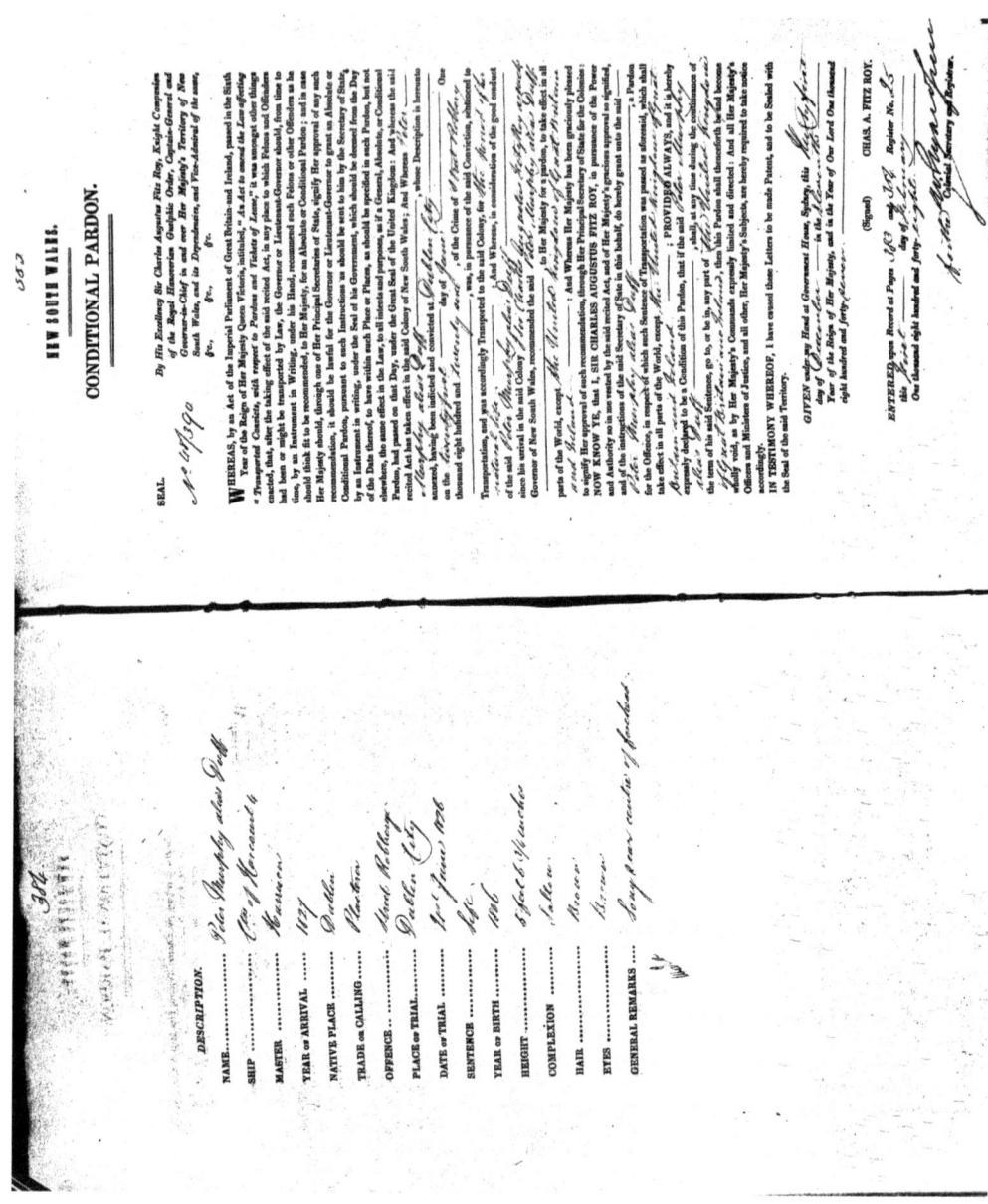

Figure 1.1: Conditional pardon for Peter 'Duff' Murphy.
(*Convict Registers of Conditional and Absolute Pardons*, 1788–1870, New South Wales, pp. 384–85)

Figure 1.2: Kangaroo Point, 1858, by Silvester Diggles. (QAGOMA)

flow, Kangaroo Point was mostly used for leased accommodation and workshops for Evan Mackenzie's boiling-down works and tanneries.[53] The area also accommodated the Kangaroo Point Ferry, R Davison's store, the Bush Commercial Hotel, Campbell's Boiling Down Works and the North Brisbane Ferry. Kangaroo Point became home to Constable Peter Murphy and his family, including his two daughters, Margaret and Elizabeth.[54]

Constable, and later District Constable, Murphy was assigned to the Kangaroo Point township, so he resided in and policed the same area. On Saturday 5 June 1847, George Gray was brought before the police magistrate charged with having concealed himself in the pig house on Mr Slavin's premises under suspicious circumstances. As was reported in *The Moreton Bay Courier*, 'It appears Constable Murphy saw the prisoner at Kangaroo Point, and questioned him as to what brought him there.'[55] Murphy was informed that Gray was delivering a message for one Mrs Potts and, as Gray indicated he had delivered the message, Constable Murphy ordered him to go home. However, instead of heading in the direction of the ferry, Gray ran away and hid in the pig house. He was discovered and placed on a ferry boat 'with orders to the ferryman not to bring him back again unless he had a pass' as Gray was a 'leaver'.[56] On the following morning, the proprietor, Mr Slavin, discovered a bundle of clothes in the same place the prisoner was found the night before, and the articles were identified as the property of William Wilson. Gray was found guilty of larceny below the value of £5 and sentenced to a term of six months to be worked in irons. Similarly, in July 1847, Murphy prosecuted a case of indecent exposure in the area. William Murray was summoned to appear before the magistrates on 20 July and was 'charged with indecently exposing his person at Kangaroo Point on the previous day'. However, 'The defendant did not appear, and the case being substantiated by Constable Murphy, he was fined £5, which was subsequently paid', so Murray avoided a prison term or a spell in the 'gangs'.[57]

Given the transient nature of the working population, the

new township of Kangaroo Point hosted a number of hotels where predominantly men were housed in close proximity. Such conditions inevitably contributed to an array of crimes that ranged in severity and sometimes extended beyond indecency and petty theft. On 26 March 1848, Constable Murphy was summoned to a grisly scene. At around 8 am, a man named George Cummings was in his boat on the river, when he:

> discovered the lower part of the trunk and the legs of [a] body, with a portion of the intestines attached, lying on a mud-bank at the bottom of the garden of a person of the name Rankin. Within a few yards of these remains, the upper portion of body and [arms], with other portion of intestines attached, but wanting the head, was found on the mud-bank, beyond Rankin's garden fence. Both portions of the body were found between high-water and low-water mark.[58]

The body remained by the river until the chief constable arrived a few hours later, and constables Murphy and William, along with a man named Copson, conducted a search in the area.[59] Around 12 pm, while passing one of the buildings across from WM Sutton's Bush Commercial Hotel, situated at the corner of Gipps and Ferry streets, they observed a dog coming out from the hotel's side gate. When they went to investigate, Copson made a gruesome discovery: 'in some long grass amongst the joists, he discovered a human head'.[60] One of Sutton's employees, William Fyfe (also spelled Fife), a ticket-of-leave man from Forfarshire, was sweeping the hotel's verandah at the time. Fyfe was a cook at the hotel and had been hired by Sutton on 23 March 1848. He had been in Australia for 21 years after arriving as a convict on *Guilford (7)* in 1827 from Scotland, where he was a baker before being convicted of housebreaking in Aberdeen and sentenced to 14 years' transportation. The convict indent described him as 5 feet 7¾ inches tall with black hair, hazel eyes and freckles. He was literate, 28 years old at the time of his transportation and had one child.[61] Fyfe identified the head as belonging to Robert Cox, a sawyer. He had met the deceased man Cox on 24 March, and they had spent that day and the following day drunk. Cox was last seen alive around 7 pm in Sutton's hotel kitchen on Saturday 25 March. Following a forensic examination of the hotel and the yard, constables Murphy and Williams discovered some clothes and a knife in the bloody water of the hotel well. Further, under the floorboards of one of the sleeping rooms, they uncovered a large quantity of blood. The soil was still moist and children's shoes discovered under the boards were also filled with blood. Fyfe was the occupant of the room at the time and was connected to the clothing evidence, so, a week later, he was committed for murder at the Central Criminal Court in Sydney.[62]

In June 1848, William Fyfe was charged with two counts. The first was for having 'murdered Robert Cox by inflicting with a knife wounds on the right side of his chest, neck and belly'. The second was the same as the first with the addition that 'the offence had been committed with a sharp instrument', but the instrument was not described.[63] The solicitor-general conducted the Cox case on the part of the Crown, while Chief Constable Fitzpatrick and Constable Murphy gave expert evidence. Following a day and a half of proceedings, the jury deliberated for about half an hour and returned with the verdict of guilty. Fyfe maintained his innocence, but, on 4 July 1848, less than a month after the trial concluded, he was executed in Sydney.[64]

The murder at the Bush Commercial Hotel was extraordinary even for a post-penal settler town. The majority of Murphy's time was occupied with more mundane cases, including property offences and offences against good order, such as drunkenness and indecent exposure. One such property offence case was heard on 24 August 1848 in the central criminal court following the search of a house in South Brisbane owned by Henry Currie, which was conducted by Constable Murphy and others. Currie was charged with stealing from a dwelling belonging to Thomas Baylen, a carpenter residing in Russell Street. On the night of Tuesday 4 July, Baylen came home to find his door had been forced open and that he was robbed of £18 5s in various currencies, notes, orders and silver sovereigns.[65] The following Saturday, Currie's house, which was located 100 yards away from the plaintiff's, was searched and orders in Baylen's name were found. The remaining sum was found the next day when the defendant's water closet was searched. The defence maintained that there was no clear evidence Currie was the thief as he lived with three other people, and he was found not guilty.

Figure 1.3: View from Bowen Terrace across to Kangaroo Point, 1851. (State Library of Queensland, 66243)

In July 1850, Murphy investigated another notable case of a house robbery. On the night of 15 July, the house of a man named Duffy in Kangaroo Point (Figure 1.3) was burglarised. The thief entered through the window and abstracted a £1 note and three penny pieces. The police court proceedings show that 'the suspicion of District Constable Murphy fell upon a ticket-of-leave holder named Isaac Thomlin (convict ship *Mount Elphinestone*), and finding the gentleman at the Police Office, where he was making modest request to be allowed a pass to remain in Brisbane, Murphy took the liberty of searching him'.[66] Murphy found the notes, which were positively identified by Mrs Duffy by the peculiar way they were folded and by some remarkable stains on them. Murphy also examined the forensic evidence at the scene and matched Thomlin's boot print to one found near Duffy's house; a nail missing from one of the boots had left a characteristic impression in the soft soil. The defendant was sentenced to six months in an ironed gang.

In the time between these two cases, Murphy's family grew as his sons Peter and John were born in 1848 and 1850 respectively. The family expanded their land holdings and purchased a garden allotment in the parish of Ipswich in 1847.[67] The Brisbane Police also underwent organisational changes and expanded over this period. In 1850, the police force comprised a chief constable, a district constable in Kangaroo Point, eight constables, a clerk and a watch-house keeper. As evidenced in the July robbery case, Murphy took over as district constable of Kangaroo Point in 1850. During the same year, the *Act for the Regulation of the Police Force in New South Wales* provided for the establishment of a colonial police force headed by an inspector-general and supported by a network of provincial inspectors. The proclamation of the Act ended the locally organised police forces in New South Wales as well as the domination of the police force by the magistracy.

The Last Years

In January 1850, Samuel Sneyd replaced William Fitzpatrick as chief constable. Less than a month before Fitzpatrick's dismissal, he was 'severely censured' by the police magistrate for not responding to a call of alarm and staying in bed due to a late shift the night before. The alarm was raised by a local squatter who was concerned about a missing bullock and perceived threats made by a group of Aboriginal Australians camped near Kangaroo Point. The military assembled along with a few constables, and shots were fired, resulting in flesh wounds to four Aboriginal men who were treated at the hospital the next day. The missing bullock turned up a short time after the affray.[68] As Sneyd took command of the force, the cases for breach of conduct by police appeared more regularly in the local newspapers, earning him the moniker 'Snatch-em'.[69] District Constable Murphy, who served as acting chief constable while Sneyd was transferring his family from Goulburn, also brought a complaint about breach of conduct to the police magistrate on 5 January 1850. Murphy claimed that constables Hore and Sparkes had neglected their duty and been intoxicated, and *The Moreton Bay Courier* reported that the charges were 'proved on oath, and corroborated by the testimony of Dr Ballow, Mr Dowes, and other witnesses', and both constables were dismissed.[70] The newspaper also indicated that 'Sparkes had confined a man in the watchhouse for drunkenness, where he himself was more intoxicated than the prisoner'.[71]

Murphy's job became increasingly more complex as he and the constables he managed struggled with the increasing demands of their positions. In 1853, Constable James McGuire died on duty while executing a warrant at Durundur. McGuire's partner, Constable James Tredennick, was in turn charged with neglect as he left McGuire and proceeded to Durundur by himself. Murphy had to replace McGuire and execute the warrant with Tredennick. Then, on 21 January 1853, Murphy himself was charged with having been drunk.[72] In June, District Constable Murphy was again charged by Chief Constable Sneyd at the police office with having been in a state of intoxication at the ferry wharf in Kangaroo Point. As this was a repeat offence, the bench sentenced him to pay a fine of £5, a substantial portion of his pay at the time of £95 16s 3d per annum, or roughly £1 8s per week.[73] Murphy tendered his resignation following the hearing, which was accepted.[74]

Land sale records and police court coverage show that Murphy relocated to Ipswich, and from the 1860s onwards he presided over the local police court. Murphy died of disease of the heart on 6 April 1878 at Charters Towers when he was 72 years old, and was remembered as 'a highly respected colonist'.[75]

Peter 'Duff' Murphy turned to crime to survive in a time of hardship, as did many of his fellow destitute working-class Irishmen. Throughout the eighteenth and nineteenth centuries, the variability and seasonality of casual labour in urban centres across the British Isles resulted in high rates of pauperism, vagrancy and destitution. The construct of a habitual criminal grew in popularity during the Victorian era alongside the developing class of criminals who turned to crime for a living, as they were depraved and unable to commit to an honest day's work. The most incorrigible criminals in the United Kingdom were sent to Australia. Initially, Murphy's fate was no different from the 160,000 men, women and juveniles transported to the shores of the Australian colonies. Murphy's young partner in crime, Christopher Monks, disappeared into obscurity. William Fyfe, the murderer Murphy apprehended, gained notoriety for all the wrong reasons during his 20 years in the colonies and was hanged for a gruesome murder. In 'The Last Fleet', Barry Godfrey and David Cox argue that 'Many former convicts found it difficult to remake their lives after gaining freedom and often reappear in court and other records as vagrants and petty offenders'; however, the majority of recidivists committed a range of petty offences that were dealt with summarily, and comparatively few convicts were reconvicted in the higher courts.[76] Murphy and the handful of men who formed the first convict police forces across New South Wales took the relative success of resocialisation further as they became assigned servants and ticket-of-leave men. Against all odds, Murphy graduated from being 'a noted Mud Islander' and a thief to a policeman and 'a highly respected colonist'.[77]

2

A Career Policeman

Samuel Sneyd

> The vigilance of the new regime soon made [1840s] Brisbane too hot to hold many of the loose characters by whom it had been infested. A marked change soon became apparent; courts of petty session, courts of request, and other necessary details were brought into successful operation and the then embryo city became a model of good order and the abode of a thriving and industrious community of free settlers.
>
> 'John Clements Wickham Obituary'[1]

BY 1850, EIGHT years on from free settlement, a young Brisbane was attempting to move away from its convict past and towards separation from southern governance. Retail outlets and pubs had emerged around the community, and convicts who had earned their freedom stayed and made a life for themselves in the 'northern reaches' of New South Wales. Brisbane was, at this stage, a place where you could purchase luxury goods, such as Congou and Hyson skin teas, coffee, rice, sugars, soap, candles, pickles, spices, first-rate cigars and a few sheep, without difficulty.[2] However, it was still a relatively small town with bushland beyond the convict windmill (Figure 2.1), and a wide, slow-flowing river at its middle. In 1850, as the local governance grew in complexity, public fears of abuse of power by the local magistrates continued to intensify and a new police Act, the *Act for the Regulation of the Police Force in New South Wales*, was passed in an attempt to stop fledgling corruption.³ The Act effectively ended the domination of the police force by the magistracy, albeit for a short time. In the wake of the new Act, Brisbane Police welcomed its third chief constable, Samuel Sneyd.

Figure 2.1: Ferry from the South Brisbane reach, 1850, sketch by Conrad Martens (1801–78). (Royal Historical Society of Queensland Photographic Collection, P53277; digital copy of P4415)

'Deployed to Australia'

Samuel Sneyd of Hanley, Stoke-on-Trent in Staffordshire, England enlisted with the 4th Foot Lancaster King's Own Regiment for a service period of 21 years at the age of 18.⁴ In the regiment, he was initially paid a nominal daily wage of 1p, although up to half of a penny was deducted from his wage for items such as daily rations, replacement clothing and medical services. By 1847, the British Government had decreed that a soldier must receive at least 1p per day regardless of any deductions.⁵

In 1831, a detachment of King's Own soldiers travelled with each of the 31 convict ships bound for Australia to guard the prisoners during the journey. Once they arrived in the colony, the soldiers were tasked with maintaining order among the convicts, chasing down escapees, restoring order and taking charge of working parties.[6] In September of the same year, at the age of 22, Samuel left the United Kingdom as a guard on the Sydney-bound convict ship *Asia*.[7] The four-and-a-half-month journey was tedious for both convicts and soldiers, and the day-to-day routine was only varied by 'plots and fights amongst convicts, courts of enquiry, inspection of men's equipment, trouble with women and catching sharks'.[8] Upon arriving in the colony, Sneyd immediately took on a law enforcement role as, according to *The Moreton Bay Courier*, in the unruly early days of New South Wales, he was one of the men selected from the regiment to suppress bushranging in the colony.[9] He joined the Mounted Police and soon rose to the rank of sergeant-major of the Goulburn Division and was earning 2s 4p per day.[10] Five years after he arrived, and with his career in law enforcement well established, Sneyd met Irish-born Catherine 'Kitty' Mulcahy, whom he married on 23 February 1837 in Dapto, near Wollongong. As Sneyd was a Baptist and Kitty was a Catholic, this was an unusual religious union at the time.

From the genesis of a convict security force, the New South Wales policing model evolved to cope with the changing population and the development of towns by separating the police into distinct districts. In 1838, the Military Mounted Police, which was established in 1825 and focused on the Bathurst and Hunter River areas, where bushrangers were considered to be particularly troublesome, was enlarged and divided into three patrols headquartered at Goulburn, Armidale and Bathurst.[11] At a meeting of the New South Wales Legislative Council in November 1839, the governor and colonial secretary were anxious about the excessive cost of the police for the preceding financial year. Councillor Richard Jones said he 'had not the slightest doubt that a great part of the mischief which existed in the country districts arose from the negligence of the Police Magistrates', and Councillor Alexander Berry agreed with him, adding his further thoughts that 'the Police was not worth half what was paid for it' and that 'the Mounted Police were to blame' for much of the crime in the colony as he 'found that during the past year they apprehended some 350 bushrangers, but as soon as they were taken the rascally constables let them escape again'. Berry went on to attribute some blame also to the council, stating that 'the Bushranging Act was no better than the English Vagrant Act. A man, a regular cutthroat, took the bush, was captured, sent to an ironed-gang, and escaped to the bush again.'[12]

Sneyd saw his fair share of both convicts and bushrangers during his service life in the colony. On 21 September 1839, Sergeant Sneyd of the Bowen's Hollow Police assisted Sergeant Moore, commander of the Mounted Police at Mount Victoria, in capturing three notorious bushrangers near the Vale of Clwyd. The men committed 'great depredations' on the settlers around Mudgee and Dubbo, and had been 'the terror of the whole neighbourhood for four months'.[13] Samuel Sneyd's reputation as a mounted officer of worth was further proved a month later when he tracked down three more desperate bushrangers who had attacked the premises of Mr Brown, a few miles from Hartley, and 'robbed the place of every article of value they could lay their hands upon'.[14] Sneyd shot and killed one of the bushrangers before capturing the remaining two.

Sneyd (Figure 2.2) accepted the position of chief constable in Brisbane in December 1849. He subsequently retired from the military with an annual pension of £18 5s. The chief constable position was gazetted on 1 January 1850, waged at £70 per annum, which was only a fraction of the pay received by the commanding officers in the London Metropolitan Police, the only centrally organised English police at the time. Samuel was in Sydney at the time of his appointment and his wife and family were in Goulburn. On 2 January, he asked for permission of the colonial secretary to remain in town while he awaited the arrival of his family.[15] This request was approved, and the family travelled up to Brisbane together on the steamer *Tamar* and arrived in early January. The position of chief constable included the provision of a house, which allowed Samuel, Kitty and their seven children, aged from 1 to 13, to make Brisbane their home.[16]

Figure 2.2: Portrait of Samuel Sneyd ca. 1880.
(Courtesy of Sneyd Family Archive, JOL Neg. 946)

Brisbane's Third Chief Constable

Sneyd's first year as chief constable brought a range of societal developments, including the proclamation of the first circuit court, the employment of an official letter carrier and the completion of Customs House. The settlement was spreading outward from the inner streets of Brisbane town, with funds invested in infrastructure to allow the greater movement of people across the town and beyond. In mid-1850, the military, who had overseen the convict settlement and stayed to keep the peace, withdrew from Moreton Bay.[17] By the end of the year, Brisbane's population had reached around 3,150 and was growing. In order to keep up with the expanding police district, in 1850, the force was divided into distinct districts and beats with a district constable and a chief constable to supervise them. During 1850 and 1851, along with Samuel Sneyd, new chief constables were recruited for Gayndah (Bartholomew Bannister, an experienced Mounted Police officer), Wide Bay (Sergeant William McAdam) and Maranoa (Sergeant William de Renzy of the Sydney police).[18]

There was no police manual available at this time, so the official training these new recruits underwent is unknown. Recruitments were made from soldier ranks and from those already holding a police rank, emphasising experience while attempting to ensure uniformity of police practices across the districts.[19] Before Sneyd's appointment as chief constable following the new police Act, the Moreton Bay District had been under the stewardship of Police Magistrate John Clements Wickham since 1843. Wickham was charged with the 'general interests of government within it, and the Representative of the Governor within its limits', and his force comprised of Chief Constable William Fitzpatrick and a small group of conscripted men.[20] Wickham showed much sympathy and understanding in his police work and exercised his authority judiciously. This attitude earned him the confidence of the settlers and helped develop a positive image of law enforcement officers in early Brisbane.[21]

Sneyd was duly sworn in and assumed his duties on 14 January 1850.[22] He had already been allotted the duties of inspector of distilleries and a week later he became inspector of slaughter houses, and of cattle intended to be slaughtered in the police district of Moreton Bay.[23] The Brisbane Police Force at the time comprised of District Constable Peter 'Duff' Murphy, watch-house keeper Constable John Booth and nine constables.[24] Given the small number of police on the ground, Sneyd and his constables were kept busy with Brisbane's array of crimes and criminals.

Duties

During Sneyd's nine-year tenure as chief constable from 1850 to 1859, the duties of his office were extremely varied. As the second highest government representative in the district, Sneyd was tasked with executing the orders of the New South Wales Colonial Secretary and he reported to five different colonial secretaries during his time in the force. In his additional post as bailiff of the court of requests, Sneyd's direct superior within the court system was Police Magistrate Wickham. Wickham reported to the colonial secretary, but he was not in control of other government officers in the district. Sneyd divided his time between his regular policing duties, such as keeping the peace and catching miscreants on the streets, and making appearances in court. He also oversaw the sale of unclaimed property, the estates of the deceased, and property seized from cancelled ticket-of-leave holders. These sales were frequently advertised in newspapers such as the *New South Wales Government Gazette* and *The Moreton Bay Courier*:

> THE undermentioned articles of unclaimed pro-perty, now in possession of the Police of this District, (supposed to be the property of the late Mrs. Cheadle,) will be sold by public auction, at the Police Office, Brisbane, at 12 o'clock, on Monday, the 1st of April, unless previously claimed, viz. :-
>
> 1 cedar box; 2 pair sheets; 4 gowns; 4 gown pieces; 7 towels; 6 yards calico; 3 night gowns; 1 pair boots; 3 shawls; 1 white jacket; 1 apron; 2 yards brown holland; 2 pair gloves; 4 night caps;

> 3 pair stockings; 1 pillow slip with sun-dries; 1 pair shoe brushes; 1 hair brush; 1 tooth brush; 1 pair side combs; 1 petticoat; 1 shift; 4 books; 1 habit shirt.
>
> By order of the Police Magistrate,
> SAMUEL SNEYD,
> Chief Constable [25]

By the mid-1850s, Sneyd only had eight constables to police the flourishing town. This lack of police resources resulted in public fears that the forces in the districts were insufficient. This fear increased when, in June, rumours abounded that the detachment of soldiers stationed in Brisbane was to be immediately withdrawn.[26] As reflected in the newspapers at the time, it was feared that the withdrawal of the small detachment might bring serious consequences, for the 'offences against the laws [were] passed but unpunished in consequence, notwithstanding the recent establishment of a Circuit Court'. In particular, the public were concerned that the magistracy would be ineffective without the police presence required to enforce the laws:

> A judge may try, and a jury may judge, but neither the judge nor the jury can be efficient without the constable, because if the constable cannot apprehend the criminal, the functions of the judge and jury are idle – a very simple reason. Now we would ask what constabulary protection is there in these districts. Some seven or eight constables in Brisbane; a few more in Ipswich; one or two at Drayton, and at Warwick, Gayndah, Maryborough, and in the far west of Maranoa – an extent of territory equal to many European kingdoms.[27]

In addition to the insufficient number of constables on the streets to preserve life and protect property with the efficiency expected, the larger social and political issue of separation from the colony from New South Wales was gaining momentum. The movement towards separation was initiated at a squatter-led meeting in Drayton in July 1850 where a Darling Downs committee who demanded 'financial separation with exiles' was formed. The agitation for separation and discontinuance of transportation surged, and meetings and counter meetings were held in Brisbane and Ipswich.[28] Despite the political turmoil, it was business as usual for the local force as crime continued to interrupt the day-to-day life of colonists. A notable case at the time was the robbery of the overland mail on 12 January 1851, which caused great anxiety within the community. At 9 am, mailman Thomas Southern started his run from Ipswich and shortly afterwards returned with the story that two armed men had stuck him up and robbed him of all the valuables from the mailbags. This included cash and money orders to the value of £395. Unfortunately for the mailman, local man William Moir was out looking for his master's horses and saw Southern meet two accomplices in the bush. Six days later, Chief Constable Sneyd apprehended John Murphy (alias Sullivan), who had attempted to pass some of the stolen orders at the Victoria Hotel. In addition to the criminally inclined mailman and Murphy, Joseph Bull, William Crabb and James McClaren were also arrested in connection with the robbery. Information gained by Sneyd from the prisoners also helped him locate a portion of the stolen goods hidden under a bridge at One-mile Swamp at Woolloongabba.[29] As the instigator of the crime, John Murphy was sentenced to 15 years of hard labour on the roads or on other public works. The conduct of the chief constable and his ordinary constables was found to be praiseworthy and a £20 reward (around one quarter of a constable's annual salary) was approved to be shared between them.[30]

By 1 March 1851, Brisbane's population had grown to 3,575, which increased the burden on the local police. The town's expansion also increased the tension between the colonial settlers and the local Aboriginal Australians as land was seized for residential and commercial development. Clashes between the two groups and police intervention were often reported in the local papers. *The Moreton Bay Courier*

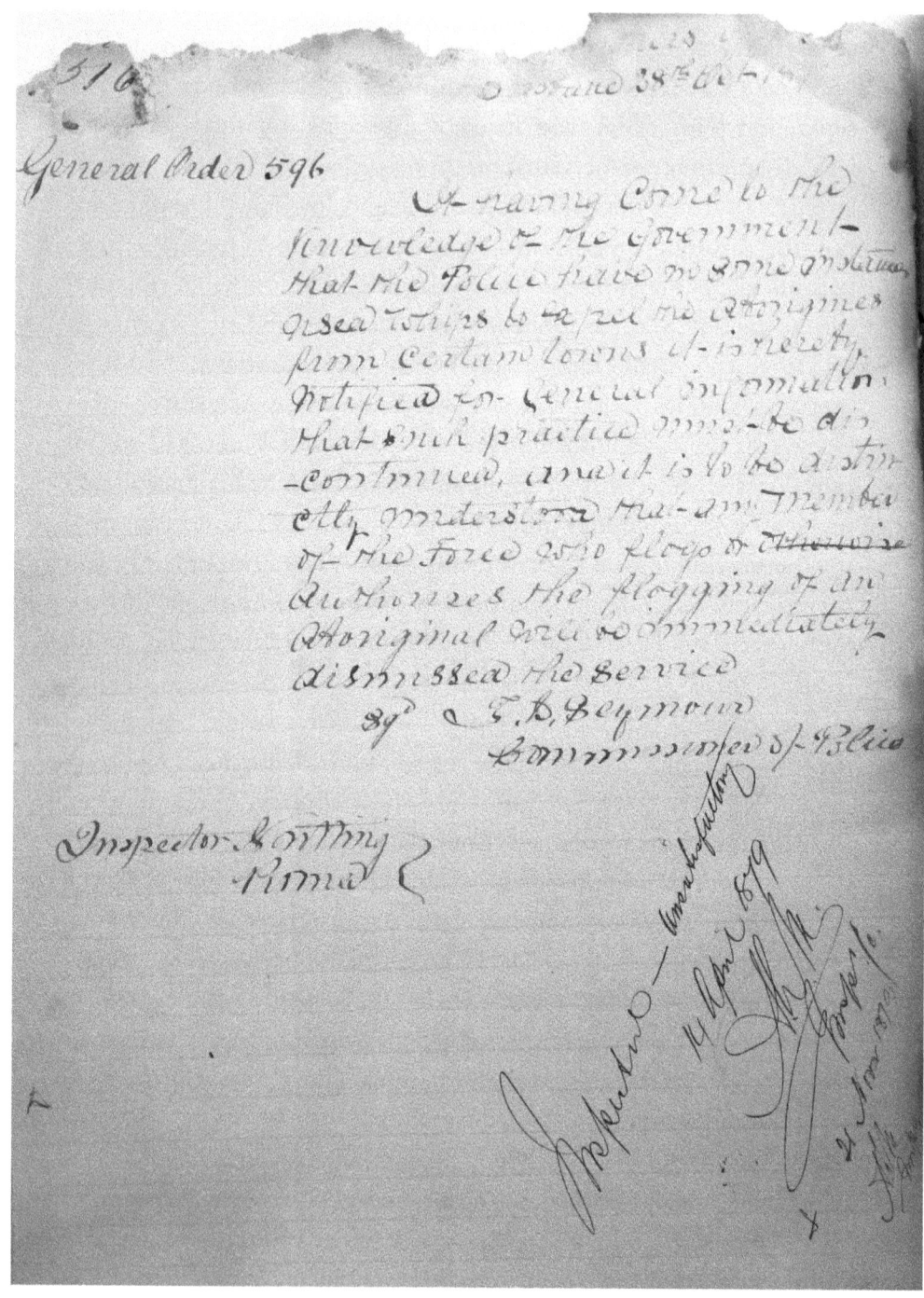

Figure 2.3: Commissioner of Police *General Order 596*, 28 October 1876. (Queensland State Archives, A/36338)

reported one such clash between Sneyd's police officers and a group of Aboriginal Australians on 12 June 1852. An article in *The Moreton Bay Courier* from the Burnett District correspondent outlined how 'a report was brought into town by Constable McAlister that a native black had broken open the door of a person named Salisbury, near Breakfast Creek, and that when the constable sought to apprehend the delinquent, about twelve blacks attacked him and his assistants, one of them throwing a tomahawk; in consequence of which they came to town for protection'.[31] In response, Chief Constable Sneyd and two mounted constables proceeded to the south side of Breakfast Creek, with District Constable Murphy and four other constables going before them on the north side to the camp. By the time the police arrived on foot, the camp had dispersed, and Murphy's party destroyed what remained: 'the vacated gunyas of the blacks, with the spears and other articles abandoned by them, were burnt'.[32] Mistreatment of Aboriginal Australians throughout the colony persisted well into the nineteenth and twentieth centuries. In October 1876, Commissioner David Thompson Seymour issued *General Order 596* (Figure 2.3), which addressed instances of the police using whips to 'repel the Aborigines from certain towns'. Disappointingly, the memo does not specify which town's police contingent practised this treatment. Seymour ordered that the practice be discontinued and emphasised that it was 'to be distinctly understood that any member of the Force who flogs or authorises the flogging of an Aboriginal will be immediately dismissed from service'.[33]

The Ellis Case

The social stratification codified in the *Servants and Masters Acts* saw members of the working class subject to abuse in both Great Britain and its colonial dominions, and crimes against servants were often heard in the courts.[34] The most ferocious and scandalous crimes committed against citizens in England were widely reported in Australia by the larger papers such as the *South Australian* and *The Sydney Morning Herald*. In February 1851, one of 'the most shameful cases [was] heard at the Old Bailey in England'. Prominent attorney George Sloane of the prestigious Middle Temple, who was also director of the Church of England Assurance Institution, along with his wife, Theresa, were charged with having been 'wilfully neglecting to supply Jane Wilbred, an infant of tender years' – whom they had hired from the local poorhouse – 'with sufficient nourishment for her support, by which she became ill'. In addition to neglecting Jane, there were counts against the Sloanes for 'assaults by beating with a shoe, stripping her to the waist, and exposing her to the weather, and forcing her to eat her own excrement'.[35] Alerted by rumours among the other servants in the temple, a colleague of Sloane's found the girl living in vile squalor. Fed almost nothing, she weighed only 59 pounds (26 kilograms). Due to a technicality relating to the burden of proving the girl's 'tender years', the Sloanes were found not guilty on most counts and were each sentenced to a mere two years in prison. The Sloanes were condemned by a horrified English community and the case specifics were closely followed by the Brisbane community.

In late October 1852, Brisbane was shocked by a similar story in its local news when it was reported that 'charges of most wanton and cruel ill-treatment had been preferred against Mrs. Jane Ellis, wife of a turnkey at the Brisbane Gaol, by Isabella McEvoy, a girl who had been living with her as a servant'.[36] *The Moreton Bay Courier* reported that the case bore a striking resemblance to the Sloane case, which had created much excitement in England in February the year before. The Brisbane case was astonishing in its cruelty. The court heard that Isabella, aged around 15, was routinely stripped, strung up by her arms so only her toes touched the ground, and beaten with a stick or whip for long periods. After a particularly dreadful week of beatings, Isabella ran away on Friday 15 October, returned the same day while Mrs Ellis was out, and then ran away again. She hid under a neighbour's house until the Sunday night when she asked the neighbour, Mrs Hardgrave, to send for the chief constable. Sneyd took her to his house and fed her supper, after which Mrs Sneyd and Mrs Wright, who occupied a portion of Sneyd's house, examined her injuries. Subsequently, on 24 October 1851, Jane Ellis was indicted to appear in court on 21 May 1852, which resulted in her being charged with 'having unlawfully and maliciously committed a series of assaults upon Isabella McEvoy [first count], and with having tied the said Isabella McEvoy up by her arms to a beam of wood [second count]'.[37] After much deliberation, the jury found Jane Ellis guilty on both counts, and she received a sentence of 14 months' imprisonment for the first count and 10 months for the second. The prisoner was committed to the custody of the sheriff, and she was sent to serve her time at the Parramatta Gaol in New South Wales. There were no additional references concerning the fate of poor Isabella McEvoy after the court case, which is a rather despairing statement about the sensibilities of the time.

Tragedy and Triumph
The following year was marred by a tragedy within the local police force. In January 1853, Constable Thomas McGuire, who had five years' experience in the colony, died under unfortunate circumstances. As mentioned earlier, McGuire and Constable James Tredennick were sent to Durundur at the head of the Brisbane River to execute a warrant on Henry Waintling for the assault of station owner Duncan Campbell. The two mounted constables left on a Monday afternoon and it took them several hours to reach Mr Griffin's station at the Pine River, where they spent the night. On the way to Durundur the next day, they came across a group encamped on the road and stopped for rest and nourishment. When Tredennick prepared to carry on with the journey, McGuire told his colleague to go without him and said that he would follow. Tredennick reached Durundur but grew concerned when McGuire did not arrive by nightfall. The next morning, Tredennick went looking for his colleague and met some men leading McGuire's horse, which they had found wandering on the road. Following a thorough search, Tredennick and the men found McGuire's body,

which had been badly burnt by a recent bushfire. Coroner Dr Swift and Chief Constable Sneyd held a magisterial inquiry and found that McGuire must have fallen from his horse while intoxicated, then suffocated as his body was consumed by the bushfire. Thomas McGuire was formerly a soldier, and had been a police constable for five years. He was generally thought of as being a good officer and a very inoffensive man. Since Thomas left behind a wife and two children, *The Moreton Bay Courier* reported, 'it is to be hoped that, notwithstanding the apparent breach of duty for which such a dreadful penalty has been paid, some allowance will be made to [McGuire's family] in consideration of the long service of the deceased'.[38] The blame for McGuire's death was mostly attributed to James Tredennick as he had separated from his colleague, and he was subsequently charged with neglect of duty and fined 20s (£1).[39]

In late March 1853, considerable excitement swept through Brisbane when it was reported that nine convicts had escaped from Norfolk Island in an open boat and had arrived in Moreton Bay after washing up on the beach at Amity Point (Figure 2.4). Chief Constable Sneyd visited Germans' station (present-day Nundah) to give warning lest the convicts should land on that side of the river. Three of the convicts were caught quickly but the other six evaded capture until a month later when the police received information about their location. On 2 May, a group including William Duncan Esquire, Richard Sheridan of the customs department, Chief Constable Samuel Sneyd, and eight volunteers and constables went downriver to the spot where the convict's boat had been left at the river mouth. With the assistance of Indigenous guides, the group tracked the runaways until they came across the convicts about 8 miles from Brisbane at 12 pm the following day. The group was anxious to ensure the runaways would not escape again and 'immediately rushed upon the pirates, and ordered them to lay down their arms, which they did without resistance, whereupon they were handcuffed, and marched back to Brisbane'.[40]

Figure 2.4: Amity Point Pilot Station in Moreton Bay, 1847. (Mitchell Collection, State Library of New South Wales, FL3175450)

The Bluestone Rum Case

While many cases, such as that of the Norfolk convict runaways, concluded with a wholly favourable outcome in police work, others ended questionably or even bordered on a miscarriage of justice. One such case was the wanton murder of Stephen Swords at Kangaroo Point in January 1854, which became known as the Bluestone Rum Case or the Kangaroo Point Murder. On 21 January, Stephen Swords, Tom Burton, Jack Hanley and Tom Dunn finished work at Douglas's soap-making works and retired to Mercer Tavern where they settled in to drink rum for a few hours. Later that evening, all four very drunk fellows staggered to the soap works hut and passed out. In the morning, Swords was found lying unconscious from a blow to the head. Burton was beside him in a state of befuddlement with the murder weapon, a large piece of wood, near his hand. When District Constable Anderson arrived at the scene after Hanley reported the crime hours later, he found Burton with the assault weapon. With this evidence and Hanley's testimony, Anderson arrested Burton for assault and subsequently murder as Swords died in hospital. The case was not closed, however, as Chief Constable Sneyd questioned the evidence and, after interviewing the other men and witnesses, formed a different opinion about the identity of the assailant. Burton, who had no recollection of the event, was almost convinced of the crime and the community was willing to condemn him as he was regarded as a rough and unforgiving man. However, due to Sneyd's diligence, in addition to a number of more credible witnesses, Burton was released and Jack Hanley was indicted for the murder of Stephen Swords instead. Hanley was found guilty and hanged in January 1854.[41]

The Wage Question

In the early 1850s, gold deposits were discovered in Bathurst, which caused a population rush and inflation in the town centres due to the influx of cash. As the previous cases demonstrate, the town's growth attracted migrant and seasonal labour, which promised anonymity to escaped prisoners. In 1853, 1,500 immigrants arrived in Moreton Bay, which put further strain on the infrastructure and resources, including the police.

At the end of March 1854, 13 members of the Brisbane and Ipswich police petitioned the colonial secretary for a rise in wages, complaining that the cost of living in Brisbane outstripped that of Sydney and that their allowances did not cover the expense of escorting prisoners to Sydney:[42]

> [Summary of] Petition of Constables and Peace Officers for Town and District of Ipswich: Several have been such for many years, respected by superiors & inhabitants for zealous and good conduct – greater vigilance and zeal required with increasing population. Mention scarcity of labour, house rent has in last 6 months risen 100%, provisions and necessities of life similarly affected. Impossible for Petitioners to support themselves and families in manner looked for in servants of government upon pay received. Petitioners pay only 5/6 except in one instance 6/3 per day – that of ordinary labouring man in District is from 7/6 to 8/- respectfully request increase of pay.[43]

This petition recommended an increase in pay for the chief constable (12s per day), district constable (9s per day) and ordinary constables (8s per day) and argued that 'the Constabulary in all other parts of the world receive higher wages than the labouring classes but in this Province the reverse is true'.[44] Three months later, on 29 June 1854, the officers escalated their requests and appealed to the governor-general in Sydney to consider the salary increase to enable them to provide for their families.

The petition outlined that to support a family consisting of a husband, wife and two children, officers required more than the average wage of £8 5s per month to cover food, clothing and accommodation. Samuel must have found supporting a wife, eight children and a servant to be challenging even on his wage of £16 8s per month, although he may have managed to do this by supplementing his police income with his army pension and property investment.[45] In March 1852, Samuel invested in land and purchased a lot encompassing 36 perches on Adelaide Street for £22 10s. He received the title deeds in early 1853, and later built Stoke Cottage on the site, which had four rooms, plus a kitchen, servant's room, laundry, store, stable and water tank.[46] To supplement their income, the family of nine with seven children under 12 likely lived in a house provided by the government and rented out the Adelaide Street accommodations. In July 1853, William Mayne, the inspector-general of police in Sydney, agreed to look into only two of the five sections of the petition: the cost of supporting and educating families and the pressure on constabulary arising from extra escort duty expenses. He expressed his irritation at the 'seemingly unreasonableness of the petition and his great regret that Captain Wickham did not consider it his duty to discourage rather than recommend the petitioners'.[47]

The Final Years

At the beginning of 1856, Sneyd's large family was still living in their government-supplied house. Towards the end of the year,

Sneyd purchased an allotment of 3 acres and 20 perches on a street that later bore his name at Bowen Hills for £30 1s 3p.[48] Despite the increased wages and upward social mobility, Sneyd and other constables like him were unable to afford the passage home to visit the families they left behind. Sneyd's children never met their maternal or paternal grandparents, or their aunts and uncles, and Sneyd could not return home when his 87-year-old father, whom he had not seen for 26 years, passed away on 20 September 1856 at his home in Hanley, Staffordshire.[49]

The next few years were difficult for Sneyd personally and professionally. In 1856, in addition to receiving the news of his father's death, Sneyd concluded the year with policing local political upheaval. On 20 November 1856, a 'great' public meeting at the courthouse convened by Mr Wickham, the government resident, saw the specifics of the separation of the northern districts debated, which put further strain on the police.[50] In 1857, Sneyd experienced significant difficulties with the constables under his control as several prisoners escaped from custody. In August 1857, constables James Tredennick and Terence Rocks were executing a warrant for arrest of an Aboriginal man named Nelson at Logan, who was wanted on suspicion of the murder of a woman named Fredrika Klumpp and her son Gottlieb. The constables succeeded in finding and arresting Nelson but he escaped on their way back to Brisbane. Both officers were indicted for misdemeanour despite the dire circumstances of transporting the prisoner.[51] The policemen had been away for a fortnight and managed to apprehend Nelson at Mr White's station, and they reported that they 'brought him as far as Boggo Scrub, three miles from Brisbane, when he escaped from them'.[52]

In his testimony, Constable Rocks stated they got as far as the Logan River, which was too deep to cross. The constables tried to seek an alternative route before returning to the river to cross. They left their horses hobbled and took their swags, but they lost their way and had to walk 4 or 5 miles. Fatigued, they reached Jimboomba at 6 pm, but then lost their way in the dark and had to light matches to find the road. The constables arrived at Mr White's station around midnight and were exhausted. According to Constable Tredennick's statement, Nelson's escape occurred on the journey back to Brisbane:

> We then went on to where the blackfellow bolted. I never observed any deficiency in the way he was secured. When he bolted he let fall his bundle, and made both our horses shy. When I got off my horse to go after him I had not strength to run. My limbs were so stiff with walking and wading on the Tuesday night that I fell down directly trying to run. I do not think that any two constables could have exerted themselves more than we did.[53]

The lives of Chief Constable Sneyd and his policemen were made even more difficult when Brisbane and Ipswich were ravaged by a flood in May 1857 following eight weeks of light but continuous rain, which made travel within and between the towns impossible. These floods and the lead-up to them were remembered in the local *Brisbane Courier*: 'There had been a strong fresh in the river for several weeks, and during a portion of this time all vehicular traffic between North and South Brisbane was suspended as the horse-punt at Russell Street was unable to cross on account of the strong current.'[54] The floods in Brisbane and Ipswich disrupted court sittings as witnesses could not get to the courthouse and police officers were unable to go and retrieve them. *The North Australian, Ipswich and General Advertiser* stated 'that the remands were rendered imperative on the part of the Crown, owing to the flooded state of the creeks, and the consequent detention of material witnesses'.[55]

Rowboats plied the streets in the centre of Brisbane town and the entire low-lying area from Elizabeth Street to the river was a muddy lake. At South Brisbane, 'one could stand on a hill at Cordelia Street near Boundary Street and see an unbroken sheet of water stretching from Melbourne Street to Tribune Street'.[56] Montague Road from

Stanley Street to the Brisbane River was under water, as was Stanley Street and most of the scrublands at Oxley. Consequently, on the streets, police work involved wading through filthy water and, in more unusual circumstances, officers were required to lay a number of charges against residents who allowed their pigs to roam the streets in contravention of the 23rd clause of the town's *Police Act of 1838*. As reported by *The Moreton Bay Courier*:

> [In two cases] the defendants, who lived in the lower part of Elizabeth-street, pleaded that if they had not let their pigs loose, the animals would have been drowned, for the rains had flooded their allotments; and besides, they had since taken the precaution of killing the pigs, in order to prevent anything of the kind occurring in future. The charges against them were accordingly withdrawn. The Bench took occasion to observe that, in this wet weather, great injury was inflicted upon property by pigs being allowed to roam at large.[57]

In 1858, Chief Constable Sneyd suffered a heartbreaking and difficult personal setback when Kitty, his wife of 21 years, passed away suddenly from a severe fit of epilepsy on 25 July when she was only 46 years old. She left her grieving 47-year-old husband with the care of their nine children, the youngest only three years old. Her death and the tale of her burial were lamented most eloquently in *The Darling Downs Gazette and General Advertiser*:

> Poor Sneyd has been bereaved of an affectionate wife, and a family of nine children are left motherless. An additional sorrow was inflicted upon the widower on the morning of the interment. Through some unexplained reason it was found upon the corpse reaching the Catholic burial ground, that the priest, Dean Rigney, had been there, and after reading prayers over the empty grave had taken his departure. Poor Sam, like most other English Protestants, naturally felt the omission of reading the burial service over the body of the departed, as a want of respect, and, as it was learnt,

upon a gentleman going in search of the Dean, and found that he would not return. Mr. T. Warry, one of the mourners, read a portion of the Protestant burial service at the entrance gate of the cemetery, after which the company, who had congregated in large numbers out of respect to the family, dispersed, commenting very freely you may depend, upon the strange proceedings of the morning. I may just mention that although Mrs. Sneyd was of Catholic parentage, she had previous to her death expressed a wish to be interred in the Episcopalian burial ground. Her husband and family belongs to that religious body but the very Reverend Gentleman Mr. Yeatman, who officiates at the head of that Church in Brisbane refused to permit the request to be complied with.[58]

Despite the aforementioned display of sectarian strife, Sneyd was a popular and well-respected member of the Brisbane community, who rallied to support him during this difficult period of his life. On 11 August 1858, a contingent of Sneyd's fellow townsmen gave him a purse of £110 as a well-merited mark of their esteem for him as a police officer. The government resident and many of the magistracy were among the donors. When making the presentation, Mr Thomas Warry announced, 'Mr. Sneyd has been in the public service since 1827 as a soldier and a peace officer, the greater portion of his time having been spent in the colony. It will certainly afford him great satisfaction to find that whilst he has secured the approbation of his superiors in office, he has discharged duties, which rarely lead to popularity, in such a way as to secure the approbation and goodwill of the public.'[59]

The year continued to gain positivity for Sneyd when, in November 1858, his eldest son, William Hartley, married Miriam Wakefield and Sneyd himself wed Margaret Hyland, with whom he had a further six children.[60] Sneyd's family continued to grow and, half a year later, he purchased another allotment in the parish of Enoggera of 20 acres 2 roods, adjoining Enoggera Road and Alderson Street, where he built a home called Westwood.[61]

Figure 2.5: Brisbane, 1859, looking south along Queen Street from the corner of Edward Street. (State Library of Queensland, 8299)

In late November 1859, Sneyd resigned from the position of chief constable of Brisbane (Figure 2.5). According to a report on his resignation in *The Moreton Bay Courier*, 'The injury inflicted on his constitution by hard bush-work both night and day, in former years, [had] told upon him lately to such a degree that he [had] not been able satisfactorily to perform his night duties, and he accordingly made up his mind to resign his office.'[62] At the same time as Sneyd resigned from the force, the responsible post of governor at the new fit-for-purpose jail at Green Hills (present-day Petrie Terrace) became vacant. Sneyd was appointed as Gaoler of Her Majesty's gaol with his wife, Margaret, as matron.[63] At 48 years of age, and after almost nine years in service to Queensland as chief constable, Sneyd had left a legacy of good management that the policing of the state could lean on. Sneyd was also well respected by the public, as *The Moreton Bay Courier* expressed: 'As a public officer, Mr. Sneyd has made himself deservedly respected for the integrity of his character, and the ability with which he has discharged his duties.'[64] Samuel Sneyd died in 1885, but left children and grandchildren to carry on his name and good work as several of his children and then grandchildren followed his example and worked in government service in both the prison and postal systems.

Sneyd's service history exemplifies a common path that many military men followed in the early decades of the Australian colonial establishment. Military experience in Great Britain often translated into a posting in the colonies that afforded officers a promotion and a pay rise. As the paramilitary model of policing pioneered by the Irish Constabulary was deemed ideal for frontier patrol, men with military experience were in high demand and nascent colonial law enforcement organisations actively sought out ex-soldiers to bolster its ranks. After his successes in the rural mounted police, Samuel Sneyd was promoted to chief constable of Brisbane's police force in the mid-nineteenth century, a time when the colonial centre was rapidly expanding. Brisbane's economic and social development was followed by the diversification of the judiciary system and, eventually, the penal system, which led to the construction of the Brisbane Gaol in 1859. Coinciding with Queensland's separation from New South Wales, Sneyd resigned from the local police after almost a decade of arduous and continuous duties punctuated with personal losses and deteriorating health. Despite the trials and tragedies of law enforcement in colonial Brisbane, Sneyd, a career policeman, continued to serve the public and the force until the end of his life in his position as jailer.

3

Queensland's First Detective

Samuel Lloyd

Brisbane, my present capital, must resemble what Boston and the other Puritan towns of New England were at the close of the last century. In a population of 7,000 we have fourteen churches, thirteen hotels and twelve policemen.

Sir George Bowen[1]

IN 1859, QUEENSLAND gained political freedom by separating from New South Wales, but it inherited a policing system controlled by a corrupt magistracy and badly in need of reform. At the time of separation, the settled area of the colony was divided into 17 districts, each with its own police force under a chief constable who took orders from the local magistrate. However, as the population grew and the colonial landscape diversified, the policing network expanded to include the Mounted Border Police, the Native Police and the Volunteer Force (cavalry and infantry). As the colony became more established, Queensland Parliament, as a separate organisation, sought to standardise the colony's policing establishment and curtail power abuse and passed *An Act to Consolidate and Amend the Laws Relating to the Police Force* (also known as the *Queensland Police Act*) in 1863. To begin this process of standardisation, Police Constable Samuel John Collis Lloyd, an experienced detective from the Victoria Police, was invited to lead the newly formed detective office in Brisbane. When Lloyd arrived in Brisbane with its 'atrociously kept shops, and houses few and far between with bullock teams frequently blocking the thoroughfares', he found a town, and a police force, in need of innovation.[2] Under Lloyd, the new Queensland Police Force was organised and regulated following the Irish forces, and its officers were distinguishable from the volunteer units by their uniforms: a dark blue jacket and top with a forage cap. The *Queensland Police Act* took effect on 1 January 1864, a year when Lloyd and his nascent force, along with the Brisbane community, were tested by a series of natural and manmade disasters.

'A gentleman's son'

Samuel Lloyd was born in County Cork, Ireland in 1829, and was listed as an indentured apprentice in the Cork merchant navy aboard the vessel *Margaret 128* from May 1840 to May 1844.[3] In 1850, when he was 21 years old, he married 19-year-old Eliza Ann South, a milliner from Waterford, and their daughter Isabella was born the same year. By 1854, the Lloyds had immigrated to Australia and Constable Lloyd had joined the Victoria Police, although he resigned three years later.

In 1858, following a recommendation by the superintendent of Geelong Police, Lloyd reapplied to join the force. On 22 September 1858, he was sworn in again to 'well and truly serve our Sovereign Lady the Queen, in the office of Constable, without favour or affection, malice or ill-will'.[4] However, on 3 December 1864, Lloyd resigned from the Victoria Police for good following his appointment as sub-inspector of the Detective Branch of the Queensland Police. The superintendent of Carisbrook, where Lloyd was stationed for the final years of his service with the Victoria Police, was sorry to see him leave: 'Det. Lloyd is a zealous, efficient and attentive man and will be a great loss to the Service. I regret exceedingly his leaving the force and more particularly this district as I am of opinion that his place will not be easily filled.

I have never had occasion to find the least fault with him during the period I have been in charge of this District in three years.'[5]

Lloyd left a legacy of 'extremely good and very efficient' conduct with the Victoria Police as in 1864 alone he had received three awards.[6] In March, Detective First Class Samuel Lloyd, along with Senior Constable Bennett at Talbot, was awarded a sum of £1 to acknowledge their expertness and diligence in the arrest of Ah Hui, an escaped prisoner.[7] In May and June, Lloyd received £2 10s for zeal and activity in recovering a mob of cattle rescued from a pound paddock. On 29 October, Lloyd was awarded a further £5 in acknowledgment of his attention in the arrest and prosecution of Matthew King, who was sentenced to five years' imprisonment for cattle stealing.[8] Most Victorian land was occupied by squatters and pastoralists, so stock killing and cattle stealing were endemic. *An Act for the Better Prevention of Cattle Stealing and the Sale of Stolen Cattle*, or the *Cattle Stealing and Prevention Act*, of 1853 provided a penalty of £50 and costs for possession of stolen skins or carcasses, and £20 or 12 months' imprisonment for working or using cattle without consent of the owner.[9] Regardless of earlier attempts to criminalise the common practice of cattle duffing, considerably more offences occurred than subsequent arrests. Police found it difficult to contain the stock-stealing situation in the vast and sparsely settled countryside, and it was difficult to obtain a guilty verdict from juries, who likely may have been involved in a bit of cattle duffing on the side themselves.

Queensland Police Act (1863)

Like Victoria, the nascent colony of Queensland experienced difficulties in managing crime in the 1860s. Between 1861 and 1864, Brisbane town's population more than doubled from 6,051 to 12,551, which put a significant strain on the existing police resources. In an attempt to improve the situation, Colonial Secretary Robert Herbert proposed a bill to consolidate the laws relating to the police in May 1862. The key departure from the existing organisation was

Herbert's recommendation to appoint a paid officer to superintend the police of the colony, which was similar to the structure used in Victoria. In 1862, the department was increasing rapidly, and the expenses in connection with its operation amounted to £50,000 for a force of just over 20 men.[10] In today's equivalent, this would amount to a staggering £5,904,687. In comparison, the present-day London Metropolitan Police with a contingent of 30,000 men has an operational budget of £47,000,000.[11] The colonial secretary provided economic justification for the reform: 'by having an officer responsible for the management of [the police] department, a saving of several thousand pounds, would [...] be effected in the supply of stores, the pay of constables, and in many other matters'.[12] The pay of constables was fixed when the goldfields broke out and 'everything was very dear', so an entry-level constable received 5s 6p per day, and those of a higher grade received 6s 3p per day, which is roughly between £212–260 per week in today's equivalent.[13]

Robert Herbert's proposed bill also intimated collusion and nepotism within the existing organisation: 'as long as [the constable] was well behaved in his own district, and pleased his own magistrate, he had nothing to fear'.[14] This issue was not limited to organisations in Brisbane, as earlier overseas forces had also experienced rampant corruption of local magistrates. For example, in 1812, Dublin citizens presented a petition to the Lord Lieutenant of Ireland complaining about the conduct of the police magistrates, including their connection with gambling houses. The petition also exposed the magistrates' 'improper use of police horses and supplies, and employment of paid constables as "domestic and menial Servants"'.[15] However, those in opposition to the bill feared the proposed changes would 'throw more patronage into the hands of the Government'.[16]

Following Herbert's bill, the Queensland Parliament proposed that an efficient person to control the police of the colony be appointed from the outside: 'The person appointed should be some person fully acquainted with the working of the Irish or

Melbourne constabulary. [As] it was well known that the Melbourne constabulary was one of the most efficient in the world – equal, perhaps, to the Irish Constabulary.'[17] After much debate, the newly established Queensland Parliament passed the *Queensland Police Act* in 1863, which established a centrally organised colonial force and placed it under the commissionership of David Thompson Seymour. This appointment marked the beginning of an independent era of local policing.[18] Lieutenant Seymour was from Ballymore Castle, Galway, and had joined the British Army at the age of 25. Though he lacked direct Irish constabulary experience, he was of military pedigree. Seymour's father was a high-sheriff and a lieutenant-colonel of the Galway Militia.[19] Seymour arrived in Brisbane with a detachment of the 12th (East Suffolk) Regiment of Foot in 1861, and within a year he became an aide-de-camp to the colony's first governor, George Bowen. Seymour was officially appointed as police commissioner in July 1864, and he inherited 150 foot and mounted officers along with 137 native mounted police. From the moment Seymour took office, he began to shape the force into a colony-wide body. Finding that no written instructions had ever been released for the guidance of the police commissioner, Seymour issued *Rules for the General Government and Discipline of Members of the Police Force of Queensland*, which were based on the Victorian police model and the Royal Irish Constabulary regulations.

On 1 January 1864, 26 new ordinary (general duty) constables took to the Brisbane streets with vigilant guardianship of person and property as one of their key principles. The newly appointed Queensland constables took an oath 'to see and cause Her Majesty's peace to be kept and preserved, and to prevent, to the best of his power, all offences against the same'.[20] Absence of crime was considered the strongest evidence that could be given of the complete efficiency of the police. However, this task proved to be especially difficult in Brisbane given the low ordinary police to population ratio of 1 police officer to 600 inhabitants.

1864: Highs and Lows

The Queensland Police Detective Office began operating on 1 December 1864, 11 months after the inauguration of the Queensland Police Force, and Samuel Joseph Lloyd was placed as the officer in charge (OIC). The number of detectives in the office was nominal, as it was not a separate department within the force, and was drawn from the best police officers in Brisbane. There were two classes of detectives: detective constable first class and detective constable second class. Employed only on a part-time basis, the detectives spent their remaining work hours carrying out ordinary police duties. They received no extra pay despite the complicated nature of their work and the long, arduous hours they often worked during criminal investigations. Between 1864 and 1867, Lloyd was OIC of the Detective Branch, and sub-inspector for Brisbane, with an annual salary of £200. There were only two other men employed to work alongside him, who were also employed on ordinary duty.[21] With the resources already stretched, the nascent force was not well equipped to respond to extraordinary circumstances such as natural disasters.

In February 1864, heavy floods inundated the colony (Figure 3.1). Brisbane residents were accustomed to being flooded in a downpour 'because of the many waterholes and the creek flowing between, and roughly parallel with Queen and Adelaide Streets' and 'Shops with cellars on Queen Street frequently found stock inundated and many buildings stood on small stumps to keep floor levels out of the water.'[22] Despite this, the colonial infrastructure in the town was not able to withstand major flooding. The central streets of Brisbane primarily consisted of the penal settlement buildings, such as the old prisoners' barracks on Queen Street, which were repurposed as the new colony's parliament.[23] Queensland's own Parliament House in George Street was not built until 1865. The female convicts' barracks (where the General Post Office is located today) had been turned into a store and home for the volunteer fire brigade. Most of the buildings were timber with shingle roofs, and were therefore vulnerable to the elements. In *Australian Pioneers and Reminiscences*, Nehemiah Bartley describes the sudden and devastating 1864 floods: 'a hurricane blew. The river rose fifty feet in twelve hours at Ipswich. A heavy lifeboat was blown over like a hat for two hundred yards on the beach at Moreton Island [...] Boats were rowed in Mary Street.'[24] The following month, the water gradually rose on Sunday 20 March, and after midday 'Albert street, from Alice street to Charlotte street, was totally impassable, and many residents in Frog's Hollow were compelled to leave their houses and furniture to the mercy of devastating elements.'[25] Due to the expansion of the population and industry in the settlement, the floods of 1864 were far more devastating than those that had come before.

Figure 3.1: View down Charlotte Street to Old Frog's Hollow during the flood of 1864. (State Library of Queensland, 22130)

The situation worsened later in the year when Brisbane was ravaged by fires, which presented further challenges for the colonists and the police. On 4 September 1864, a major fire broke out at the

Little Wonders shop on Edward Street. Constable Blake, who was on duty at the time, was the first to discover the blaze at about a 1.15 am. The constable was walking his beat 'when his attention was attracted by observing an unusual light in the shop known as the "Little Wonders", which was kept as a place of business for the sale of books and miscellaneous articles, by a person named Marriott, who used to be the proprietor of a book-stall in Queen-street'.[26] Constable Blake tried to break into the store with the assistance of some passers-by but was unsuccessful. The fire spread to the adjacent building belonging to Mr Bulcock, which stored a quantity of corn, potatoes and vegetables. When the Number One Fire Brigade clad in red shirts, along with 40 members of the Volunteer Fire Brigade (led by Mr Cutbush), arrived on the scene, they were also unable to extinguish the fire. The men focused on securing the neighbouring wooden structures, and Leck's photographic gallery was saved by pouring a tank of water over it. Eventually, Mr Bulcock's building was torn down and the fire contained. A significant section of one-storey buildings along Edward Street, known as Refuge Row, was burnt to the ground. Little Wonders, the epicentre of the fire, was insured for £350.[27]

The next day, shortly after midnight, an alarm of fire was raised in the city once again. *The Brisbane Courier* reported the event in detail:

> suddenly awakened sleepers were excited to a fever of anxiety by the breaking out of flames in a house situated on Bowen Terrace, directly opposite Kangaroo Point. A living stream of people rapidly poured through Queen and Ann streets across the Gas Company's reserve, and along the river bank, to the scene of disaster. Arrived there amongst the crowd, we learned that the house on fire was a new one on the eve of completion for Mr. R.R. Smellie, head clerk of the A.S.N. Co's Brisbane agency. It was a wooden structure of fair proportions, and had not been delivered by the architect and contractor to the proprietor but was to have been so delivered this week.[28]

According to the *Brisbane Courier* coverage, several members of the Citizens Fire Brigade, again led by Mr Cutbush, battled the blaze: 'Members of the Volunteer Artillery Company of the Fire Brigade No 1, and of the city police force did their best to raze the burning building and to clear the ground.'[29] The magisterial inquiry following the disaster found that the fire was caused by a person or persons unknown.[30] Mr Smellie was not as lucky as Mr Marriott, the owner of the Little Wonders shop, as his new house was not insured.

On 1 December 1864, another fire broke out on Queen Street and destroyed 50 tenement buildings, including two banks, three hotels and four drapery establishments. Just before 8 pm, a blaze was observed in the cellar underneath Stewart and Hemmant's store. The news was quickly conveyed to the police station, and 'the fire bell pealed forth loud notes of alarm'. When the available force arrived at the scene, 'the doors of the doomed building were broken in when it was found that the whole interior was one vast sheet of flame'.[31] Cutbush's brigade and a detachment of the 12th Regiment, headed by Lieutenant Mair, arrived at the scene 'and rendered material assistance in keeping a clear space for the men who were working with an energy and fearlessness that deserves the utmost praise'. *The Brisbane Courier* also noted that the 'Police rendered good service'.[32]

The number of small houses destroyed by the fire was impossible to determine, but the newspaper reported that 'the whole of the shops in Albert-street from Stewart and Hemmant's down to Ballantyne and M'Nab's coach factory, which latter place escaped almost by a miracle, were destroyed'.[33] The insurance companies suffered great losses: Pacific Fire and Marine Insurance Company, the Queensland Insurance Company and the Sydney Insurance Company each lost around £1000 in damages to their office buildings. The fire destroyed much of the east block between Albert and George streets, including prominent buildings such as the Victoria Hotel, the Union Bank and the Sovereign Hotel. The total loss of property has been roughly estimated at £60,000. An inquest following the disaster showed the fire originated at the Stewart and

Hemmant drapery store.³⁴ In the aftermath of the fire, the insurance companies paid out tens of thousands of pounds to cover the losses. Mr Hemmant's stock alone was insured for £10,000.

Figure 3.2: Great fire in Queen Street, Brisbane, 1864.
(State Library of Queensland, 125754)

An article in *The Brisbane Courier* the next morning depicted the scene of destruction that greeted Brisbane residents:

> at dawn of day, the scene of the late fire presented a desolate appearance. The site on the previous day occupied by a long line of shops, which, if not particularly handsome or imposing, still were the centre of the retail traffic of Brisbane, was nought but a smoking heap of ruins. Occasionally, when a burnt through beam gave way, a dull hollow sound of falling bricks might be heard, raising a cloud of dust.³⁵ (Figure 3.2)

The goods that were rescued were all piled on the street outside the ravaged structures and guarded by policemen and soldiers, as well as volunteers (Figures 3.3a and 3.3b). Three men were injured by falling roofs, which they were trying to pull down to stop the blaze from spreading to nearby structures.[36] Considering the extent of the fire, the casualties were few, and most of the injuries sustained were not of a serious nature. As reported in *The Brisbane Courier*:

> four men and a boy were taken to the Hospital. Mr. Cutbush, one of the sufferers, sustained a severe wound in the throat, and was insensible for half an hour. On his coming to, the wound was dressed, and a speedy recovery is anticipated. The other cases were, as far as could be ascertained, simply bruises. Many narrow escapes were witnessed, but fortunately no life was lost.[37]

Figure 3.3a: Stereoscopic views of the 1864 Brisbane fire.
(State Library of Queensland, 30115 01)

Figure 3.3b: Stereoscopic views of the 1864 Brisbane fire.
(State Library of Queensland, 30115 03)

In his musings, a *Brisbane Courier* reporter noted that the responsibilities conferred on policemen and soldiers alike during the fires induced thirst and, contrary to the regulations, 'in their natural desire to quench [their thirst] as speedily as possible the absence of water had overcome their repugnance to fermented and spirituous liquors, and the consequence was, that neither they or their firearms were for any length of time in a position that would excite much admiration in the mind of a martinet'.[38] The article also singled out and praised a lone volunteer who kept watch and ward opposite Messrs Morey and

Forbes' drapery establishment, where he had been stationed on the evening of the fire. According to the report, the man was 'deaf to all the blandishments which were temptingly placed before him, in the shape of illicitly obtained beer, porter, or champagne, as to partake of them would have necessitated his departure from his post. He marched on his beat with as much circumspection as if he were on parade, and many attempts to get him to disobey orders were made in vain.'[39] Professional and volunteer efforts proved effective as the police court reports for December 1864 and January 1865 do not show any cases of looting.

Daily Police Business

Despite the disasters that plagued Brisbane in 1864, day-to-day police business proceeded as usual, with cases of drunkenness and assaults dominating the city police courts. On 5 December 1864, Cosmo Morris, James Wilson, James Dunne, Henry Jordan and William Green appeared before the police magistrate and were each fined 10s for drunkenness.[40] This case was followed by James Thompson, whose offence was drunkenness aggravated by violent and disorderly conduct, for which he was fined 40s. On the same day, Robert Cook was brought before the magistrate on suspicion of being of unsound mind (charged with lunacy) but he was discharged. In a summons case of Farrell v. Quigley, the defendant was fined 20s for assault and 4s 6d costs (or seven days in the cells in default).[41] On 26 December, Peter Dougall was fined 20s for using obscene language. Dougall was later fined 25s for destroying government property in an attempt to escape from the lock-up.[42]

While dealing with the fires and floods, and the day-to-day petty crime committed by the colony's citizenry, Detective Inspector Lloyd also had to process some strange offences. One such case was of 'Larceny by a Servant' on 1 October 1865, in which William Rennie was indicted at the supreme court, criminal session for feloniously stealing 36 volumes of books and one photographic album while working as a clerk for bookseller George Slater (Figure 3.4 shows one of the maps printed by Slater). Mr Slater

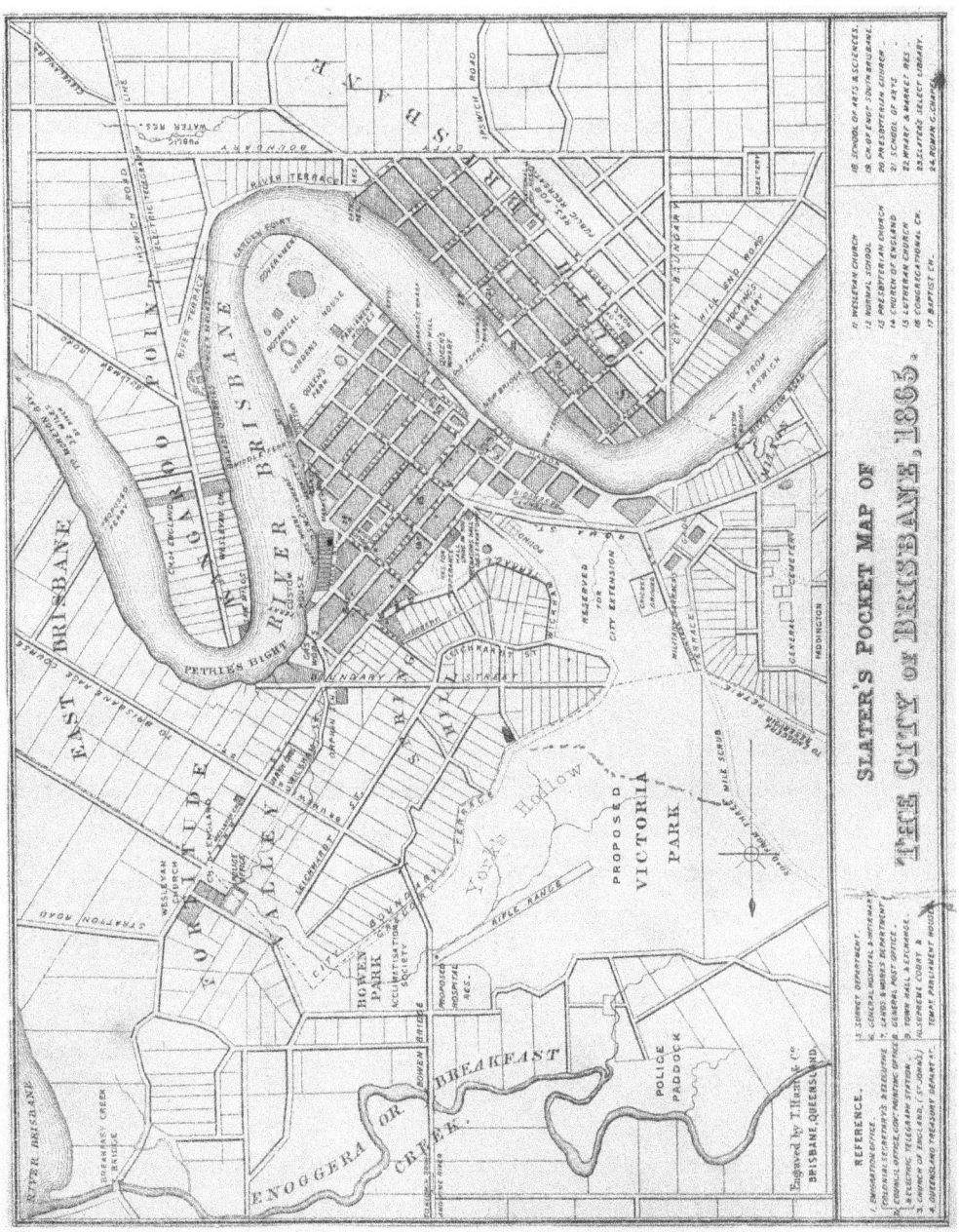

Figure 3.4: Slater's pocket map, 1865. (State Library of Queensland, APA-59, Nicholson Family Photograph Album)

was suspicious of Rennie's behaviour and went with Inspector Lloyd and Mr Tevlin, the landlord of the City Arms Hotel where Rennie lodged, and searched Rennie's bedroom, where they found 36 books on a table. Rennie admitted they were Mr Slater's, and that he had taken them, but said he had only taken them to read. The jury found the prisoner guilty, with a recommendation for mercy, and he was sentenced to be imprisoned in Brisbane Gaol for 12 calendar months.[43]

Despite the disasters that plagued the city in 1864, municipal infrastructure kept developing and, on 29 November, businesses in Brisbane were illuminated by gas for the first time. This advancement aided policemen in witnessing crimes that previously would have occurred under the cover of darkness. For example, around midnight on the night of 21 December, W Thornton, chief inspector of distilleries, and Sub-Inspector Lloyd watched James Behan conveying a keg of spirits into the George Street Hotel on Edward Street. Lloyd then gave Behan in charge to the watch house. A few days later, Behan was brought up on remand at the central police court on a charge of illegally conveying spirits upon which the duty had not been paid. He pleaded not guilty. It was elicited in the cross-examination of Thornton that the prisoner had received authority to methylate spirits in bond (investors in authority bonds had a right to claim their bonds' yield directly from the net profit of the business). The case was adjourned with bail set at £100 and two sureties at £50 each.[44] The outcome of this intriguing case was not covered by the newspaper as it was postponed until after Christmas Day.

As the municipal amenities in the colony improved, and the population continued to grow, the number of businesses in Brisbane rapidly expanded. This afforded fraudsters and swindlers abundant grounds for criminal activity as 'the success rate of these crimes depended on the existence of ignorant or credulous persons' in addition to a population large enough to provide criminals with anonymity and therefore help them avoid detection.[45] In one such case investigated by Sub-Inspector Lloyd, a young man named William BM Innes (also Ennis) was charged with using worthless cheques throughout the colony. The police had been watching Innes for some time, and, when he arrived in Brisbane from Rockhampton, Innes was arrested by Constable Robert Kilfedder, an experienced policeman with previous service in the Irish Constabulary.[46] However, as *The Brisbane Courier* reported, the arrest did not proceed as planned:

> Innes was arrested, and when within a few yards from the lock-up, he was seen holding a small phial at his mouth. It was snatched from him by the constable who had hold of him, but too late, for he had drank nearly all of its contents. He was immediately placed in the lock-up office, and Dr. Hobbs was called in; but, as he had taken prussic acid, nothing could be done to save his life, and he died in about twenty minutes.[47]

At the inquest into the Innes case, Sub-Inspector Lloyd deposed that he knew the deceased six years previously when Innes worked as a bank clerk in Sandhurst, Victoria. The jury returned the verdict of *felo de se*.

'Crime Triumphant'

On 6 June 1866, His Excellency the Governor sanctioned an award of £50 from the Police Reward Fund to Sub-Inspector Samuel J Lloyd for his diligence in procuring convictions in certain important cases.[48] However, not all were convinced of Lloyd's diligence. In a letter to the editor published in *The Brisbane Courier* on 30 July 1867, Samuel Clifford aired some grievances and laid allegations against the Queensland Police detectives in general and Samuel Lloyd specifically. In his piece titled 'Police Obtrusiveness and Defectiveness', Clifford opined that 'improper obtrusiveness on the part of a police force is an undue interference with the immunities which should be enjoyed equally by the inhabitants of every free country'. His complaint stemmed from the fact that upon his cousin's sudden death from a fit that resulted in a fall and suffocation while unconscious, the property of the deceased was secured by the police until a claim came for its collection. Clifford asked readers, 'Are you content to entrust the safety of your chattels, and the disposition of your effects, to any individual policeman who may force himself into the position of the administrator?'[49] These sentiments reflect that the legitimacy and honesty of the young colonial force was still very much under question three years after its inception, particularly because of the high turnover of its recruits.

The strict rules of police service (which allowed little personal time), exhausting duty and the hostility of the general public towards police officers all contributed to an extremely high turnover rate during the first decade of the force's existence. The majority of recruits throughout the nineteenth century were younger sons of farmers, semiskilled workers and labourers whose work days were mostly unregulated. The term 'labourer' covered a wide range of employment within the unskilled, and often rural, work sector. The *Register of Members of the Police Force, 1856–1917* shows recruits with 'labourer' entered as a previous calling dominated Queensland Police ranks. By the end of 1864, 14 per cent of the men sworn in to the force had either been dismissed or quit. By the end of the decade, 114 men (half of the men sworn in in 1864) had left the police force.[50]

In addition to questioning police interference in his *Brisbane Courier* letter, Clifford questioned the integrity of the force. Clifford laid out allegations of incompetence and neglect of duty against Detective Lloyd and his men using examples of unchecked crimes, such as shops open on the Sabbath, 'a ruffianly attempt to violate a young woman in her bed-chamber', burglary of a property in Gregory Terrace, and 'a capital crime perpetrated in the city, a few weeks ago, upon a girl of tender years'.[51] The day after Clifford's letter to the editor, another article by a 'Sufferer' appeared in *The Brisbane Courier* and added a gang of marauders who destroyed 'poor Mr Macpherson's house and crops only a few miles outside of Brisbane' to Lloyd's personal oversights.[52] Both authors believed that Detective Lloyd's ineffectiveness was not due to personnel shortages, inadequate training or poor quality of men in the force, but instead to Lloyd's social standing. As Clifford asserted, 'it seems that some of our police officers are too "high-minded" for their positions, and consequently above performing the duties of their office. They are sporting "gentlemen", who would be degraded by arresting – and whose hands would be sullied by contact with a criminal.'[53] Lloyd's personnel file does not reflect any official complaints against him; however, he was transferred to the Wide Bay District from 1867 to 1892, which could indicate that there was some substance to these allegations.

Wide Bay District (1867–1892)
Following his rural transfer, Samuel J Lloyd was promoted to inspector second class in October 1868, and in 1869 he was appointed as inspector of distilleries in the Wide Bay District.[54] Lloyd also frequently gave expert witness statements and prosecuted cases at the Brisbane Central Police Court and the supreme courts across Queensland. More so, in 1870, Lloyd received a commendation and a monetary reward for the police work in the district under his command in the case of the murder of Patrick Halligan. Homicides were rare in the mid-nineteenth century, averaging at two guilty verdicts per year at the time of the Halligan case.[55] Halligan was found shot through the chest in scrubland near Rockhampton on 25 April 1870, and a reward of £300 was offered for any information that would lead to the apprehension or conviction of the murderer or murderers, and a free pardon to an accomplice not actually the murderer.[56] In October, Alexander Archibald and George Charles Frederick Palmer were charged with Halligan's murder after the considerable reward and free pardon offered by the colonial secretary induced Archibald to confess to the murder. Palmer was arrested by the

police on Archibald's advice, though he stated that he was about to turn himself in.[57] On 11 October 1869, Palmer was indicted for the wilful murder and initially pleaded not guilty, but he later confessed to the crime.[58] In his confession, Palmer stated that Archibald incited him to 'stick up' Halligan on the victim's way back from the diggings, and that Archibald provided him with firearms for the purpose. Both Palmer and Archibald, as well as their co-defendant, Williams, were found guilty of murder at the Rockhampton District Court and executed in November 1869 at the Rockhampton Gaol.[59] According to the *Queensland Police Gazette, General Order 439*, 'His Excellency the Governor in Council [was] pleased to award to Inspector S. J. Lloyd, the sum of twenty-five guineas, in recognition of his services in the apprehension and prosecution of the late G. F. Palmer, concerned in the murder of Patrick Halligan.'[60]

The remainder of Inspector Lloyd's time was preoccupied with prosecutions for horse stealing and escort duties, such as escorting gold nuggets from the diggings to the bank at a main centre for exchange into banknotes, which were then taken back to the goldfields. It was the officer's duty to supervise the sergeant and the men escorting the valuables 'to satisfy himself as to the vigilance of the men and the security of everything connected with the treasure and the conveyance'.[61] Just before Christmas in 1879, Inspector Lloyd escorted an unusually large amount of gold from Gympie to Maryborough, a total of 7,246 ozs 9 dwts 6 grs, along with 3,000 sovereigns (US$9,000,000 in present-day monetary equivalent).[62]

The arduous, and sometimes dangerous, work and the harsh climate of the Wide Bay District took a toll on Lloyd's health. Throughout much of September and October 1884, he was confined to his room suffering from rheumatism, and in November he had a severe rheumatic attack.[63] In January 1885, Lloyd was visited by the police surgeon, who recommended complete rest, so Lloyd applied for six months of extended leave to go to the southern colonies.[64] Inspector Lloyd punctuated the rest of his time in Maryborough with short trips to Brisbane until his final transfer back to the Metropolitan District in 1892.

Return to Brisbane

In 1892, Inspector Lloyd returned to Brisbane and again took charge of the Detective Branch. Three years later, amid economic and social unrest in the colony, Police Commissioner Seymour stepped down, and William Parry-Okeden took command of the force. In his first report to the parliament, Parry-Okeden indicated that he found 'the detective force required thorough reorganisation, and it was considered best to establish a Criminal Investigation Branch in lieu; and those detective officers whose services were retained were absorbed into the regular police, receiving equivalent ranks and pay'.[65] Following this, in May 1896, *General Order 678* was issued, stating that members of the police force attached to the Criminal Investigation Branch (CIB) would always, when on ordinary duty, appear in plain clothes, and that they would only appear in the regulation uniform when required to give evidence in the police or other courts, subject to special instructions that their officer might see fit to issue.[66]

On 1 July 1895, the Detective Office was separated from the workings of the ordinary police and became known as the CIB. (Figure 3.5 is a list of the first 'detectives' in the CIB.) In January the following year, First Class Inspector Lloyd was, subject to the control and authority of the commissioner of police, charged with the government direction and superintendence of the CIB across several police districts.[67] However, one month later, Inspector Lloyd was superannuated and Sub-Inspector First Class James Nethercote took charge of the new branch along with a detective senior sergeant, four first class detective sergeants, a second class detective senior constable, an acting third class detective sergeant and two third class detective constables. These detectives were drawn from the uniformed ranks and selected based on their natural aptness or predisposition towards detective work.

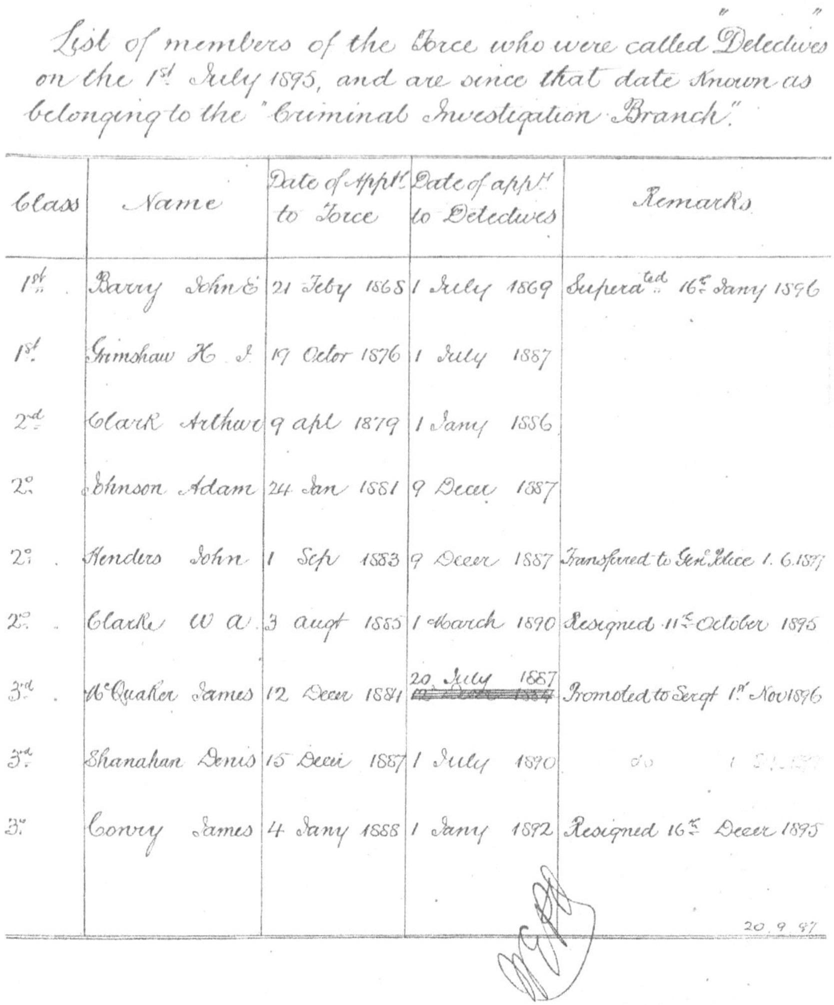

List of members of the force who were called "Detectives" on the 1st July 1895, and are since that date known as belonging to the "Criminal Investigation Branch".

Class	Name	Date of Appt. to Force	Date of appt. to Detectives	Remarks
1st	Barry John E	21 Feby 1868	1 July 1869	Superannuated 16th Jany 1896
1st	Grimshaw H. J.	19 Octor 1876	1 July 1887	
2d	Clark Arthur	9 apl 1879	1 Jany 1886	
2°	Johnson Adam	24 Jan 1881	9 Decer 1887	
2°	Henders John	1 Sep 1883	9 Decer 1887	Transferred to Genl Place 1.6.1897
2°	Clarke W. A.	3 augt 1885	1 March 1890	Resigned 11th October 1895
3d	McQuaker James	12 Decer 1881	20 July 1887	Promoted to Sergt 1st Nov 1896
3d	Shanahan Denis	15 Decr 1887	1 July 1890	do
3°	Conroy James	4 Jany 1888	1 Jany 1892	Resigned 16th Decer 1895

20.9.97

Figure 3.5: Members of the force who were called 'Detectives' on 1 July 1895. (Queensland Police Museum Collection)

Of the 10 men who formed the CIB, 'half were from Ireland [including Lloyd] two from England, two from New South Wales, and one from Scotland; five out of ten men had previous law enforcement experience, including metropolitan [city police] forces'. Detective Sergeant John Henders, for example, had served with the Dublin Metropolitan Police, and Detective Constable Second Class

William Archer Clarke had worked with the London Metropolitan Police.[68] A year after the reorganisation, Parry-Okeden was pleased to report that between 1896 and 1897 convictions in the supreme and district courts more than doubled, which he attributed to the increased efficiency of the CIB.[69]

In support of *General Order 678* and its provision for officers to appear in plain clothes when on ordinary duty, ex-Inspector Lewis stated in his evidence to the royal commission that he did not believe in detectives wearing uniforms or disguises.[70] Lewis said, '[His] experience was that the better men were known the more information they got.'[71] This sentiment was shared by senior police officers in Victoria who were at the time 'advocating an increased detective function for ordinary police, and increase in the number of men patrolling in plain clothes'. Inspector Henry Cawsey in particular was a strong advocate of increased plain-clothes policing, and commented that the 'thief cannot know where the plain clothes man is [...] a plain clothes man may pop up at any moment'.[72] In 1906, the desirability of increasing the numbers of plain-clothes police and having them work the city beats 'irregularly and contrawise to the uniformed men', was one of the key recommendations of a royal commission established to investigate the organisation of the police force in Victoria.[73]

The CIB was initially housed in the manse belonging to St John's Cathedral as the church property was sold to the Queensland Government in 1901. Specialised training was not offered immediately after the branch was reorganised. However, in his report for 1897, Parry-Okeden detailed new developments that aimed to increase the education levels of the men in the service: 'It will be seen that every effort is made to teach the police their duties, so as to fit them to perform their work credibly and to maintain discipline.'[74] Following this report, a weekly Wednesday night class of instruction in general knowledge and police duties was introduced, which was attended by all the members of the force stationed at the Police Depot, as well as by all recruits. At the time, recruits completed drill training, including squad and company, physical and dumbbell; fatigue work as required; and read aloud each afternoon. Those men deemed suitable were also taught to ride and maintain a bicycle. In addition, from 1895 onwards, the Police Museum was used to instruct recruits in the various methods employed by criminals.[75]

Queensland Police Museum

The Queensland Police Museum was established on 27 November 1893. Mr Finucane, Chief Clerk of the Queensland Police at the time, signed a memorandum on behalf of Commissioner Seymour that instructed all police officers to send in items of interest concerning crimes and suicides. Initially, the museum consisted only of boxes of evidence, which expanded into a glass cabinet collection in 1895 and then a small room. The collection was by nature eclectic. The exhibits in the museum were 'a painful reminder that criminal instincts, slumbering in the hearts of men, like extinct volcanoes, belch forth at times in full eruption'.[76] On the right of the entrance door, lethal weapons used in the various murders committed in the colony were arranged on a long shelf. An article about the Police Museum in *The Brisbane Courier* described these objects and the crimes they related to:

> A photograph of the neat grave in which sleep the mortal remains of poor Rudolf Weismuller, murdered at Mooraree on the 5th of April, 1892, and his blood-stained garments, recall the recollection of the effort of the brave German youth to better the lot of his family and himself by emigration to our shores, and the inhospitable fate he met with. Now 6ft. of earth are all too wide to hold their shattered hopes. Equally sad is the fate of the French hermit, Gervaise Dubroeca. Here is a picture of his lonely camp in the scrub, where he made baskets. Here the pole on which he hawked his wares to our doors, and here a small piece of a broken penknife found embedded in his neck, sole witness of the bloody deed, sole relic

left by the unknown assassin. An evil-looking face is that of G. F. Blantern, hanged for murdering Flora McDonald at Marlborough, on 8th May, 1893. Above the photo of the murderer hangs the axe with which he perpetrated the deed.[77]

These objects were initially housed at the Petrie Terrace Depot and police officers were required to see the display as part of their training. There are only a few objects from the original collection left as some items were transferred to the Queensland Museum in the 1930s, but the rest have disappeared over the last 125 years. A fake gold nugget from 1894, 'a cunningly wrought imitation gold nugget made from brass', currently on display is the oldest original object still in the collection.[78]

In the latter half of the nineteenth century, policing organisations across the Australian colonies underwent a series of reforms aimed at professionalising law enforcement bodies. Lloyd's police service spanned nearly half a century, consuming his skills, knowledge and, eventually, his health. Lloyd joined the Victoria Police in 1854, a year after it was established, but resigned from his post in Carisbrook a decade later and joined the Queensland Police Force the same year the *Queensland Police Act* was promulgated. Rising through the ranks, Lloyd's life was shaped by his experience as a policeman. His extensive and varied service with detective offices in Victoria and later in Queensland contributed to the development of a key element of the force: the specialised detective unit. Following 32 years in service to the Queensland Police Force, and 42 years of employment 'under the most gracious Sovereign Lady Queen Victoria', Inspector Lloyd applied to retire. He was superannuated on 19 February 1896 at a pension of £450 per annum.[79] Samuel John Collis Lloyd died on 24 May 1909 in his residence at 45 Brown Street, New Farm.[80] He was survived by his wife, Eliza Ann.

4

Beat Policing

Thomas Tyrrell

> The constable, though frequently acting on specific orders applicable to the occasion, is very generally, in the execution of his duty as a peace officer, called upon to act on his own responsibility; he therefore requires discretion, intelligence, decision, and perfect command of temper.
>
> 'Constables', *Manual of Police Regulations for the Guidance of the Constabulary of Queensland*[1]

THOMAS TYRRELL WAS born in 1838 in Maynooth, County Kildare, Ireland.[2] He served with the Royal Irish Constabulary, stationed in County Tyron, for three years before resigning in June 1865.[3] Soon after his resignation, Thomas departed for Queensland aboard the *Venilia*, and he arrived in Brisbane in October 1865.[4] On 7 February the following year, when he was 28 years old, Thomas Tyrrell was sworn in to the Queensland Police Force. At the time, applicants with previous police or military service were favoured by the colonial forces. Thomas Tyrrell was an ideal applicant for the Queensland Police: single, literate, free of bodily complaints and with previous police service in Ireland.[5]

Recruitment

The Queensland Police were moulded to be symbols 'of the aspirations and ideals of colonial authorities seeking to fashion a more stable and cohesive society'. Further, as Victorian police historian Dean Wilson argues in his chapter on symbolism in early policing, of the symbols of state power, the police were perhaps the most significant.[6] Policemen ensured the town laws were enforced by continuous presence on the streets through day and night duties. Under the *Queensland Police Act* (1863), persons appointed to the force were sworn in for one year in the first instance, during which period they could not voluntarily leave the force, but, when they had served a year, they were allowed to leave after providing three months' notice.[7] However, constables could be discharged for unfitness, or dismissed for negligence or misconduct.[8]

Recruitment and training took place in Brisbane at the Police Depot on Petrie Terrace, despite complaints from country hopefuls of their inability to travel to Brisbane. All candidates for admission into the police force had to submit an application in their own handwriting, along with 'such testimonials as they may have' at 9 am on a Wednesday at the Police Depot.[9] If they were considered suitable, they would be accepted for training. The *Queensland Police Act* (1863) provided a lengthy list of disqualifications for applicants looking to be admitted into the force, although the Queensland Police entrance specifications were more lenient than those of the Irish Constabulary. The age limit, for instance, was significantly higher and the physical parameters were not as strict or precise. In consequence, an applicant had to be of sound constitution, able-bodied and under the age of 40 years. They also had to be 'of good character for honesty fidelity and activity', not been convicted of any felony, nor be a hired servant, and they could not have kept 'a house for the sale of beer wine or spirituous liquors by retail'.[10]

The age cut-off for applicants became stricter in 1864. According to the new set of regulations, candidates eligible for the force had to be under the age of 30, as opposed to 40, unless they had previously been engaged in police duty, in which case they could be admitted up to the age of 35. Twenty-eight-year-old Thomas Tyrrell, with his previous police experience, ability to read and write, and basic knowledge of arithmetic, as well as his bachelor status and record clear of previous convictions or questionable associations of any kind, met the strict entrance specifications. The recruit register does not list Tyrrell's physical details, but to be successful a candidate had to measure 5 feet 8 inches without boots and 37 inches across the chest.[11] These entry requirements were adopted from the manuals of the existing police forces of Dublin and London.

Upon joining the police, the recruits were disenfranchised. Queensland Police regulations stated that both officers and men were to observe neutrality in political matters so to preclude partisanship, as it was deemed that 'when a man becomes a partisan his utility and efficiency as a policeman is, to a great extent, lessened'.[12] Queensland policemen also had to apply for and obtain the commissioner's permission to get married. The Irish forces, Royal Irish Constabulary and the Dublin Metropolitan Police had analogous regulations; however, the colonial forces were not as prohibitive in their rules nor as strict in their enforcement. Before 1866, a constable in the Queensland Police Force had to have served for at least two years prior to seeking permission to marry. In comparison, the members of the Royal Irish Constabulary had to be in service for up to 10 years before petitioning the authorities. The rationale for this rule was that the commissioners took into consideration the difficulties constables would face if they married young and without sufficient means to sustain a family. They observed that men who married young often accrued debt and were unfit to carry out their duties with zeal, spirit and impartiality. Chief Commissioner Lake of the Dublin Police required a man to produce £30, and his wife to do the same, to enable them to furnish and keep a house, as all married men were stationed separately from the barracks.[13] Commenting on the regulations of the Irish Force, the Governor of Upper Canada, Sir Francis Bond Head, mused that the first thing 'Cupid has to teach a Dublin policeman is to put by a sixpence, – to repeat the operation sixteen hundred times, and *then* apply for his license.'[14]

For constables wanting to get married sooner, there was a degree of flexibility. Despite Police Commissioner Seymour's *General Order 212*, which indicated that permission to marry would not be granted to constables until after three years of service in the force, Constable Tyrrell married Maria Molloy at St Stephen's Cathedral in Brisbane on 24 February 1868, less than two years after joining the police (Figure 4.1).[15] Maria was also from Ireland and had arrived in Brisbane on *Venilia* (sailing from Plymouth) in October 1865.[16] The ceremony was witnessed by David Graham and Eleanor Molloy, Maria's sister. The bride and groom were both listed as 25 years old, but, according to baptismal records, Thomas would have been 30 by this time. Maria and Thomas had five children in fairly quick succession, with four living past childhood. They had three boys (John Thomas born in 1869, William in 1871 and Robert Alexander in 1873) and a girl, Fanny, born in 1875. Their second daughter, Caroline Ellen, was born in 1878 but passed away two years later.[17]

Police Depot and Training

When Tyrrell joined the force, recruit training took place at the Police Depot. The men received drill and service training during their probation period, which varied considerably but averaged to roughly three weeks. The men who were not sworn in but were eligible to join the force were retained on the list of supernumeraries and called upon when new recruits were required. These men resided across town where allocated in government-provided accommodations. During their probationary period, supernumeraries received a pay of 3s per day.[18]

In the 1860s, the main police station was in the old hospital building (Figure 4.2) on the corner of Ann and George streets, facing the river on the North Quay side.[19] Between 1875 and 1885, the police were housed at the Victoria Army Barracks on Petrie Terrace. The complex included the main building, where the mounted and foot constables on duty at Petrie Terrace, Paddington

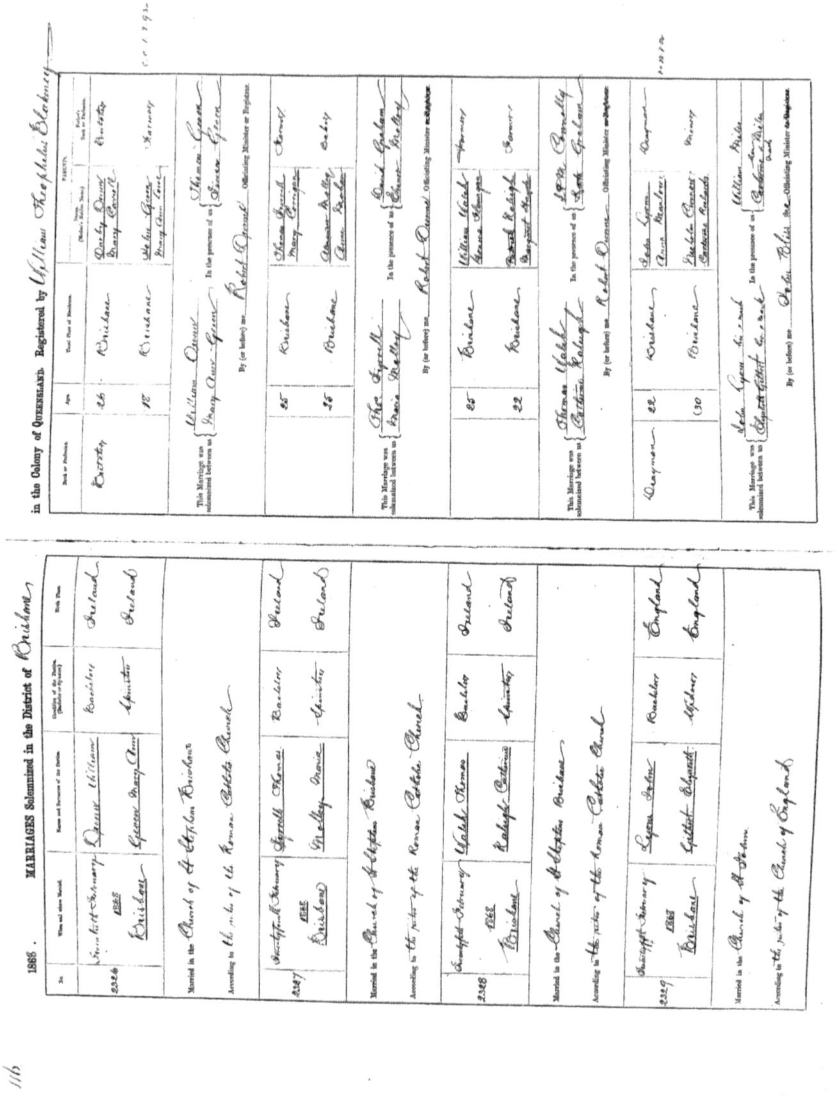

Figure 4.1: Marriages solemnised in the District of Brisbane in the Colony of Queensland by William Theophilius Blakeney.
(Births, Deaths and Marriages Queensland, 1868/B/2327)

and Red Hill resided, the commissioner's house, and the officers' mess building, which was occupied by the inspector of the detective force (Inspector Lewis at the time). The parade and drill routine grounds were also within the barracks walls. In 1885, the Police

Depot was moved to be next to the old Brisbane Gaol building on Petrie Terrace and the Victoria barracks were handed back to the National Guard. Built in 1860, the Brisbane Gaol was the first building on Green Hill, and was a grim and imposing edifice. Its two wings were three storeys high and hosted 72 cells arranged back to back, which opened onto balconies with iron railings and external staircases. During the police reconstruction, one wing of the jail was demolished and the second wing was converted into police barracks. In 1883, the prisoners were moved away from the central city area to Boggo Road Gaol across the river.

Figure 4.2: Brisbane General Hospital, George Street, Brisbane, 1865.
(Queensland State Archives, 1442595, Digital Image 5830)

In the training conducted at the depot, the objective in all exercises in drill and the use of arms was 'to make the force effective, and not to make it approximate in its character to a military body, further than by introducing the promptness and uniformity of action attained in such bodies'.[20] The period recruits spent at the depot varied until a compulsory term of three months was introduced by Commissioner Parry-Okeden in the 1890s. Even then, as the recruits' register shows, the period between being sworn in and the first transfer was regularly under one month. In some cases, constables received their first transfers the same day they were sworn in; however, this practice was confined to the years when the force was extremely understaffed.[21]

Tyrrell was promoted from supernumerary to constable on 6 March 1866 and was stationed in Brisbane, the largest police establishment in the colony (later Moreton, Division A) for his first few years.[22] He was single upon joining the force, and so resided at the barracks scattered around Brisbane, where a strict daily routine was in place. All constables, with the exception of those employed on night duty, rose in the morning no later than 6 am. The next half hour was allocated to getting dressed and arranging their rooms with the bedding neatly folded, and the rooms swept and set in order. The men had their breakfast at 8 am, dinner at 1 pm, and tea or supper at 6 pm. At 9.30 pm, men who were not on duty went to bed, 'and all lights and fires, except such as are authorised to be kept up during the night, [were] extinguished by ten o'clock'.[23]

The *Dublin Metropolitan Police Alphabetical Register, Register of Members of the Police Force, 1856–1917*, as well as the *Applications for the Police Force 1866–1894* for Western Australia, list most recruits' previous occupation as 'labourer', and many recruits had worked in the rural sector. Likely as a result of this, the 1869 *Manual of Police Regulations for the Guidance of the Constabulary of Queensland* specifically emphasised that 'no poultry, cows, horses, goats, pigs, or other animals, are to be kept by the police without permission'.[24] As mentioned in Chapter 3, there was an extremely high turnover rate during the first decade of the forces' existence.[25] In 1864, 223 men were sworn in to the force, but by the end of the year 15 men had been dismissed, 13 had resigned and 3 were discharged. Drink-related breaches were a major factor in men being dismissed from the force. On 5 September 1867, Constable Richard Riley (reg. no. 187) was fined 5s for 'disobedience of orders by bringing liquor into barracks after 11pm and causing a disturbance', and Constable Thomas Archibald McArthur (reg. no. 1717) was fined 10s for falling asleep on duty.[26] The Queensland Police Force internal records show a policeman was liable to a fine of £2 for the first offence, or less depending on the severity of the infringement, £3 and a warning for the second offence and dismissal for the third. In the first four years of the Queensland Police Force's existence, an average of 80 new recruits were added annually to the ranks, with a considerable dip to 38 in 1869.[27]

Regulations and Extraneous Duties

As a whole, police regulations across the British Empire in the nineteenth century were constructed in such a way as to instil obedience and order. In discussing a beat constable as a social symbol, historian Dean Wilson describes how the 'shaping of the police constable into the symbolic representative of a benign and rationally applied central authority was to be achieved through the strict regulations of appearance and conduct'.[28] The first Queensland police manual stressed the importance of a constable commanding respect 'by all classes'. The constables were directed to be extremely cautious in their demeanour, to never smoke in uniform, 'and by sober, orderly, and regular habits' be 'ready zeal to execute the lawful orders and commands' of their superiors.[29] These 'lawful orders and commands' ranged beyond ordinary police duties and made the Brisbane city policeman a jack-of-all-trades. In addition to preserving the peace and preventing crime, colonial police officers in Brisbane were expected to fill gaps within the civil service system. Their list of extraneous duties contained between 50 and 80 tasks well into the twentieth century and included: 'summons-serving, acting as Clerks of Petty Sessions, rangers of Crown lands, inspectors of Slaughter-houses, district registrars of births, deaths, and marriages, and bailiffs of Courts of Requests'. As the 1865 *Report of the Commissioner of Police* asserted, none of these duties were 'legitimately those of constables'.[30]

The extraneous duties carried out by the police occupied much of their time and took their attention away from crime prevention and detection. For example, on 18 May 1864, James Lovett appeared to answer a summons for breaching the *Towns Police Act of 1855* when he was ordered to pay a total of 10s (a fine and costs of court) for depositing manure on North Quay.[31] In another summons, Dr Hugh Bell, the visiting surgeon for Brisbane Gaol, vaccinator, and medical officer for the police and Aboriginal Australians, whose surgery was registered on Adelaide Street, appeared before the bench.[32] He was summoned 'for suffering a dunghill on his premises to become so as to have caused an offensive smell on the 2nd December', a fine and dry day with north-easterly winds and a maximum temperature of 48 degrees in the sun.[33] Dr Bell explained that the stables were being cleaned in his absence and without his knowledge, and the case was subsequently dismissed.

Uniform and Equipment

On ordinary police duty, Brisbane constables were equipped with batons. Pistols were standard issue but only carried when it was probable that firearms would be required, such as on prisoner or gold escort duties.[34] The men were supplied with 20 rounds of ammunition, and, in the event of ammunition being unaccounted for, 3p for every missing cartridge was deducted from the constable's pay.[35] If more rounds were needed, a written statement as to how and when these were expended was required. The regulation-issued sword and carbine were not for use on ordinary police duty, but for riot control and ceremonies.

The foot police wore a blue wool or serge jacket and trousers with a brimmed cap. The annual clothing allowance for constables consisted of a tunic, tunic undress, a pair of dress trousers, two pairs of undress trousers, two caps, four white covers for caps and two glazed covers, two pairs of boots, and four shirts. Biannually, ordinary constables and sergeants were issued a great coat, and an oilskin cape triennially.[36] In the 1880s, the police cap was replaced with a black helmet, which was not a popular choice among the ranks due to its tendency to cause collapse from sunstroke. In addition to their batons, pistols and uniform, each member of the foot police was furnished at the expense of the government with a rifle, pouch belt, waist belt and frog, number and letter, manual of police regulations, extracts from acts of parliament, handcuffs and a duty badge.[37]

The Beat

Ordinary police duty consisted of walking a beat. In Brisbane, each beat was committed to the care of a constable and consisted of a series of streets and roads. A constable was 'responsible for the security of life and property, and for the preservation of the peace, and general good order within his beat during the time he is on duty'.[38] The beats were divided into day duties – 5 am to 1 pm and 1 pm to 5 pm (12 hours in total) – and night duties – 5 pm to 9 pm and 9 pm to 5 am. Brisbane night-duty beats comprised four sections: three on the north side and one on the south side of the Brisbane River (see Appendix C: Brisbane Night Duty Beats).[39]

As a general rule, constables worked their beats with their right hand next to the houses. Sergeants and senior constables in charge of sections worked the beats in the opposite direction, with their left hand next to the houses. Constables on night-duty beats walked on the inside of the footway near the houses quietly to avoid disturbing the inhabitants. The Queensland beat instructions repeated almost verbatim the instructions for other forces, such as the Dublin, London and Victorian police regulations:

> The Dublin constables on day duty were advised to keep near the curb-stone, but by night next to houses, while all accessible places be patrolled in due order on night duty. In a manner similar to his fellow London Metropolitan patrol constable, a Dublin policeman was responsible for checking doors, windows, gratings, cellar flaps and fanlights for unauthorised access.[40]

The average speed for beat duty patrol was set at 2.5 miles per hour (5 miles per hour for horses unless in pursuit), which enabled constables to see every part of the beat in the time allotted; 'and this they [were] expected to do regularly, so that any person requiring assistance, by remaining in the same spot for that length of time, may meet a constable'.[41] The predictability of the beat times and routes was its strength and also its weakness. Melbourne police beat changeover was at 5 am, so 'many burglaries in Melbourne's central area occurred at five o'clock in the morning'.[42] The weakness of the beat system's predictability was exemplified in one story from Melbourne when 'a well-known Melbourne criminal had informed a senior constable exactly where and when all the men on the beat in one section of the city could be found at any given time'.[43] Brisbane's changeover also occurred at 5 am.

In addition to preserving peace and deterring crimes, the beat system also served as constant surveillance for the men on duty, as senior officers frequently performed unscheduled checks of beat constables to ensure their behaviour was regulated. The police on duty were forbidden to gossip idly with each other, or with any persons, especially female servants at houses on their beats. *Punch, or the London Charivari*, a weekly British humour magazine, satirised the policeman's love of gossip with female cooks and servant girls and showed that the attraction was mutual. A cartoon published in 1853 asked, 'What article of dress are Cooks most attracted to?', and answered with 'The Pelisse'.[44]

Policing Brisbane Streets

Queensland's population experienced dramatic growth through the 1860s and 1870s. In 1863, there were 61,000 residents in the colony, and by 1874 the population had reached 163,000.[45] In 1864, Brisbane town's population formed 17.1 per cent (12,551 persons) of the colony's total population.[46] Despite the rapidly expanding population, the city's police presence totalled 26 ordinary constables, 3 sergeants and district constables, and

1 chief constable.[47] At full strength, the police to population ratio amounted to 1 policeman to 483 persons. Incorporating shift work and sick leave, the ratio was closer to 1 policeman to 1,000 persons. According to the *Queensland Statistics*, there were just over 1,400 persons taken into custody in 1864, with 1,000 of these apprehended on a charge of 'drunkenness'. Throughout the nineteenth century, drunkenness or drunk and disorderly conduct were the most numerous misdemeanours. The earliest attempts to codify and regulate public order in the Moreton Bay settlement go back to 1838 when Brisbane constables were granted powers to arrest any person 'found drunk in any street or public place, and also all loose, idle, drunken, or disorderly persons who [a constable] shall find between sunset and 8 am lying or loitering in any street, highway, yard, or other place, not giving a satisfactory account of themselves'.[48] A subsequent Act in 1855 added a number of offences to the list that Brisbane constables had the power to arrest persons for, which were indicative of the mid-1850s city life and its common activities:

> Selling gunpowder, squibs, or rockets; hoisting or lowering goods of any description carrying carcase of newly slaughtered meat without a cloth covering, or carry the same for sale without covering; placing line, cord or pole across any street to hang clothes on; placing flower-pots in upper windows without protection; throwing anything from the roof of house into any street; blacksmiths keeping windows or doors opening into any street open at night; burning rags, bones, cork, &c., within one hundred yards of streets.[49]

Offences against good order, such as drunkenness, loitering and swearing, featured prominently in criminal statistics. By the mid-nineteenth century, a myriad of charitable societies and movements aided in popularising Victorian middle-class values as the 'golden standard', or the socially desirable set of norms and behaviours.[50] These included the National Temperance League and the Sacred

Heart among the Roman Catholics, which promoted teetotalism; a variety of hospital funds, such as the King Edward's Hospital Fund and the London or Dublin Lying-in Hospital, which raised money through donations, concerts and lotteries, and other medical societies; schools; missions; and mechanics institutes. As was the case in the policing of Britain at the time, a significant part of policing the colony stemmed from 'the desire to inculcate new standards of behaviour among the urban masses'. The police became 'vital cogs in this new moral machine' as the law was adapted to encompass moral standards.[51]

In addition to preventing crime, nineteenth-century police officers were tasked with enforcing moral laws, and monitoring and curtailing undesirable behaviours. Soon, the majority of daily activities in the town were regulated. These ranged from damaging a public building to extinguishing a street lamp, and from bathing near or within view of a public wharf to installing awnings on shops and houses, with penalties ranging from £1 to £20.[52] Police also enforced trading hours. The penalty for operating outside of these hours, such as on Sundays after 10 am, was £3. The fine for assaulting or resisting police in the execution of duty was set at £5. The *Police Act of 1838* did not provide for imprisonment as a form of alternative punishment because the first Brisbane jail was only opened in 1850.[53] The *Police Act of 1855* reflects the change in custodial punishment as the fine for assaulting police was replaced with a sentence of six months' imprisonment.[54]

To accommodate for the increasing population of the colonial capital (Figure 4.3), which had grown to over 20,500 by the mid-1870s, the number of ordinary policemen in the colony more than doubled between 1864 and 1874 from 176 men to 392.[55] In 1874, the total strength of the Brisbane Police Force was 134 sworn men (92 constables, 22 senior constables, 13 sergeants, 5 senior sergeants, 1 sub-inspector second class and 1 inspector first class) and 1 native trooper.[56] Native Mounted Police numbers, whose jurisdiction was outside of the Brisbane metropolitan district, remained mostly the same.[57] *The Commissioner of Police Annual Report for the Year 1874* noted a minor increase by 6 men, from 163 to 169, for the Native Mounted Police.

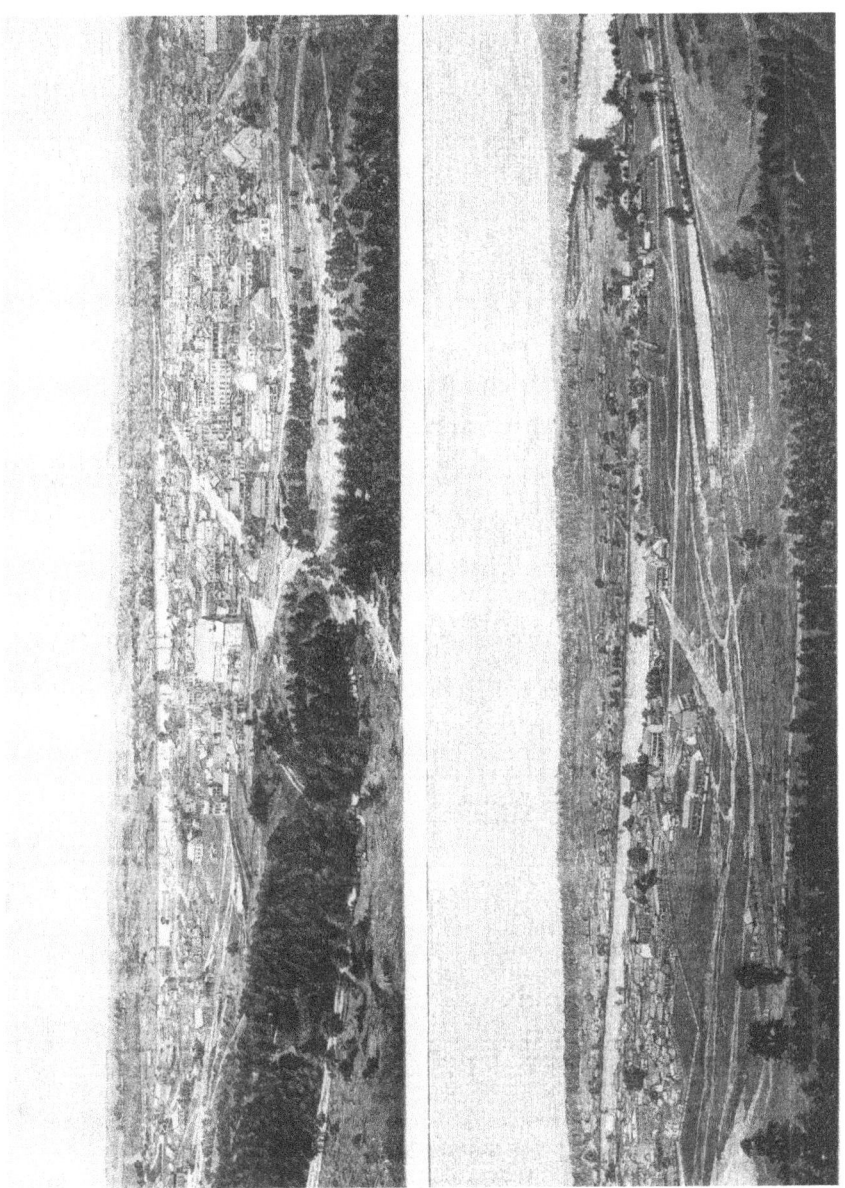

Figure 4.3: Brisbane, the capital of Queensland, 1865.
(State Library of Queensland, 19422)

Drunkenness and Disorderly Conduct

Throughout the nineteenth century, the majority of a patrol constable's time was occupied with arresting drunks and vagrants, breaking up fights, and enforcing trading hours and the city's by-laws. Similar trends were observed internationally across major urban centres at the time, including Dublin, New York and London.[58] In 1875, the Dublin Police took 23,055 persons into custody and summarily convicted 13,346 of these offenders for drunkenness. Similarly, in 1875, the New York Board of Police Justices reported that 'almost one-half [36,091 with 24,786 males] of the total number of cases disposed of in the Courts (81,032 total arrested), were cases of intoxication, and it is estimated that these and other cases which are directly and indirectly due to the use of intoxicating liquor constitute 75 to 90 per cent of all the business of the police courts'.[59] In London, 8,333 constables made 72,606 arrests in 1875, with 14,926 persons apprehended for drunk and disorderly and 16,050 for drunk and incapable.[60] As Table 4.1 shows, Brisbane policemen were similarly occupied. In 1864, 26 constables made over 1,400 arrests, with 1,000 persons taken into custody being charged with drunkenness.[61] By the mid-1870s, the number of men and women arrested on the charge mirrored Dublin, New York and London trends.[62]

	1864	1866	1868	1873	1876	1880	1882	1884
Against Person	102	94	70	178	216	204	316	814
Against Property	175	195	76	77	125	164	197	324
Drunkenness	1,000	976	487 (86)	942 (181)	1,411 (211)	1,049 (256)	1,160 (228)	1,479 (380)
Under *Vagrant Act*	141	91	81 (53)	159 (73)	283 (87)	349 (159)	445 (210)	-
Sub-Total	1,418	1,356	1,706	1,610	2,333	2,181	2,556	2,997
Total for Brisbane Bench	1,418	1,495	1,241	1,830	2,758	2,306	3,125	3,335

Table 4.1: Return of persons taken into custody or investigated by the Brisbane court of petty sessions from 1864 to 1884 (women taken into custody are indicated in brackets).[63]

Constable Tyrrell's first calls for assistance reflect the trend of arrests for drunkenness. On 5 March 1866, Tyrrell was called to assist James Lee, a resident of South Brisbane, who had fallen from an 11-foot-high wall in William Street, opposite the old Corporation Ferry. *The Brisbane Courier* reported that Lee was 'picked up insensible by Constable Tyrrell, whose attention was drawn to the accident by some persons who witnessed it'.[64] Lee, who was under the influence of drink at the time, was taken to the hospital with two severe cuts on his head and injured legs.

The high rate of misdemeanours related to drunkenness likely resulted from the numerous opportunities to overindulge offered by the array of public houses, shops, hotels and brothels in the city centre. Queen Street, Adelaide Street, Albert Street, North Quay and their immediate vicinity, such as William Street, stand out for the number of drunkenness and petty assault charges, arrests for vagrancy, and a variety of offences against good order, such as using obscene language and indecent exposure. The commercial district of the city was also inviting to thieves of various denominations, from pickpockets to hotel robbers. On 8 March 1866, Constable Tyrrell was passing Queen's Wharf and arrested George Wilson for picking pockets. The central police court reported that 'An immigrant per the Legion of Honor, [had been] lying on his box in the Queen's Wharf on Monday evening, when he felt some one pulling a handkerchief out of his pocket. He got up and caught hold of the prisoner, and shouted out "police".'[65] The victim stated that he had a large sum of money in his pockets at the time, and the prisoner was sentenced to six weeks' imprisonment.

The year 1866 was one of higher strain between the police and the policed as it saw rising rates of unemployment and economic hardship, which culminated in the Bread or Blood riots on 11 September that were instigated by the recently retrenched urban and rural workers alike. In 1866, 'Pastoral conditions were adverse, with the southern half of the colony in the grip of a drought which had begun during the previous year' and many men in Brisbane and the surrounding towns of Ipswich, Toowoomba, Warwick and Maryborough lost their jobs.[66] As news of hundreds of unemployed navvies heading towards Brisbane reached the local authorities, government officials were sworn in as special constables to assist the police. These special constables were paraded along William Street to show the strength of the force, despite being 'armed with nothing more lethal than badges on their coats'.[67] As the navvies and unemployed arrived in the city, and the local unemployed joined them, the government did their best to appease the band by offering rations, free passage to Rockhampton and reduced wages for railroad work. However, an agitator named Eaves felt the offer was inadequate and called for bloodshed, encouraging his fellow men to 'drive the police and fire brigade through the town with a stone in a stocking'.[68] As the situation escalated and the Bread or Blood riot threatened the sacking of Government House, the *Riot Act* was read. This action enraged the band rather than calming them, however, and the crowd soon turned on the police, showering them with stones. In his chapter on 'The Brisbane Riot of September 1866', Paul Wilson describes the action that ensued:

> The second reading of the Act had no more effect. The police were ordered to load with live ammunition. This order caused a momentary hush and the crowd fell back a little. Seizing the initiative the police charged and pushed the crowd back towards Queen Street. At the corner of George and Queen the crowd regained its courage and stood fast again and even looked as if they would push back the police. The police reformed [sic] ranks after the last charge and were ordered to fix bayonets and then to charge. At this, the crowd fell back again down Queen Street and was driven towards Albert Street where the momentum of the charge split it into sections, which in turn began to disperse.[69]

A number of stones were thrown from the crowd, and several police and special constables were injured.[70] The following month, the riot ringleaders were tried for unlawful assembly among other charges. Eaves was found guilty and sentenced to 12 months' hard labour. The local police, special constables and volunteers from the fire brigade were praised for their temperate conduct on the night, despite direct assaults and casualties.[71]

Assaulting the Police

From the 1870s to the 1890s, assaults on the police formed the second most numerous of sub-categories of assaults against a person. Alcohol was the catalyst in the majority of cases brought before the summary courts with resisting arrest, obstructing justice and assaulting the police among the more prevalent related offences. On 25 January 1875, Patrick McIvor was fined '20/ or 24 hours' for drunkenness, and £3 (or one month's imprisonment) for resisting the police.[72] The next day, Robert Marshall was charged with disorderly conduct and resisting police and also fined £3 (or one month's imprisonment).[73] On 28 January, Joseph Harrison was fined 20s or 48 hours for drunkenness, 40s or 14 days for resisting police, and a further 40s or 14 days for destroying a police uniform.[74] The extraordinarily high rate of crime against policemen on duty committed within the Brisbane central district frequently appeared on the pages of the local newspaper, *The Brisbane Courier*, in 1875. For example, on 27 July 1875, four out of six offenders charged for drunk and disorderly behaviour were also charged with assault and obstruction of justice with all offences committed on Ann, George and Edward streets.

Along with assaulting officers and resisting arrest, destroying police uniforms was a common occurrence. The force did not provide an additional allowance to replace officers' uniforms and, in 1865, a new regulation indicated that members of the force were to provide their own clothing, 'instead of its being as heretofore served out by the Government'. The reasoning behind this regulation was that 'The constables having to pay for their uniform themselves will no doubt be more careful of it'.[75] Unfortunately, as the evidence shows, it was not always in the constables' power to 'be more careful of' their uniforms.

In colonial Brisbane, there were five distinct types of offences committed against the police: assaulting a constable, resisting arrest, rescuing or aiding a rescue of a prisoner, obstructing a constable during execution of his duty, and destroying uniform. The number of cases of each type varied from month to month; however, after drunkenness and common assaults, offences against the police formed the most prominent and consistent sub-category brought before the Brisbane Central Police Court throughout the second half of the nineteenth century.

Figure 4.4: Queen Street, Brisbane, 1872.
(State Library of Queensland, 20298)

According to the *Deposition and Minute Books*, assaults and assaults on the police were a daily occurrence at the Central Police Court, with offences commonly committed at the corners of Queen and Creek streets (Figure 4.4), or Elizabeth and Albert streets. Thomas Tyrrell experienced this firsthand when Charles Stewart was charged with assaulting police while in the execution of duty.

As reported on 22 June 1880 in *The Brisbane Courier*, between 12 and 1 am on the previous Saturday night, Sergeant Tyrrell, who was on duty in plain clothes on Elizabeth Street, saw a number of people fighting and interposed, stating that he was a constable. He succeeded in arresting those engaged in fighting, but while doing so was struck by Stewart twice and knocked down. Stewart was sentenced to one month's imprisonment without the option of a fine and was charged with damaging a constable's uniform, for which he was fined 1s and ordered to pay the amount of the damage (15s). In default of payment, he was sentenced to undergo a sentence of 24 hours in the cells. The other two men involved in the affray pleaded guilty and were fined 20s each with the option of imprisonment.[76]

The following day, John O'Keefe was also charged with having assaulted Sergeant Tyrrell on the Saturday night. At around 12.15 am on the night mentioned, O'Keefe caught Tyrrell by the legs while Stewart knocked him down. At the close of the evidence in this case, *The Brisbane Courier* reported that Mr Inspector Lewis had said 'the police force was now considerably more than a third less in numbers than it was twelve months ago' and that 'there was all the more need of strengthening their hands; and he hoped when the bench found a man guilty of interfering with them in the execution of their duty they would inflict a severe punishment'.[77] The police magistrate said the bench would deal severely with cases of this kind, and he wished the government would give him the power to order flogging for larrikinism. O'Keefe, who protested his innocence of the charge laid against him, was sentenced to one month's imprisonment.[78]

'Meritorious Conduct'

Throughout his police career, Thomas Tyrrell was awarded twice for meritorious conduct. In 1872, the then senior constable received £5 for saving the life of a child at personal risk. In 1877, Sergeant Tyrrell was awarded a further £1 in recognition of his services in stopping a runaway horse at personal risk. It was a common occurrence for

Brisbane Police to have to either stop a runaway horse or save a person from getting run over as violent driving was always present on the streets, be it a horse-drawn carriage or an omnibus. The diversification of business and more accessible consumer goods resulted in a vast expansion of the volume of street traffic, especially in the final decades of the nineteenth century. This is evident from the numerous applications to the police for better control of the roads and the subsequent prosecutions for furious driving. In many cases, however, traffic control remained a general responsibility of the local authority and was only placed specifically under police jurisdiction years later.[79]

Sergeant Tyrrell, an 'old and much-respected member of the police force', retired on police pension at the end of February in 1881. *The Brisbane Courier* eulogised his departure by reporting: 'Sergeant Tyrrell has served fifteen years in the police force, and has given entire satisfaction to all those with whom his duty has brought him in contact.' The *Brisbane Courier* article continued that, while on a brief placement at Sweers Island, Tyrrell had 'contracted an illness from which he never entirely recovered, and during the last two or three years he has suffered so much from general debility to render him unfit for duty' and concluded that 'The police lose a valuable officer in him.'[80] By all accounts, Sweer's Island in the Burke district, 'a small rocky island in the Wellesley group' nearly 5 miles long and about 1 mile wide, 'skirted by rocky ridges with foul ground and patches of rocks', was not an inviting place.[81] Following his retirement from the police, Tyrrell moved to Enoggera and resided near the New Market Hotel. He was found dead in the bush at the back of his residence on or around 31 December 1886, with his cause of death listed as fatty degeneration of the heart.[82] He was survived by his wife and children.

As is evident in the biography of Thomas Tyrrell, the life of a colonial policeman was not an easy one. The round-the-clock heavily regulated duties were cumbersome and often took a toll on officers, which resulted in a high turnover during the first decade of the Queensland Police Force. However, there were benefits for the men who joined the force in its early days. For Tyrrell, immigration to Brisbane and service with the local force allowed him to get married and start a family much sooner than he could have if he had stayed in Ireland as part of the Irish Constabulary. Tyrrell received his first promotion only two years after joining the Queensland Police, which was common for men with previous service history, but, after being reduced to the position of constable in 1870, it took him another three years to advance his position once again. The Brisbane that Tyrrell policed was a fast-growing colonial capital where offences against good order, such as drunk and disorderly, larcenies, and assaults on police, were widespread. This rapidly changing colonial landscape placed ever-increasing demands on the Brisbane constables and the citizens they were tasked with policing.

5

Policing Female Criminality

Susan McGowan

> Susan Hegarty, a young woman, eighteen years of age, and described by the police as an incorrigible character, was found guilty of behaving in a riotous and disorderly manner in a public street, and sentenced to be imprisoned for fourteen days in Fortitude Valley gaol.
>
> Minor Offences, City Police Court[1]

BY THE AGE of 18, Susan Hegarty, alias M'Gowan or McGowan, was an 'incorrigible character' on a path to a 'life of crime'.[2] Her contemporaries viewed her as a depraved woman and a habitual criminal. Susan Hegarty was born in 1862 in New South Wales, and by the time she reached 18 she was of below average height (5 feet); stout; without any visible physical markers such as tattoos, scars or deformities; freckled; and had auburn or sandy hair and brown eyes.[3] By all accounts, she spent her adult life on the streets of Brisbane, mainly Albert Street and the adjoining streets, as a lady of 'negotiable affections'. Contemporary social commentators viewed criminal women like McGowan as idle, profligate, sexually depraved and vain. Susan McGowan's life and her experiences on the streets of colonial Brisbane reveal how female criminals in the colony were treated, which was often more harshly than men.

Between 1880 and 1890, Susan McGowan made 29 appearances in the police courts and prison records. She first appeared before the police magistrate in July 1880 for using obscene language in a public place and was sentenced to a week in prison in default of paying the £2 fine.[4] Later the same year, McGowan was again sentenced for behaving in a riotous and disorderly manner and spent a fortnight in the Fortitude Valley Gaol.[5] For the next decade, and the remainder of her life, McGowan was arrested for either or both of these offences annually. Her life trajectory was representative of a working-class woman's at the time, as many women were unable to secure a domestic service job or factory employment or get married. With just over 40 per cent of the Australian colonial population living in urban centres in the 1880s, these were the most readily available forms of employment, paid or unpaid, for women of this socio-economic class.[6] When faced with social persecution, these women often attempted to take control of their situation by resorting to any means available, including vagrancy. Since McGowan was already well known to the local police by the time she became an adult, it would have been almost impossible for her to break out of the cycle of petty crime.

Policing Morals and Female Criminality
In addition to detecting and preventing crime, the role of Victorian-era police organisations, including the Queensland Police Force, was to enforce certain morals and social norms valued by the middle class. These social standards unequivocally relegated women into the domestic sphere as a caregiver – 'the angel of the house'. The ideal woman in the nineteenth century was virtuous, pious, obedient, loving and nurturing. These beliefs about the role of women affected how their behaviour was policed, and female offenders were viewed as offending against both the law and their nature. As legal scholar Lucia Zedner describes, 'Notions of femininity and, no less, masculinity influenced the ways in which crime was viewed […] the result was that criminality was perceived, judged, and

explained differently according to the sex of the offender.'[7] Susan McGowan's offence records reflect the trend for morality policing, as 33 per cent of her prosecutions were for riotous and disorderly conduct, which was inevitably followed by a custodial sentence. As McGowan's records show, she became locked in the perpetual cycle of crime, conviction and imprisonment.

On 29 December 1880, 18-year-old McGowan was sentenced to 14 days' imprisonment. A week after her release, she was arrested again for 'riotous conduct' and appeared before the police magistrate on 21 January 1881. McGowan found herself before the police magistrate so soon after her release for encouraging 'larrikin' James Morrison to resist and assault Constable Glancy. As described in Chapter 4, the police were not universally – or well – liked, and were assaulted on a daily basis. *The Brisbane Courier* reported the details of McGowan's crime:

> Constable Glancy deposed that about a quarter to 7 o'clock on Thursday evening he had a man in custody in Charlotte-street; about a dozen persons interfered with him and rescued the prisoner; accused [McGowan], was in the crowd, threw a stone about the size of his fist at him, striking him on the head, and felling him to the ground. Constable Jessop said he came to Glancy's assistance, and heard the accused say, 'We'll give it to the ---; don't let the prisoner go; take him away; there's enough of you here.'[8]

McGowan was sentenced to six months' hard labour. James Morrison, the larrikin instigator of the fight, was charged with five offences: disorderly conduct, interfering with police duties, destroying police uniform (Constable Glancy's jacket was 'torn almost into shreds'), rescuing a prisoner and assault of Constable Daly (who was struck on the mouth and severely bitten on the thumb). In total, Morrison was sentenced to 48 hours for disorderly conduct and a month of hard labour for each of the remaining offences (a total of four months and two days' imprisonment).

Both defendants grievously assaulted the police, but McGowan received a significantly longer sentence. Her gender and use of a weapon both contributed to the disparity.

A week after being released from Fortitude Valley Gaol, McGowan was back behind bars. The *Queensland Police Gazette* shows she was released from Toowoomba Gaol on 20 July 1881. McGowan was not the only woman trapped in the cycle of criminality at the time. Also in July 1881, a woman named Mary Fisher was released from Toowoomba Gaol after a six-month term with hard labour for riotous behaviour.[9] A year prior, in July 1880, Fisher was convicted before the police magistrate the same day as McGowan, also for vagrancy, having spent only a week 'on the outside' following another six-month imprisonment.[10] Mary Fisher was described as 'an old offender, against whom there were forty-five previous convictions' recorded.[11] She was from Ireland, 40 years old, and, like McGowan, she was fairly short (5 feet 1 inch), stout, of sallow complexion, and had brown eyes and hair. Fisher's prison record states that the third finger on her right hand was deformed and that she had several blue spots on her right cheek.[12] As is evident in Fisher's and McGowan's records, and, as Zedner identifies, during the colonial era, women were predominantly sentenced to very short terms varying from only a few days to weeks but returned over again to the same prisons, obfuscating the 'divide between life inside and their own communities outside'.[13]

The lock-up for the city was in Elizabeth Street, with the cells occupying the back portion of the ground floor of the police court buildings. The lock-up housed both female and male prisoners, who were searched upon arrival and had their crimes or offences recorded in the books of the lock-up at the charge-room. The charge-room was connected to the cells by a dim and crooked corridor, and there was little ventilation or natural light, so the cells were dark and oppressive.[14] The cells averaged around 7 by 9 feet, and the smaller cells had no provisions for sanitation. There were three female cells and five male cells, with around seven women confined to each cell. The cells did not have benches, so the women had to sleep on the floor using two blankets: 'one to spread on the floor and the other to use as a coverlet'.[15] These blankets were never washed but were aired in the yard, folded and kept in the corridor until required.

Offensive or abusive language was a common offence that led to short-term custodial punishment. From 1880 onwards, the courts recorded the offending language, but this was not covered by the local papers. The severity of penalties for using offensive or abusive language varied, and these penalties were again influenced by the gender of the offender. On 5 April 1880, Margaret Byrnes answered a charge for obscene language and disobeying summons for the same offence. The name of the plaintiff was not recorded, though it must have been a woman as Byrnes was recorded as saying: 'You are a Bloody rotten whore and a bloody rotten cow mother calves daughter went to Sydney rotten with the disease.'[16] Byrnes was found guilty and fined £2, or one month's imprisonment with hard labour. Ellen Lightfoot received the identical penalty for obscene language in Petrie Terrace in August 1880 when she pleaded guilty to using the words 'Fuck yourself you bloody bugger.'[17] A week later, John Hirsch was tried and charged for the same offence. He pleaded guilty for saying the following on Charlotte Street: 'You bloody bugger, you bloody orange bugger bloody Irish bugger.'[18] Hirsch was fined £2 (or seven days' imprisonment) for his divisive language. This fine is consistent with the offences committed by the women, but Hirsch's prison sentence was only a quarter of Lightfoot's.[19]

Lightfoot, like McGowan and Fisher, could not break out of the cycle of criminality. She was released from Toowoomba Gaol in May 1881 after completing a term of six months for vagrancy, meaning she managed to stay out of the criminal system for two interim months. Lightfoot was from England and was 47 years old at the time of her release, which was old for a woman during the Victorian period, as the average life expectancy for a female in the

1870s to 1890s was 43 years.[20] She was only 4 feet 11 inches tall, and was stout with a fair complexion, black hair and brown eyes.[21] Similar to Mary Fisher, Lightfoot had a deformity on her right-hand index finger, which suggests that both women were previously employed in a factory.

Obscene Language and Disorderly Conduct
As women in the nineteenth century were viewed as gentle creatures who were incapable of aggression and violence, and the 'culture of sensibility' grew in popularity in the late 1800s, previously accepted modes of behaviour were refashioned as felonious. In *Wayward Women: Female offending in Victorian England*, Lucy Williams argues that utter desperation was a key reason for female violence in Victorian society: 'attacks, fights and assaults took place when women felt there was no other recourse available to them'.[22] In 1882, Susan McGowan completed two prison terms for riotous conduct. In April, in between her prison stints, she appeared at the police court on a charge of obscene language and was back in December after being charged for disorderly conduct and assault.[23] On Tuesday 5 December, McGowan was charged with behaving in a disorderly manner on Albert Street and on Friday 8 December she pleaded guilty 'to having assaulted a South Sea Islander named Jackey Sambo, by striking him on the forehead with a bottle'.[24]

McGowan was arrested twice in 1883 on her customary charges of drunkenness and disorderly conduct, but the latter charge was not substantiated and was dropped by the police magistrate. According to a report in *The Brisbane Courier*, on 11 November, McGowan and a woman named Polly White, along with two men, one identified as 22-year-old Robert Marks, drove in a cab to Hamilton where a party 'indulged pretty freely'. During the party, a 'dispute arose between the two men, who engaged in a drunken fight, while the girls stood by, urging them on to renew their efforts'.[25] However, the cab driver, William Crozier, told the court a different story: 'he saw the two men have a fight, but did not hear either of the defendants [White and McGowan] make use of bad language or conduct themselves in a disorderly manner; so far as he knew, the girls were only weeping copiously'.[26] The bench considered there was not sufficient evidence to substantiate the charge against the defendants, although, according to the *Brisbane Courier* article, 'they were no doubt guilty'.

Violence Against Women

By 1883, McGowan resided in Albert Street as a known woman of negotiable affections. Repeated assaults against her by a man named Joshua Stead, described by *The Brisbane Courier* as 'a larrikin', between 1883 and 1885 invites speculation that he was either McGowan's souteneur or boyfriend, or both. Stead was a 28-year-old Englishman of medium build (5 feet 4 inches) and had tattoos on both arms: a female figure on the right and 'MM' with a union-jack on the left.[27] In her article 'The Larrikin Girl', Melissa Bellanta asserts that 'the violence dealt out to women by rough working-class youth known as "larrikins" lends a chill edge to the history of relations between sexes in late nineteenth-century Australia'.[28] On 1 October 1883, Stead was charged with having assaulted McGowan in Albert Street. According to the report that followed, on the afternoon of 26 September, 'the accused met [McGowan] at her own door in Albert-street and struck her in the face and knocked her down, and then kicked her on the bridge of her nose, which feature was now considerably out of joint in consequence'.[29] Stead was fined 40s with legal costs, or 14 days' imprisonment.

McGowan spent a third of 1884 incarcerated and appeared before the police magistrate twice. At the beginning of January, she was charged with using obscene language in Albert Street.[30] The prosecuting policeman, Sergeant Burke, stated that the accused was a very disorderly character, and she was found guilty and fined 60s. In August, McGowan was again apprehended and charged with wilful destruction of property after damaging a hat belonging to Kate Needham. The hat was valued at 7s 6p and the defendant was ordered to pay the cost of the property destroyed and was fined an additional 5s. In 1885, McGowan was in and out of the police court a total of 10 times. She was arrested for disorderly conduct twice – once for obscene language and once for fighting – and in the remaining cases she was either a witness or a plaintiff.

McGowan was assaulted quite severely six times in 1885. In mid-January, Joshua Stead pleaded guilty to assaulting, 'a girl of ill-fame named Susan McGowan' again.[31] According to the case report, Stead accosted McGowan and accused her of getting him two months' imprisonment, knocked her down and kicked her two or three times. Stead was sentenced to two months' imprisonment with hard labour and sent to the St Helena Island Penal Establishment.[32] Two months later, McGowan was assaulted by another man named Brittan. Sub-Inspector Galbraith prosecuted the case:

> From the evidence it appears that McGowan was standing in Margaret Street when Brittan threw a stone at her, inflicting a nasty wound on the head causing her to fall on the ground. He then went up to the girl and kicked her. A crowd gathered round, and Brittan challenged anybody to fight him. Constable Devine then came up, and on going to arrest Brittan he was thrown down and his uniform torn. With the assistance of two other constables Brittan was eventually conveyed to the watchhouse.[33]

The wound on McGowan's head as a result of this assault measured three-quarters of an inch (1.9 centimetres) in length and about one quarter of an inch (0.65 centimetres) in width, which led to severe loss of blood. Brittan was sentenced to three months' imprisonment for the assault, and separately fined for disorderly conduct and destroying a police uniform.[34]

Figure 5.1: Albert Street, Brisbane, 1883: 'on the corner with Mary Street, is the Gympie Hotel'.³⁵ (State Library of Queensland, 2543)

On 22 April, McGowan was charged with the theft of a silver locket and chain from Annie Williams. The alleged witness, a barman of the Gympie Hotel (Figure 5.1), gave contradictory evidence 'at the box' and the case was dismissed.³⁶ A few weeks later, McGowan was assaulted on Margaret Street again. The accused, Margaret Corkery, hailed from England, and at 5 feet 6 inches was much taller than McGowan.³⁷ According to the report, Corkery severely beat McGowan after 'some ill-feeling created by a recent case'. Corkery was found guilty and sentenced to two months in prison.³⁸ In the first week of June, McGowan was charged with disorderly conduct and fell victim to another vicious assault. William Wade attacked her on Albert Street as she was engaged in an altercation with another woman. *The Brisbane Courier* reported that 'Wade came up and struck her in the face with a fist giving her a black eye and bruising her mouth.' However, unlike the assault by Corkery, 'Evidence was called for the defence to the effect that the accused never struck McGowan at all' and, with the bench 'inclined to give the greatest credence to the evidence for the defence', Wade was only given an unofficial caution.³⁹

Notoriety within the legal system made redress virtually

impossible, locking women like McGowan in the cycle of abuse and abusing. In July 1885, McGowan was beaten up again in Albert Street, this time by 'larrikin' James Feeney. The two constables who witnessed the assault stated that 'Feeney knocked the girl down two or three times, cutting her mouth'. Feeney was sentenced to two months' imprisonment with hard labour.[40] Brisbane Gaol records show that Feeney was from Ireland, 20 years old at the time of imprisonment, of slight build and dark complexion, 5 feet 3½ inches tall with a scar on his right elbow.[41] The records also show that Feeney was in and out of prison throughout 1885 for assaults and theft.

Despite the numerous assaults McGowan suffered, her notoriety in the system gave her a level of strength and independence in the colonial society. As cultural historian Melissa Bellanta argues, female 'rowdies' (such as McGowan), also known as 'donahs' or 'molls', had a large social role and formed a subculture of their own that was independent from men.[42] Susan Hegarty, alias McGowan, was 'a brazen larrikin girl' in her own right.

Larrikinism and Prostitution

Following her challenging 1885, McGowan's court appearances became more sporadic. In 1886, she was apprehended for vagrancy in January (released from Toowoomba Gaol in March) and again in June, and she appeared as a plaintiff in an assault case when James Feeney assaulted her again on Mary Street.[43] After assaulting McGowan, Feeney fled Brisbane. The warrant issued in his name described him as an unprepossessing young man who was clean shaven with the exception of a small moustache.[44]

While McGowan's court appearances decreased, crime in Brisbane increased during the mid-1880s. The increase was slight in offences of a serious nature, but, according to Commissioner Seymour's report in 1883, 'in those [crimes] that are chiefly comprised under the popular denomination of "larrikinism", including common assault, assaulting and obstructing police, drunkenness, obscene language, and other offences under "The Vagrant Act", the growth is very large'.[45] Arrests under the heading of 'larrikinism' in 1883 amounted to 1,036 more than those of the preceding year. In his report, Seymour included an explanation of why crimes of 'larrikinism' had increased and how they could be deterred:

> Fines and imprisonment have no deterring influence on the class known as 'larrikins'; they subscribe to pay the fines, and look on short terms of imprisonment as a joke. They are cowardly blackguards, who watch their opportunities, and never attack those who are able to defend themselves; nothing but corporal punishment will effectually put a stop to this nuisance, and it is to the influx of this class from the South, whence they have been driven by the lash, that I attribute the increase of offences I have named above.[46]

Case reports from 1883, 1884 and 1885 commonly describe male offenders as larrikins, and women that associated with them as 'girls of ill fame'. In 1888, *The Brisbane Courier* provided the following description of this type of character: 'The larrikin loves Saturday night, and in all the glory of high heels – of the French pattern – bell-bottomed pants, and bobtailed coat, decked with many buttons, he props himself against hotel walls or friendly lamp posts and bespatters the footways with his copious expectoration.'[47]

The *Vagrancy Act* introduced in 1852 was another legal measure to curtail certain behaviours, including begging, gaming, obtaining money or goods under false pretences, and soliciting. Prostitution in itself was not a crime, and prostitutes could not legally be taken into custody simply because they were prostitutes as 'to justify their apprehension they must commit some distinct act which is an offence against the law'.[48] In his annual reports for 1881 and 1887, Commissioner Seymour stated that many complaints had been made during the years of the annoyance caused by the presence of prostitutes in the streets of Brisbane. Applications had been made to the police to take steps to close brothels and other places where this class of women resided. The commissioner's view was that the only way to curtail the problem was to introduce licensing for such houses:

> as to the houses of ill-fame and similar places, the proof requisite under the existing law to obtain a conviction is so difficult as to amount almost to an impossibility, and the experience of other cities is that the closing of such places throws an additional number of the objectionable persons into the streets, and so increases the annoyance consequent to their presence. Such places will exist notwithstanding any amount of legislation to the contrary, and the best plan to adopt will be to place them under police supervision as much as possible, which might be done by licensing common lodging-houses and giving the Police power to visit and inspect them at any hour.[49]

The previous police court coverage inferred that McGowan was a prostitute but did not directly indicate so as prostitution was not a criminal offence. To be known or suspected as a common prostitute was reason enough for a notice to be issued for a medical examination under the *Act for Prevention of Contagious Diseases* (1868) and, if necessary, be admitted for compulsory treatment at the Lock hospitals. According to Clause 3 of the Act:

> Where an information on oath may be laid before any justice of the peace by an inspector or other officer of police charging to the effect that a female therein named is a common prostitute and being resident within the limits of any place to which this Act shall apply has been within fourteen days before the laying of the said information [...] be subjected to a medical examination by the said visiting surgeon.[50]

Failure to present for treatment resulted in arrest and forced conveyance to the hospital. Any female still affected by a contagious disease found soliciting for prostitution was in breach of the Act and therefore liable to be imprisoned for a term of one month on the first conviction and three months on any subsequent offence. As mentioned previously, Susan McGowan spent a third of 1884 in prison in Brisbane. She was charged under the *Act for Prevention of Contagious Diseases* in February and released after a month on 19 March. She was charged and convicted of the same offence the following month and released on 2 July after completing a three-month term.[51] Initially, the Act passed by the United Kingdom parliament in 1864 was designed for garrison and port towns to combat venereal disease epidemics.[52] However, the legislation empowered the police to apprehend women suspected of prostitution and provided for compulsory medical examinations for sexually transmitted diseases. This led to a number of malicious prosecutions, as the examinations branded women as prostitutes regardless of their background. That the Acts did not include any provisions for examination and treatment of men further highlighted the disparity in the gendered justice system. As Zedner describes, 'women, far more than men, were subjects of social definition'.[53]

Nine Holes

By the end of the 1880s, McGowan was ill and living at the 'Chinese den' in Lower Albert Street, Old Frog's Hollow. Old Frog's Hollow was an area larger than the main street space that enclosed a site from Elizabeth Street to Alice Street and George Street to Edward Street. The hollow was a low-lying area with a stream running through it, which frequently flooded with water flowing into the basements, backyards and premises of the workshops and stores. Originally, in the centre of the area was 'a swampy depression', 'a water catchment with a tidal swamp and several creeks, including an outlet around Margaret street', which was named Frog's Hollow due to 'the vocal efforts of the batrachians which made the night hideous in its neighbourhood'.[54] The streets were inundated by any high spring tide 'let alone a real flood'.[55] Old Frog's Hollow was the disreputable area of town where illegal or immoral activities were pursued by individuals of all classes and races. As local publication the *Boomerang* described it, 'Walk down Albert-street on any night in the week, if you care to venture through its suffocatingly significant aroma of opium and insanitation, and among its prowling gangs of wolf-like larrikins, and its filthy swarm of cursing slatters.'[56] Although this 'Den of Iniquity' was only two blocks south-east of Queen Street, it was a world away in terms of class.[57] As Rod Fisher describes in his article 'Old Frogs Hollow: Devoid of interest, or den of iniquity?', it was 'really the red light district of Brisbane in 1888 a rare clustering of drunkards, prostitutes, larrikins, thieves and assailants who, one way or another, lived off the visitors, mariners and new arrivals at the many boarding-houses, lodgings and hotels'.[58]

On the north side of the street there was a row of nine shop-houses under one roof between Charlotte and Mary streets, which were referred to as 'holes'. Each of the 'holes' had a narrow room at the front, which was used as a shop, with apartments behind that included a cellar. Most of these dwellings were occupied by Chinese immigrants and their families. These nine 'holes' were run-down and unsanitary, and, given the 'sickening odour' that arose from the holes, they were 'looked upon for many years as a disgrace to Brisbane'.[59] Further along from the 'holes', a drapery store on the corner of Elizabeth and Albert streets was used as a front for a gambling 'den', which was a popular place for card games such as fan tan troy.[60] While this area of immorality and criminality was labelled as the 'Chinese Quarter', records at the time show that Chinese immigrants in Brisbane did not cluster together in one location but settled in distinctive areas of the town linked to their particular occupation and consistent with that of the wider community.[61]

In addition to the Chinese Quarter in Albert Street, Brisbane had a 'Chinatown', which consisted of two or three fruit shops located close to the Roma Street Markets.⁶² In 1887, *The Brisbane Courier* reported that the Chinese market gardeners coming into the city had for some months made a practice of leaving their horses and spring carts standing unprotected outside the Chinese Quarter in the back streets for an hour or so at a time. According to *The Brisbane Courier*, the traffic authorities had repeatedly warned the cart owners against this breach of the traffic by-laws, but were always met with the reply, 'Me no savee.'⁶³ In October, Ah Fun, Sam War and Tommy Chong were selected from the group of traffic offenders and prosecuted by way of warning to their countrymen. At the police court, the three defendants pleaded guilty to the charge made by Inspector TF O'Carroll of the Metropolitan Traffic Board for leaving their horses and carts unprotected in the public streets, and the bench imposed the nominal penalty of a 10s fine and 3s 0d costs of court to be recovered by levy and distress.

Fisher's article concludes that the Chinese immigrants provided accommodation for prostitutes and had a reputation for being kinder to those women.⁶⁴ Susan McGowan's experience confirmed the former but not the latter half of the statement. In 1890, she was assaulted by a Chinese man, the same Tommy Chong charged with leaving his horse and cart unprotected. The *Brisbane Courier* report of the assault stated that 'from evidence it appeared that the defendant went into a house in Albert-street in which the woman lived, when an altercation took place between them, and the defendant struck her in the face with his fist and knocked her down'.⁶⁵

In mid-March 1890, Old Frog's Hollow was affected by floods. *The Week* reported that 'the scene in Albert street on the subsidence of the water was one of the dirtiest ever experienced there, and as soon as an entrance could be effected into the flooded premises, Mr Marshall, the town clerk, was at hand with a couple of firemen, with a hose and hydrant, ready to assist the occupiers in cleansing their premises with water from the mains'.⁶⁶ The town clerk was well supplied with disinfectants, which were applied as soon as the premises had been washed out. The newspaper report continued by saying, 'The row of Chinese shops known as the "Nine Holes," were cleaned [...] and were soon after occupied by those who on Tuesday night had to leave them. The three two-storey buildings adjoining the row, also occupied by Chinamen, were also cleaned out and disinfected. Opposite these premises a butcher's shop gave out an abominable stench, a quantity of meat having been left in it on Tuesday night.'[67] However, Old Frog's Hollow was identified as dilapidated and unsanitary even before the flooding.

According to the reports of medical health officer Dr Joseph Bancroft, following his inspection of Old Frog's Hollow with the mayor, Alderman McMaster, and General Inspector Mr Lee Bryce, the area was 'very unhealthy to the residents in the neighbourhood'.[68] Dr Bancroft carried out a series of sanitary inspections between 1887 and 1891. He reported that 'By far the largest number of trouble spots were found in the Frogs Hollow area, aggravated by serious flooding in late 1887 and early 1890.'[69] Most of the old houses in this area were proclaimed insanitary due to damp, dirt and decay. When Ellen Hayes was arrested for vagrancy, she was found 'in a small filthy outhouse' in the Chinese Quarter. The arresting constable said, 'the place is not for any human to live in. It is the filthiest place I ever saw in my life.'[70] Before arriving on Lower Albert Street, Hayes spent a year in the Magdalene Asylum in Wooloowin, and, according to *The Brisbane Courier*, 'upon leaving that institution she went to gaol for three months, then she entered the hospital, after which she went to see a friend of hers residing in the Nine Holes'.[71] The Magdalene Asylums, also known as the Magdalene Homes (or Laundries due to the services they provided), had existed since the 1760s in Ireland. These institutions were run by Catholic nuns and were established to 'care for prostitute women'. From the mid-1990s, evidence emerged of physical cruelty and sexual abuse of the inmates.[72] When arrested, Hayes was in a dreadful condition, and she attempted to drink a bottle of rum lying on a shelf in the outhouse. Sub-Inspector O'Driscoll said she should be sent to the hospital. Hayes followed the all-too-familiar downward trajectory for lower-class Victorian women.

Susan McGowan resided in the 'Nine Holes' area during the major floods of 1890, and, judging by the infrequency of her police court appearances after this time, her health was impacted by the poor living conditions. The assault by Chong in May was her last cameo in the local press. McGowan died on 29 March 1891 in cab number 271 on the way to the Brisbane Hospital accompanied by a female friend. She was taken from one of the 'holes' occupied by Ah Gee, whose house was open to the worst female characters in Brisbane. Constable Sullivan saw McGowan a month before her death and said 'she was in a wretched state'.[73] McGowan was only 28 years old when she died, and her cause of death was listed as phthisis and exhaustion. She was buried at Toowong Cemetery on 9 April.[74]

The nineteenth-century ideals about morality and the position of women in society meant female offenders were policed much more harshly than men and were given little opportunity for reform or rehabilitation. As Zedner argues in her work on women and crime in Victorian England, 'the paucity of moral powers she was thought to possess made the chance of her retrieval, once fallen, seem remote'.[75] In Britain and its colonial outposts, females were viewed as moral guardians, and societal beliefs about their innate virtue and gentility presented them as physically and morally weaker than men. Consequently, female criminals were viewed as offending against both the laws of men and the laws of nature. The punitive cycle propagated the cycle of criminality and moved the prospect of 'salvation' out of reach for many female offenders. Further, negative imagery of female criminals in the press pushed these women, who were often victims as well as perpetrators, deeper into the recesses of the criminal underworld. For women like Susan Hegarty, alias McGowan, ill-fame and habitual offending were viewed by society as irredeemable characteristics, and the cycle of criminality became inescapable.

6

Policemen as Prosecutors

James Nethercote

From 'The County of Broad Acres' –
And of large hearts, also –
This detective came to Queensland

Full thirty years ago,
'To evil-doers' once 'a terror,'
A scourge to rogue and thief,
He left 'The Foorce' [sic] when in his prime
Much to the rogue's relief,
His name with deep respect men mention,
And, thank the Lord! He draws a pension.

Ex-Sub-Inspector Nethercote, Private Detective, Brisbane[1]

JAMES NETHERCOTE WAS born in 1852 to Ann Dunn and James Nethercote, who both worked in the woollen industry, and was raised in Uffculme, Devon. According to the census of 1871, when Nethercote was 19 he resided with his parents in Wellington, Somerset, and worked as a weaver.[2] On 13 December 1873, Nethercote joined the Bradford Borough Police Force in Yorkshire, but he resigned two years later on 27 November 1875. Despite not having friends or family in the Australian colonies, James embarked on the *Western Monarch* on 9 December 1875 as an assisted migrant when he was 24 years old.³ He arrived in Brisbane on 27 March 1876 and soon after joined the Queensland Police Force.⁴

Between 1880 and 1900, Queensland judicature and the police experienced reforms aimed at standardising and professionalising the institutions, which resulted in the organised police being responsible for the detection, apprehension and prosecution of offenders. The key developments during this time were the passing of the *Justices Act 1886* and the establishment of the new Criminal Investigation Branch (CIB) in 1895. Over these same decades, James Nethercote progressed through the ranks from a detective constable to the head of the CIB and eventually a prosecuting inspector, a role that garnered him widespread respect and popularity.

Constable Nethercote

Nethercote applied to join the Queensland Police Force on 20 June 1876 and, due to his prior policing experience, was accepted the following day. He was sworn in two weeks later on 5 July.⁵ Shortly after his required service time, Detective Second Class Nethercote received permission from the commissioner to marry Elizabeth Sarah Rose Mawditt, who had migrated from Middlesex to Brisbane on *Earl Derby* in June 1879, and they were married on 6 May 1880.⁶ James and Elizabeth went on to have seven children, including two sets of twins: John William Mawditt and Charles Henry Mawditt were born on 9 September 1880, Ethel Ann Mawditt was born on 7 December 1882, Ellen Elizabeth Mawditt was born on 3 June 1884, Daisy Alice Mawditt and Lilly Edith Mawditt were born on 9 June 1886, and James Philip Mawditt Nethercote was born on 20 June 1892.⁷

In his application to join the Queensland Police, Nethercote showed he had served for two years in the Bradford Police in West Riding, Yorkshire. His character references described him as steady, intelligent and industrious. The Borough Police Office in Bradford verified that Nethercote joined the local force on 13 December 1873 and resigned on 27 November 1875, and indicated that his conduct was 'very good' (Figure 6.1).⁸ Nethercote's prior experience

Chapter 6: Policemen as Prosecutors 121

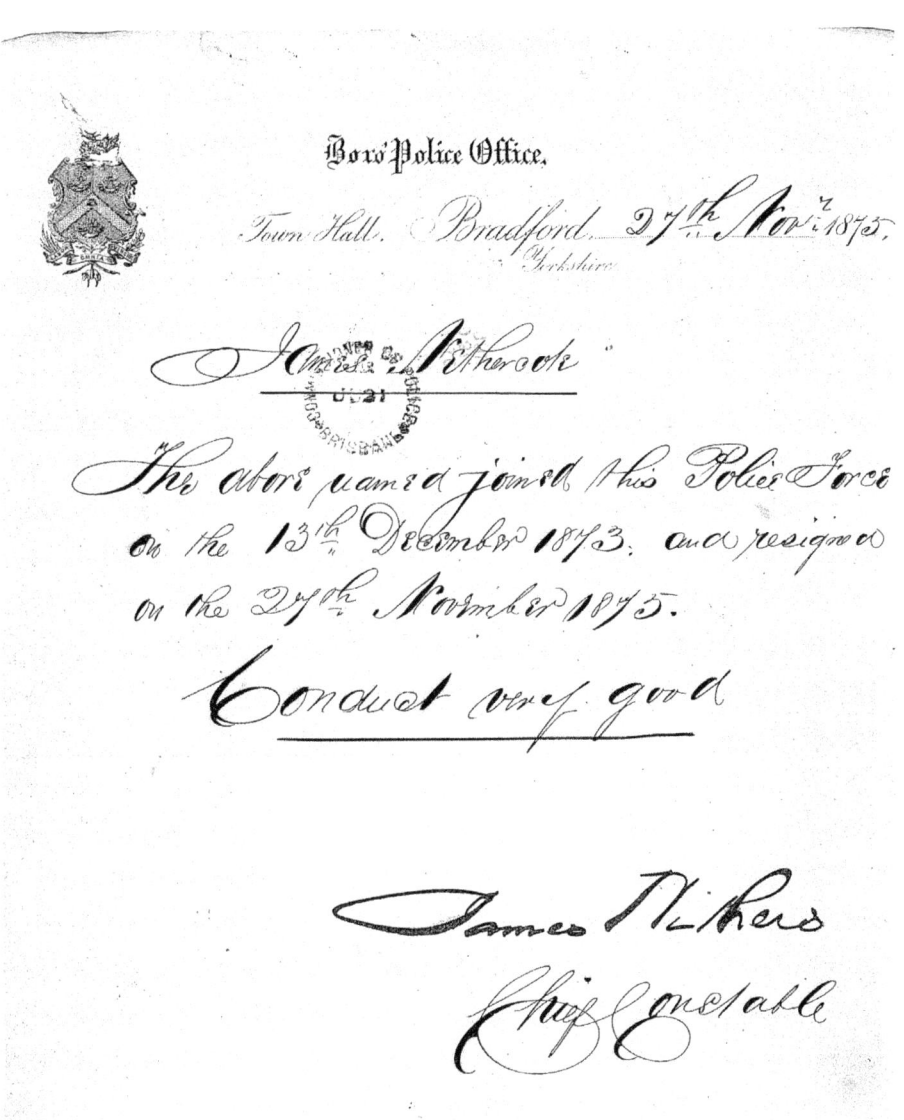

Figure 6.1: James Nethercote, Borough Police Office service record, Bradford, Yorkshire. (Queensland State Archives, 2258)

in the English police gave him a competitive advantage in the colony. Migrants of varied backgrounds sought employment in the colonial police force using references from parish clergy, country gentlemen or former employers as it was a means of gaining a firm hold in the new country. A position in the Queensland Police Force offered reliable pensionable employment and a secure income. Aside from work on the railways, the police force was the main form of government employment and 'few other male permanent occupations had such an insatiable thirst for new recruits'.[9]

When Nethercote joined the force, the police entry conditions emphasised neutrality and the unacceptability of political partisanship within the ranks. In taking their oath, supernumeraries swore that they were not members of any secret order or society, excepting the order of Freemasons. Nethercote himself was a member of the Freemasons' Victoria Lodge in Brisbane. He was initiated in March 1892 and maintained his membership with this lodge until he was transferred to Charleville in 1905 where he joined the local lodge.[10] The Victoria Lodge was established in 1867 and was initially located in the Masonic Hall on Queen Street. By the time of Nethercote's initiation, it had relocated to the Freemasons' Hall in Alice Street.[11] The *Freemasonry Membership Registers for Brisbane* shows that 50 members born between 1840 and 1860 listed their occupation as 'policeman'. However, the swearing-in certificates for the Queensland Police ranging from July 1890 to December 1892, and April 1893 to March 1900, which include 700 recruits, list two men belonging to the Order of Odd Fellows and one member of the Loyal Orange Lodge but do not list any recruits identifying as Freemasons. This inconsistency in records may be due to the way the question was posed on the certificate: 'Do you belong to any Secret Society?' At the turn of the nineteenth century, the Freemasons were not viewed as a secret society.

Brisbane Detective Office

Given his previous police experience in a town force, Nethercote was first assigned to the Brisbane Detective Office as a plain-clothes detective.[12] As has been evident in the biographies of officers examined in earlier chapters, candidates with law enforcement experience progressed through the ranks much faster than those without any previous experience in the system. Nethercote received his first promotion to detective second class in August 1879 and was further promoted to detective first class in July 1885. Over his three decades of service, Nethercote progressed through the ranks quickly and became a fixture in the city police court, initially supporting and later prosecuting a range of cases.[13]

Prior to his promotion to the commissioned officer rank, Nethercote successfully convicted a variety of crimes in his time as a Brisbane detective. In April 1886, he was involved in an exciting case of 'serious defalcations' by Mr EB Holt, a manager of the Bank of New Zealand, Sydney Branch, who suddenly disappeared. Initially, the detectives could not find anything amiss in the bank books. However, further investigation showed Mr Holt had embezzled £1,400, and *The Western Star and Roma Advertiser* reported that 'public interest in the matter [ran] high in Sydney, and the wildest rumours were circulated as to the amount of Holt's financial transactions, the climax being reached in statements that the deficiencies amounted to £250,000'.[14] The manner in which Holt left Sydney was also widely speculated about. *The Western Star and Roma Advertiser* reported there was 'reliable information that on Thursday 18th instant, Mr Holt waited on a well-known shipping firm and urgently applied for a passage for a friend by the barque *Cynisca*, which was to sail immediately for Valparaiso'.[15] According to another rumour, Mr Holt boarded the Northern Railway of New South Wales disguised as a Roman Catholic priest named Father Res. He apparently stopped in Toowoomba on his way to Brisbane with the intention of sailing for London on the RMS *Dacca*. On the way to Brisbane, Holt changed his name to

Rev. John Payten, and he was watched at every port by the local policemen. When he reached Brisbane, he changed his disguise and name once again, and presented himself as 'Mr Tinks', a tourist, at the Transcontinental Hotel.[16] On 9 April 1886, Senior Detective Nethercote and Detective Wyer arrested Holt at the hotel. Upon searching his bedroom, the police found three bags of sovereigns containing £200 in gold and a bill of exchange on London for £500. After the search, Holt, still wearing his clerical hat, was escorted to the watch house by the detectives.

Economic Fluctuations and White Collar Crime
The case of EB Holt's embezzlement reflects the emerging prevalence of white collar crimes occurring towards the end of the nineteenth century. As the economic structure evolved and the number of private businesses in the service sector expanded, instances of theft and misappropriation of funds by bank and post office clerks increased, and there was a 'mushrooming in attempts to defraud and embezzle'.[17] Embezzlement cases from across metropolises, such as London, Dublin and Toronto, in the late 1880s and the 1890s show that employees took sums small and large as opportunities presented themselves, including light-management, machinations or 'bad' investments. Unlike the thefts carried out by the lower criminal classes, most of these crimes were not motivated by hardship or need.[18]

The railway boom of the 1880s boosted the economy and benefitted local hospitality businesses, but it also provided the means and opportunity for a greater variety of property crime. In April 1887, Edward Stenhouse was arrested at Messrs Howard Smith and Sons Wharf for suspected theft of jewellery from the Australian and Longreach hotels. According to the *Maryborough Chronicle, Wide Bay and Burnett Advertiser*, 40-year-old Stenhouse had 'been in Brisbane but a few weeks, and his career in the city during that period, although containing nothing sensational, may not be without interest'. This was because £200 of stolen property was recovered following his arrest.[19] Before his arrest, Stenhouse had confided in his housemates and offered to leave for Sydney together; however, as the men suspected Stenhouse also stole from them, they reported him to the police. While Stenhouse was preparing to leave the city under the cover of joining an opera company in Melbourne, detectives Nethercote, Grimshaw and Clarke intercepted him, and his extensive baggage, at the wharf. According to the newspaper report, 'The arrest was made very quickly, and Stenhouse looked miserably foolish as each watch was abstracted by Grimshaw.'[20]

The economic boom of the 1870s and 1880s was followed by a financial downturn, labour unrest and associated strikes. As wool prices collapsed and labour conflict increased, the police had to intervene to prevent a corresponding rise in crime.[21] The financial collapse was particularly hard on the Brisbane banking sector. In his book, *The Making of a Metropolis*, Brisbane historian John Laverty states that 'the absolute failure of a considerable number of financial institutions and the reconstruction of many others seriously reduced banking facilities available to businessmen' and this created an actual shortage of currency.[22] The result of this banking crisis was a steep decline in business, employment and income in the colony.[23] These changes of fortune were reflected in the rising numbers of charges for larceny and petty theft reported in the police court section of *The Brisbane Courier*. In particular, prosecutions for larceny of food and clothing items from shops and houses were distressingly frequent, and charges for vagrancy, neglected children and child desertion increased.[24] On 15 January 1891, Henry Proudfoot was summoned for defaulting on a bond of £50, a bond he entered into for a man named Wilson. Wilson was ordered to agree to support his wife and family or go to jail some months prior. Instead, while Proudfoot supported his family, Wilson left the colony.[25]

Predictably, with the dwindling prospects and economic insecurity residents faced, Brisbane's population began to drop and the construction of new dwellings halted. In 1890, an 'industrial war' was declared as workers at the Australian seaports demanded better conditions and went on strike. The problem increased the following year when shearers also went on strike after the Shearers' Union refused to sign an agreement with the Convention of Pastoralists.[26] These widespread naval and shearers' strikes crippled the main colonial exports.

In addition to the economic disaster, in 1893, Brisbane saw significant flooding as the strong summer south-easterly winds brought clouds laden with heavy rain. The storm broke over Cairns at the end of January. In early February, Queen Street was inundated by 7 feet of water, and residents had to use boats to move within and around the town (Figure 6.2). *The Brisbane Courier* had 40 feet of water in their offices. Victoria Bridge, which connected north and south Brisbane, was flooded (Figure 6.3), and the Indooroopilly Bridge was entirely washed away by the current and debris. The city transportation was further disrupted as 'all ferries stopped running on Friday evening [3 February] and every one of the wharves in Brisbane [were] inundated over the sheds to a considerable depth'.[27] In *A River with a City Problem*, social historian Margaret Cook describes how in February alone 1,026 millimetres of rain were deposited at the Brisbane Regional Office, which was 'Brisbane's highest ever recorded monthly total'.[28]

By the first weekend of February, much of the city was affected. *The Brisbane Courier* reported that 'all the low-lying portions of Fortitude Valley [were] completely inundated. Two vacant allotments in James-street [were] completely submerged, and the water in places [was] over the road. Various other low-lying places of this suburb (especially in the vicinity of the Waterloo Hotel) have suffered in a similar way. The old racecourse at New Farm was under a sheet of water.'[29] The Chinese gardens bordering Ithaca Creek in the Enoggera and Ashgrove districts were also flooded, with 'the flood water having covered the gardens for […]

Figure 6.2: Intersection of Queen and Edward streets during the 1893 flood. (State Library of Queensland, 84889)

Figure 6.3: Victoria Bridge during the 1893 flood. (State Library of Queensland, 67645)

three days'. The newspaper declared that the gardeners would be 'very heavy losers' as any vegetables that withstood the force of the floodwaters would be 'found to be rotten after the water has subsided'.[30] Enoggera and Musgrave roads were severely damaged and bus drivers experienced great difficulty travelling over them. By 5 February, all the principal streets of South Brisbane were submerged along with Albert Street on the north side of the town. Attempts of burglaries were reported daily, and the police were 'entirely unable to cope with the difficulty'.[31]

Criminal Investigation Branch

Throughout the early 1890s, Nethercote was stationed in Roma Street. Following a successful run of promotions, he was appointed as sub-inspector first class in 1892 and took command of the Detective Branch. After the reorganisation of the detective force in 1896 and the establishment of the CIB, Nethercote was transferred into the CIB, and he was in charge of the branch between February and July 1896. Prior to his transfer, Nethercote's file shows that he received four awards for his service. Two of these were for detection and arrest (1886), and one was for 'working up a case under difficult circumstance of conspiracy' (1891).[32]

During his time at the CIB, Sub-Inspector Nethercote made numerous appearances in the police court as, within the nineteenth-century common law court representation system, policemen came to act as prosecutors.[33] The city police court coverage in the local press shows Nethercote provided witness statements in nearly 300 cases, ranging from bigamy to suspected murders, as well as a myriad of property offences such as cases discussed earlier in this chapter. Prior to his promotion to sub-inspector of the Detective Branch, Nethercote gave evidence as an arresting constable rather than a prosecuting one. As a result, Sub-Inspector Nethercote was an experienced investigator, as well as an efficient and well-respected prosecutor at the police court. At this time, the administration of Queensland's justice system was multi-tiered and directly derived from the common law and statutes of England. Schematically, the main levels were the courts of petty sessions (there were 28 courts throughout the colony that provided summary jurisdiction), district courts (with criminal and civil jurisdiction covering non-indictable offences), circuit courts (also known as assizes in England) and the supreme court (the highest court in Queensland), which heard appeals on capital cases and possessed both civil and criminal competence.

Justice System
Police and Summary Courts

The courts of petty sessions were presided over by a magistrate or a justice of the peace or both. Justices of the peace were appointed by the governor and granted summary jurisdiction to hear petty criminal matters in the first instance without a jury. A majority vote of the court was sufficient for conviction except in capital cases, where, unless five members of the court held the accused guilty, the matter was reserved for Royal decision. The criminal and civil courts operated along the lines of military courts and resembled a court martial in composition and procedure. The only sentences the court could inflict were death for capital offences and corporal punishment, usually flogging, for other offences. The Moreton Bay penal settlement had its own scourger who delivered corporal punishments and was also a convict.[34] In practice, if not in statute, the courts of petty sessions were divided into five branches: the police court (for prosecutions commenced by police), the summons court (for prosecutions and proceedings for ejectment commenced by private prosecutors), the traffic court, the petty debts court and the water police court.

The powers of justices of the peace and police magistrates in petty sessions were initially codified in the *Act to Regulate Summary Proceedings before Justices of the Peace* in New South Wales during 1835 and 1850, and ultimately in the *Justices and the Magistracy Act* in 1886.[35] The 1886 Act 'provided for the appointment of the Peace and police magistrates in Queensland', and for 'matters in courts of petty sessions to be heard and determined "by two or more justices in the summary manner".³⁶ Section 30 of the Act mentioned 'Stipendiary Magistrates' (magistrates awarded a salary for their services) and equated their powers and functions to two or more justices.³⁷

The justices of the peace and police magistrates responsible for the administration of these courts also performed a wide range of duties as representatives of the central government in outlying parts of Queensland, such as acting as electoral officers, registrars of births, agents for the Lands Department, and customs, immigration and quarantine officials. The only legal training or instruction many of these early magistrates received was through watching proceedings at the circuit courts, or by utilising manuals such as JK Handy's 1869 *Queensland Magistrate's Guide*.³⁸

District Courts

The next tier in the Queensland judicial hierarchy was the district courts. In 1850, Brisbane was included in the list of regional centres at which a circuit court would be conducted by a visiting judge of the Supreme Court of New South Wales, and Mr Justice Therry was the first judge to hear cases in Brisbane. At the time, the colony was divided into three administrative districts: metropolitan (Brisbane, Ipswich, Toowoomba, Warwick), northern (Rockhampton, Bowen, Clermont and surrounding towns) and western (Dalby, Condamine, Roma) districts. In line with the colonial parliament statutes, the Metropolitan District Court was to be held in Brisbane six times each year at intervals of one to three months.³⁹ At the regional locations, the district courts were held four times a year. In 1861, Ipswich, Toowoomba and Maryborough were proclaimed as circuits or circuit courts, also known as assizes, and the Queensland *Supreme Court Constitution Amendment Act* provided for the admission of barristers and solicitors. Subsequently, the *District Court Act* of 1858 was amended and the administrative districts were reconstituted in 1875 as the southern, central and northern districts. The courts heard both civil cases (up to £200 damages value) and criminal cases; however, only non-indictable offences were tried and the courts were initially excluded from hearing some crimes such as blasphemy, perjury and bribery. Criminal matters at the district courts involved a trial by jury and the courts had the power to try indictable offences that did not carry the death penalty.

Circuit (Assizes) and Supreme Courts
In 1850, a circuit assize court was established in Moreton Bay, which allowed serious criminal cases to be heard in Brisbane during routine visits by a Sydney-based judge. In his opening address at the first proceedings, Judge Therry emphasised the court would 'be useful, not only for the punishment of crime, but for what is more desirable, for its prevention, by deterring those who may be now hesitating on the brink of crime from plunging into its commission, when they are aware and assured that there is now as easy a mode and as effective a machinery for bringing criminals to justice in Brisbane, and throughout the wide district of Moreton Bay'.[40] On the first day of proceedings, 18 May 1850, 'after the crier had called upon all jurymen and witnesses to attend, the Clerk of Arraigns read her Majesty's ordinary proclamation against vice and immorality, and the names of the jurors were then called over'.[41] Of the 48 individuals summoned, only one failed to answer, but they arrived at the court a few minutes afterwards. The business of the court on the day mainly consisted of property offences, such as theft.[42] Further, in 1855, the *New South Wales Constitution Act* established a constitution for the colony and introduced a new system of responsible government based on the Westminster model.

Indictable and capital offences were heard at the next court level, the supreme court, which was the highest court in Queensland and operated from the chapel of the old convict barracks in Queen Street. Similar to the district courts, the supreme court had civil and criminal jurisdictions, and the cases heard included murder, manslaughter, infanticide, rape and sodomy, along with capital offences like treason, bribery, arson and perjury. Similarly to the assize sessions, the supreme court judges had to travel on circuits in towns that did not have permanent judges. The circuits were divided after 1875 into the southern and northern circuit courts, with the Brisbane territory forming the central criminal court. The circuit for the northern supreme court included Townsville (established in 1874), Cooktown (1875), Charters Towers (1883), Mackay (1884), Normanton (1887) and Cairns (1889), and additional circuits were established at Roma in 1888 and Bundaberg in 1890. The selection of circuit towns and the decision to establish a supreme court at Bowen (which was transferred to Townsville in 1896) was partly an attempt to appease separatist sentiment among the citizens in northern Queensland. The supreme court proceedings continued to be heard at the convict barracks in Queen Street. However, due to inadequacies in the chapel building, such as poor ventilation and a lack of windows, in 1878, provisions were made to relocate the court. A new court building situated in George Street was designed by Francis Drummond Greville Stanley, the colonial architect, and opened by Chief Justice Sir Charles Lilley in 1879.

Policemen as Prosecutors

Prior to the establishment of an organised police force and courts that were presided over by paid, stipendiary magistrates, the common law justice system was victim-led. The responsibility and costs of prosecuting rested with the victim, and it was therefore only accessible to the wealthy. Private prosecutions were expensive, and, as the propertied classes such as the industrial capitalists expanded, so too did extra-legal groups and private prosecution societies. These were organised 'to defray the high costs of prosecution and to gain access to the criminal justice system of the period'.[43] For those in the lower classes, due to the limited accessibility of the judiciary, many misdemeanours were resolved within the local community using infrajudicial methods where decisions or agreements were reached under the direction of a well-respected member of the community.[44]

Members of prosecution societies pooled their resources by 'signing a formal charger agreeing to pay an initiation and annual subscription fee for the purpose of meeting the expenses connected with the investigation, apprehension, arrest and prosecution of offenders who committed crimes against their property'.[45] Organisation and membership of these private societies were advertised publicly to encourage participation, as well as to deter potential offenders. In the absence of an organised police force, private prosecutors and associations for prosecutions frequently offered rewards to facilitate faster apprehension of 'depredators', and constables (or 'thief takers') traded information with victims of theft for a reward.[46] This practice led to speculations that amateur and professional thief takers derived their income from 'blood money' – the money received from successful apprehensions, prosecutions and 'from rewards paid by the gratified victims of convicted thieves and robbers.'[47]

As the nineteenth century progressed, and societies were influenced by the ideas of utilitarianism and humanism, the legal and penal systems became more 'rational and systematic'.[48] In Britain, these prosecution societies continued to function throughout the nineteenth century, despite the professionalisation of the judiciary (including representation) and police forces.[49] The only statutory qualification necessary for judicial appointment was five years standing as a barrister or solicitor in the United Kingdom or one of the eastern Australian colonies, although appointees usually had extensive experience through practising law.[50]

The private societies that emerged over the course of the eighteenth and early nineteenth centuries, in which members organised to support each other in times of need, migrated with their members to the colonies. One such friendly society, the Ancient Order of Foresters, opened a branch in the colony of Victoria in the late 1840s, and a further branch named Court Fortitude in Brisbane in 1859. Rather than exclusively defraying prosecution costs, this friendly society provided financial and social support to members and their families in times of hardship. Members who experienced unemployment, sickness, death or disability could rely on the assistance of the society to ensure they and their families were cared for. The Ancient Order of Foresters was one of the largest affiliated orders of friendly societies and was governed by a district body and composed of local branches or courts. It was established in Britain in 1834 as a splinter group of the Royal Foresters, which dated from 1790, and, according to the *Queensland Heritage Register*, 'its tradition is linked with the mythology of Robin Hood and this is reflected in the ritual, regalia, hierarchy and names of the individual courts'.[51]

These societies processed significant funds, and their clerical members could not always resist temptation. On 18 November 1896, Alexander Bell, an accountant and a secretary of Court Fortitude in Brisbane, was charged in the central police court with embezzlement as it was alleged that he embezzled a sum of £300.[52] The police presented a total of six charges of embezzlement and two charges of falsification of books. Sub-Inspector Nethercote prosecuted the cases, as he did hundreds of others following his promotion to the CIB. The local press covered over 400 cases prosecuted by Nethercote, the majority of which were property offences including embezzlement, larceny and forgery.

Crime and Prosecutions

As described in Chapter 4, Queensland's population experienced dramatic growth through the 1860s and 1870s. The overall population of the Australian colonies also experienced an increase of 20 per cent, from 1,145,585 in 1860 to 1,390,043 in 1865.[53] The majority of colonial police forces were centralised by 1865, which is reflected in the spike in charges for offences against order from 7.8 to 142 per 10,000 persons. This was a 1,820 per cent increase in the number of individuals charged for disorderly behaviour, obscene language and drunkenness. Rather than being the result of a sudden crime wave or population increase on the colony or national level, this marked rise in charges and convictions was due to the continuous presence of foot policemen on the streets. Further, as the court system shifted from private prosecutions with the associated financial burden falling to the complainant to public prosecutions by the police, bringing formal charges forward was no longer a deterrent, and there was a significant increase in the number of offences heard (Table 6.1).

	Charges	Convictions	Discharged	Committals	Charges (per 10,000 persons)	Conviction Rate (%)
1860	903	866	37	0	7.8	95.9
1865	20,639	13,583	7,035	21		65.8
1870	24,155	17,915	6,230	10	142	74.2
1875	40,537	30,217	10,317	3		74.5
1880	27,327	21,023	6,301	3	121.4	76.9
1885	69,911	57,218	12,669	24		81.8
1890	70,264	56,344	13,895	25	221.3	80.2
1895	29,190	22,007	7,175	8		75.4
1900	76,080	64,497	11,558	25	201.6	84.8
1905	77,882	67,301	10,561	20		86.4

Table 6.1: Offences against order for Australia, national statistics, summary courts only. (Supplied by Barry Godfrey, Liverpool University)

The establishment of the CIB in 1895 facilitated a similar increase in cases and convictions as compared to the previous year as the number of cases increased by 34 per cent.[54] Police court convictions rose by 51 per cent, and the supreme and district courts experienced an astonishing increase in convictions of 130 per cent.[55] Commissioner Parry-Okeden attributed the rise in cases and convictions 'to the increased efficiency of the Criminal Investigation Branch [rather] than to an actual increase in serious crime'.[56]

The Royal Commission

Despite the notable increase in prosecutions and convictions facilitated by the restructuring of the Detective Branch in 1896, the

CIB remained quite small. At the time of the *Commission of Inquiry of 1899 into the Criminal Investigation Department and Force*, the CIB strength stood at only eight men.[57] The strain began to show, and the prevailing sentiment was that the work of the detective service was far from satisfactory. The woeful mishandling of the notorious Oxley and Gatton murder cases in 1898, a few months after Nethercote handed over command of the CIB to Inspector Urquhart on 29 April, confirmed that the CIB was not meeting expectations. Both cases received extensive coverage in the local newspapers as well as in the inquiry. The description of the Oxley murder case proceedings given in the inquiry report illustrates the crippling level of bureaucracy and the desensitisation of the force to the trauma of victimisation.

On 14 December 1898, Frederick John Hill reported to Acting Sergeant Small that his 16-year-old son was missing. The acting sergeant recommended Hill should go to Brisbane to inquire at the police department. The subsequent inquiry report stated that 'Hill reported the matter the same evening to Constable Rayner at Nundah. After being bandied about from police office to police office, he came finally to the Criminal Investigation Branch.'[58] The CIB did not open an investigation as they were not responsible for searching for missing friends (the term used for missing persons cases) in the country, and the father's anxiety and continuous expressions of disbelief in the boy's having gone away voluntarily fell on deaf ears. The report deemed that Mr Hill 'was entitled to more consideration at the hands of Sergeant Shanahan, who, according to Mr Hill, was brusque and rude to a degree'.[59] Although it became apparent the boy could have been led away by a man unknown, the chief inspector held a photograph of the potential suspect in his possession for four days before making use of it 'either by publication in the *Gazette* [*Queensland Police Gazette*] or otherwise'. At its conclusion, the report determined that the Oxley case established the fact that some members of the police had an imperfect comprehension of their duty to the public, especially because the chief inspector's excuse for not pursuing the case was that 'it was holiday time'.⁶⁰

'Holiday time' also prevented Inspector Urquhart of the CIB from executing his duties and going to the scene of a mass murder of a family in Gatton. The murders, which were committed on Boxing Day 1898, initiated an avalanche of public outrage and condemnation:

> Words are too weak to express one's horror of the fiendish slaughter which has taken place. Three members of a highly respected family, a brother and two sisters, have been murdered at Christmastide, when life was at its brightest, and when they were in full possession of every faculty. We begin to ask what manner of creature is loose amongst us. In the crowded centres of the old world it is not so much a matter for astonishment that abominable crimes are committed, for the sinks of human iniquity are alive with hideous vermin. But that a quiet country district in a colony containing less than half-a-million souls should be the scene of such a murder as that perpetrated at Gatton makes the hair stand on end.⁶¹

Even though a telegram was sent by the sergeant at Gatton Station on the morning the bodies were discovered, in 'some unaccountable way' the telegram remained unopened until 9 am the next morning.⁶² This oversight was due to a lack of proper provision made for the receipt and opening of telegrams over the holidays. The murders were further ignored by the inspector of the CIB for another day, for he was 'content to let the matter rest, as there was a rumour that the matter was a hoax'.⁶³ Having confirmed the homicides had indeed taken place, Urquhart reported it to the commissioner, but further postponed his travelling to the crime scene until the following morning.

Predictably, the Gatton and Oxley murders remain unsolved. The inquiry report recommended the removal of Sergeant Shanahan and Inspector Urquhart from the Queensland Police Force. However, rather than being removed from his position, Inspector Urquhart (who had taken over the CIB from Nethercote despite having never served with the detective office) was further promoted to inspector first class in 1904 and was placed in charge of the Brisbane police sub-district (Figure 6.4).[64] Nethercote, on the other hand, was promoted to inspector second class but transferred to Charleville less than a year later in October 1905.

Figure 6.4: Senior police officers in the Brisbane district, 1904. Left to right (back row) Sub-Inspector Henry Ross, Sub-Inspector Charles Savage, Sub-Inspector James Geraghty, Sub-Inspector Hugh Malone; (front row) Inspector John White, Chief Inspector Alexander Douglas, Commissioner William E Parry-Okeden, Inspector Frederick C Urquhart, Inspector James Nethercote.
(Queensland Police Museum, PM1884)

Charleville

On 8 October 1905, *Truth* published a piece titled '"Pink Peter," Pub Prosecutor. Impales an Inspector'. The newspaper claimed that 'Pink Peter', the nickname given to Peter Airey, who was elected as the Labor representative for Flinders in 1901, was 'at the bottom of Inspector Nethercote's transfer to Charleville'.[65] The police commissioner's note on the article relating to the transfer in Nethercote's file states that it was his decision only; however, Airey had been elected while Parry-Okeden was a district magistrate in the same shire. This unofficial connection between the police and the government in decision-making may be an early example of the electoral gerrymandering and complacency of the Queensland political apparatus coupled with mounting corruption that the upper ranks of the police became notorious for. Nethercote's Charleville transfer was closely timed with Urquhart's promotion to the commissioner's office.[66] This was despite the fact that the recommendations of the royal commission deemed Urquhart inept but commended Nethercote, who was initially Urquhart's superior but due to a ministerial hiccup and reconciliation of general and detective police ranks was incidentally demoted.[67]

Truth also questioned the wisdom of sending Inspector Nethercote, whose entire service had been in Brisbane and large urban centres, to a bush district. Further, according to the paper, 'there is one view of the matter, however, that people are pondering over, ever since Inspector Nethercote was man enough to come forward in the public interest and give valuable evidence before the Police Commissioner, there would seem to have been an underhand boycott silently working against him'.[68] *Truth* concluded that the promotion and the transfer out west was no promotion at all, but indeed the opposite. A decade later, an article in the newly established *Queensland Police Union Journal* classed such transfers 'to the "Siberia of Queensland"' as punishment for expressing 'one's mind in protest'.[69] Nethercote had no bush experience, knew very little of the Queensland outback and was self-admittedly a poor rider.[70] By the time of his transfer, Nethercote was in his mid-50s with over 30 years of continuous police service. Two years into his posting, he informed the commissioner his health was ailing, as he was suffering from extreme nervousness, loss of memory and debilitating eczema worsened by the climate.

In addition to the physical and psychological demands of working in the northern district, the tranquillity of Inspector Nethercote's household was undermined by the unceasing pursuits of Jack Roche, 'a plumber of about 21 years of age, the son of a Frenchman', of one of his daughters. In 1907, Roche submitted a formal complaint stating the inspector told him to leave Ms Nethercote when the two were speaking and came up very close to Roche before saying, 'you brute you ought to be castrated'.[71] Nethercote wrote a lengthy response to the complaint, which outlined what was essentially the stalking of his daughter by Roche. No action was taken against Nethercote, and, in a memorandum to Roche, the commissioner indicated that the inquiry found Roche's conduct towards Inspector Nethercote's daughter disgraceful 'and that the Commissioner cannot blame the Inspector for anything he may have said under the circumstances'.[72]

The Charleville transfer effectively ended Nethercote's police career as, on 1 August 1908, he retired from the force on medical grounds.[73] Following his superannuation on 1 August 1908, Nethercote returned to Brisbane. A year later, he was awarded the Imperial Service Medal, which was presented upon retirement to selected civil servants who completed at least 25 years of service (Figure 6.5). No longer limited by the Queensland Police self-employment restrictions, in 1910, Nethercote opened a private inquiry office in the Treasury Chambers on George Street.[74] Nethercote's PI office offered to 'collect evidence in all court cases, trace missing friends and absconding debtors, keep suspected persons under surveillance and faithfully perform anything coming within the scope of Secret Service Agency'.[75]

James Nethercote passed away on 14 April 1937 at his residence in Bertha Street, Kalinga. His primary cause of death was a sudden onset of senility, but cardiac failure was listed as the final cause on his death certificate.[76] In his obituary, Nethercote was described as 'undoubtedly one of the most efficient and popular officers in the service, every inch of a man, and a thorough gentleman, strictly honest and honourable in all his actions'. The obituary also stated that 'his kind and sympathetic nature endeared him to all sections of community and his passing has removed one of Nature's genuine gentlemen'.[77]

Figure 6.5: Portrait of Inspector Second Class James Nethercote in ceremonial uniform with Imperial Service Medal and Silver Jubilee Medal. (Queensland Police Museum, PM1641)

James Nethercote's police career in both England and Australia during a time when the police and the judiciary underwent reforms was commendable. During the latter half of the 1800s, the systems in place became more 'rational and systematic' and professionalised as the colonial society grew in complexity and was influenced by the ideas of utilitarianism and humanism. Within the new court system, procuring justice was no longer the responsibility of the victim. Nethercote joined the Queensland Police in 1876, and rapidly moved up the ranks to become a fixture in the city police court, initially supporting and later prosecuting a wide variety of cases. Nethercote was a city policeman to the core. He was stationed in Roma Street for the majority of his service but moved to the CIB after the reorganisation of the department and even briefly took command of the new branch. Throughout his career, Nethercote successfully detected, apprehended and prosecuted hundreds of offenders. However, Nethercote's career was not without controversy. Shortly after his transfer out of the CIB, the detective service came under investigation by the royal commission and the department's work was deemed far from satisfactory. In the aftermath of the commission, Nethercote was controversially promoted and posted to a rural station. This received wide coverage in the press, which questioned the wisdom of the decision and insinuated the move was retribution rather than a promotion. The apparent collusion between the colonial political establishment and the police authority in the decision to transfer Nethercote highlighted a growing corruption in the force.

7

Habitual Offending and Punishment

Charles 'Dubious' Durant

Charles Durant is a seasoned sinner with a bad record as long as a Tram Trust suburban section, but he is now where his wiry whiskers and thick thatch over the top lip will not grow for six moons. He was before Magistrate Macfarlane […] and the item opposite his name was, in vulgar words, pinching a pioneer's mansion, otherwise a tent-fly. Constable Charles Brown captured the prize in Stanley-street […] Durant denied having come by the fly dishonestly […] Charles Durant had a sentence of a sixer hard added to his record of 70 odd offences. He is now in the State Boggo road hoarding establishment, where he can't pinch people's property.

'Dubious Durant takes a tent', *Truth*[1]

ON 8 FEBRUARY 1888, Charles Durant, also known as 'Dubious' Durant, stepped out of the Brisbane Gaol into a sweltering summer day after spending a month behind bars for the theft of a carpenter's tools.[2] The weather was hot and sticky, and had already claimed several victims by heat stroke.[3] Durant had only arrived in the colony the previous year, but this diminutively statured man of 5 feet 2⅜ inches soon became one of Queensland's hardened recidivists and he spent the better part of his life behind bars (Figure 7.1).[4]

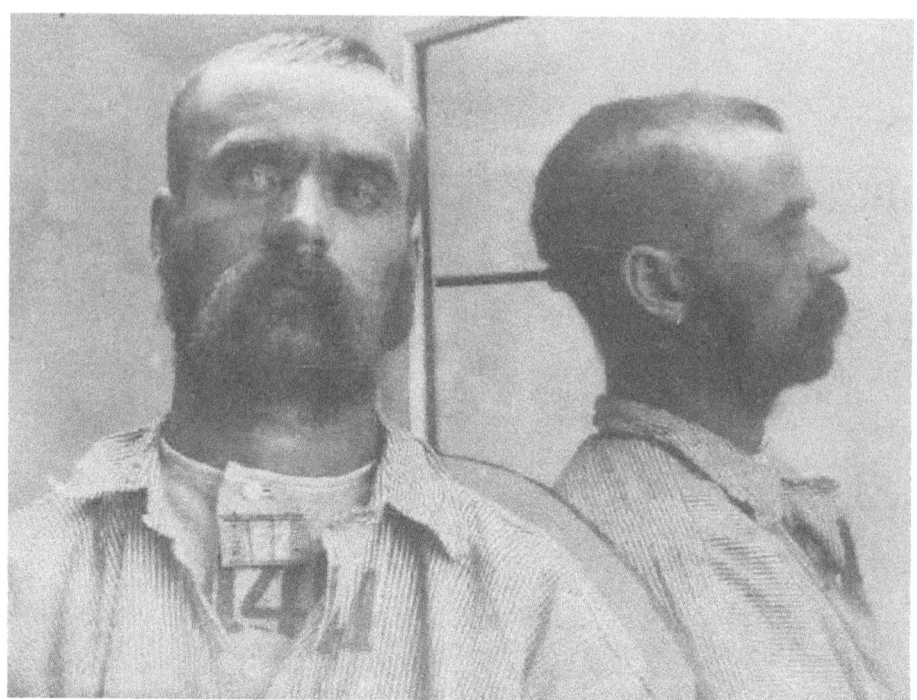

Figure 7.1: Charles Durant's mugshot, taken from Her Majesty's Gaol Entry Card, 27 March 1895. (Queensland State Archives, 18723)

In the month Durant was discharged from Brisbane Gaol, the *Queensland Police Gazette* described him as a 25-year-old native of England with a fair complexion, light brown hair and blue eyes. The *Gazette* also noted that Durant was identifiable by three dots on the butt of his left thumb, a scar on his right hand and a scar at the corner of his left eye.[5] Throughout the nineteenth century, the growth of 'scientific information about offenders – photographs, fingerprints, Bertillonage and so forth', such as Durant's unique physical features recorded in the *Gazette*, ensured offenders were easily recognised by the police upon each committal and 'highlighted the extent of recidivism'.[6]

Classifying Criminals

Before the contemporary methods of forensic identification of criminals, such as COMputer Facial Identification (COMFIT), were developed, nineteenth-century police forces around the world relied on a range of appearance-based methods of identification. One of the most frequently used methods was anthropometry, which evolved from phrenology (the analysis of cranial measurements to divine an individual's characteristics, including their proclivity towards criminality). Alphonse Bertillon developed anthropometry, also known as 'bertillonage', in 1882 as a system to identify criminals. Bertillon's system involved three kinds of signalment: anthropometrical (based on a series of specific body measurements), descriptive (such as hair colour, eye colour, and front and side view photographs) and signalment by peculiar marks (such as tattoos, scars and birthmarks). Prior to Bertillon's method of classification, a range of judicial identification techniques were used by police forces, including: the impression of the tip of the thumb (used in China); a plaster cast of the jaw; a minute drawing of the areola and denticulation of the human iris; the impression, mould or photograph of the ear, the hollows and projections of which present so great and individual variety that it is almost impossible to find two human ears exactly alike, with the shape remaining unchanged from infancy to old age; and the anatomical description of peculiar marks, such as beauty spots and scars.[7]

The Tool Stealer

Durant's movements when he was out of jail and free to roam the streets of Brisbane are largely unknown. There is no indication of where he lived when he was not in jail, although a local newspaper indicated that he stored his loot at his 'camp'.[8] In the late 1880s, Brisbane was a town of around 52,000 persons, a population large enough to offer anonymity.[9] The city centre grid, including Queen and George streets, was one of wide dirt tracks lined with grand buildings (Figure 7.2).

Figure 7.2: The wide, unpaved thoroughfares at the south-east corner of Adelaide and Edward streets, ca. 1887.
(State Library of Queensland, 202403)

Winding away from these wealthier streets and busier thoroughfares with smaller shops and bespoke businesses was a marshy, flood-prone and unpleasant area bounded by Edward, Alice, Albert and Charlotte streets: Old Frog's Hollow. While there is no record of Durant's place of residence, it is likely he would have lived in this cheaper part of town as the noxious nature of the terrain attracted the seamier side of Brisbane's inhabitants and businesses. The area's susceptibility to flooding resulted in cheap rents for poorly constructed buildings, which in turn attracted the poor and disadvantaged and made Old Frog's Hollow a place where criminal activity flourished. In the late 1880s, as many as 50 per cent of cases that came before the police court originated in Old Frog's Hollow.[10] Unfortunately, criminals in the poorer areas of Brisbane were not the only 'offenders' who appeared before the police court. Under the harshly worded vagrancy acts of 1852 and 1863, modelled on the *Vagrancy Act 1824* in the United Kingdom, beggars, as well as homeless and disabled citizens, could be arrested and sent to the nearest jail: 'Beggars – deformed, blind, or suffering from offensive or contagious diseases – [were] to be especially noticed and charged with the offence (Begging).'[11]

Durant was most frequently committed on the charge of larceny (the theft of goods), and his first nickname, 'The Tool Stealer', came from his tendency to steal easily movable and saleable items, such as tools. The 1876 *Queensland Police Manual* defines larceny as the 'unlawful taking and carrying away of things personal, or of things which have been made the subject of larceny by statute, with intent to deprive the right owner of the same'. Larceny differed from robbery, which was defined as 'an open and violent larceny from the person, or the unlawful and forcible taking from the person of another, or in his presence, against his will, of goods or money to any value, by violence, or putting him in fear'.[12] As far as the official records show, between 1887 and 1900, Durant stole tools on at least five occasions. He was convicted and imprisoned at the Brisbane Gaol for his shorter sentences (those of one to two months) and at St Helena Island Penal Establishment for the longer sentences (ranging from six months to four years). These sentences often included light labour (such as oakum picking and boot making) or hard labour (such as treadmill, shot-drill, crank, capstan, stone breaking, work on public roads or streets, and railway work).[13]

The Panopticon: Boggo Road

The penal reformers of the eighteenth century, such as John Howard and Cesare di Beccaria (the founder of penology), argued for progressive and humanitarian modifications to the prison system to align with progressive ideas ignited by the Enlightenment. Howard advocated a system of state-controlled prisons in which the regime was tough but the environment healthy. Throughout the 1770s, he visited most English and Welsh county jails and prisons, as well as the penitentiaries of Scotland, Ireland, France, the Netherlands, Flanders and Germany, and he advocated a regime of solitary confinement, hard labour and religious instruction.[14] The objective of imprisonment, Howard believed, was reform and rehabilitation, rather than purely punishment. As crime and policing historian Clive Emsley describes in *Crime and Empire 1840–1940*, 'convicts were to be encouraged to understand their place in a hierarchical society by being given work in prison, and they were to understand their wrongdoing by being given a Bible, silence and solitude in which to reflect on their behaviour'.[15] However, instead of enabling self-reflection with a view to reformation, Howard's prescribed solitary confinement, padded shoes and face masks worn in shared spaces resulted in increased rates of suicide and insanity.

In the latter half of the nineteenth century, phrenology and theories of moral deficiency propagated new forms of thinking about criminals and criminality. The shift in perception from criminality as a choice to flout social and legal values in exchange for a life of immorality and idleness to a physical and mental predisposition led to moral deviancy being almost medicalised. Early attempts to provide for the religious and moral reforms of prisoners in the nineteenth century 'gave way to rational, scientific explanations of offending and to "treatment"'.[16]

Emsley asserts that, in the mid-nineteenth century, the 'interaction of medical science with Social Darwinism fostered the new science of eugenics', which 'led to the extreme "scientific" proposals for lifetime incarceration or the sterilisation of moral defectives'.[17] According to Dr James Bruce Thomson, Perth's general prison doctor from 1858 to 1873 and a father figure to the eugenics movement, 'if these *habituées* were confined for life, the residue outside would be small, and the propagation of the criminal class prevented'.[18] Victorian moralising and the popularisation of respectability and middle-class values 'situated a criminal class in the lowest depths of the working class replete with all the vices that the respectable middle class condemned – idleness, drunkenness, love of luxury and so forth'.[19] As these theories of moral deficiency aligned with Victorian moralising, the constructs of a habitual criminal and the existence of a criminal class became firmly entrenched in the policing, penal and legal lexicons.

Accompanying the revised ideas of criminality was a change in thought as to how prisoners should be housed and guarded. According to English philosopher Jeremy Bentham, the 'origins of modern punishment' began in the late eighteenth century with his blueprint for a 'modern prison', which he labelled the 'panopticon'.[20] The scheme of the design was to allow all inmates (*pan*) of an institution to be observed (*-opticon*) by a single watchman. Bentham theorised that, as the inmates did not know when they were being observed, they would be motivated to act as though they were being watched at all times. Thus, they were effectively compelled to regulate their own behaviour. Bentham described the panopticon as 'a new mode of obtaining power of mind over mind, in a quantity hitherto without example'.[21] The panopticon served as a template for key carceral establishments, such as the National Penitentiary (or Millbank Prison) and Pentonville in London, sections of Kilmainham Gaol in Dublin, Fremantle Prison and, finally, Boggo Road Gaol in Brisbane (Figure 7.3).

Her Majesty's Brisbane Gaol, colloquially known as 'Boggo Road', opened in July 1883 on the government reserves on Boggo Road in present-day Dutton Park. Initially, the jail included a single 54-cell wing to house short-term male inmates or those awaiting transfer to the St Helena Island Penal Establishment. The conditions in Boggo Road following its establishment were poor. Prisoners speaking to the 1887 Board of Inquiry complained of filthy bedding, inadequate food provisions and outbreaks of disease. In 1887, the prison was extended, and two more cell blocks were added by 1890, bringing the total number of cells to 178.[22] Between October 1888 and August 1892, Durant spent 1,180 days in Boggo Road Gaol for seven different counts of larceny, and all his sentences included hard labour. His shortest incarceration was 30 days for possession of stolen property, and his longest was 730 days for the theft of a clock. Overall, larceny was the most common offence on the prison register, comprising 25 per cent of the total offences recorded in 1886. It was followed by 'miscellaneous', which formed 23 per cent, and assaults at 14 per cent.[23] Manslaughter and bigamy were the least numerous, with approximately one offender each out of the 762 offences recorded in 1886. English (including Durant), Welsh and Irish prisoners outnumbered Queenslanders by around two to one, and Australians from across the colonies combined to a quarter of the prisoner population, with 195 Australian prisoners recorded in 1886 (95 of whom were from Queensland).[24]

Figure 7.3: Main gates of Boggo Road Gaol, Brisbane.
(State Library of Queensland, 65256)

St Helena Island Penal Establishment

On 17 October 1892, only seven weeks after his previous incarceration, Durant was committed to 12 months' hard labour at the St Helena Island Penal Establishment in Moreton Bay (Figure 7.4) for the theft of a pair of boots.

Chapter 7: Habitual Offending and Punishment 151

Figure 7.4: Tailoring Workshop at the St Helena Island Penal Establishment. (State Library of Queensland, 220411)

Her Majesty's Penal Establishment on St Helena Island was proclaimed on 18 May 1867. The original prison comprised two wards that could hold up to 80 inmates, and single cells for a further eight prisoners. It was considered a model prison at the time, with ward walls of hardwood grooved and tongued with iron, and internal walls of thick iron wire, which allowed for constant supervision of the inmates. The prison was surrounded by a 14-foot wooden stockade wall with a 20-foot wide 'track' between it and the buildings inside. The prisoners' diet mostly included hominy and bread, and the complex grew wheat, sugar cane and vegetables, and raised sheep and dairy cattle. The *Truth* newspaper issues of 23 and 30 April 1905 featured a two-part article titled 'St. Helena: Gaol Grievances – A Convict's Chronicles'. This article outlined that the daily routine for prisoners on the island began 'at the sound of a bell at 6 am except the dairymen, cooks, and some few others who have to rise much earlier'. The article also informed readers that the prisoners' days were separated into 8 hours of work, 13.5 hours in the cells or wards, and 2.5 hours in the yards. In addition to these general facts about the penal establishment, the article asked readers to ponder the life of the criminals across the bay: 'How many of those who go down to the Bay to take their pleasures ever think as they pass the pretty island of St. Helena of those confined in this the chief penal establishment of Queensland, of the dreary monotony of their daily existence, of the hearts fretting for liberty?'[25]

In the 1880s, the prisoner population on St Helena increased to over 250 men and conditions on the island began to improve. In addition to work, the prisoners were allowed leisure time, which included reading, and the prison library was open for lending on Saturdays. The prisoners' diet became more varied and included bread, maizemeal, meat (on Wednesdays and Sundays), vegetables, and a small allowance of sugar, salt, rice and milk. Sick prisoners also received arrowroot (made into one pint), oatmeal (made into one-pint gruel) and gill's milk (a quarter of a pint). Extra rations, or 'indulgences', for good conduct were issued to prisoners completing hard labour and included half an ounce of tea and two ounces of sugar daily, as well as a weekly two ounces of tobacco.[26] Offenders under solitary confinement subsisted on bread and water only.

The 1887 Board of Inquiry into the conditions of the penal establishment found 'there was very little of a penal character in the life at St Helena. The labour imposed was in no sense heavy; it was much less so than that done every day in the bush, on the rail-ways, or in free workshops.'[27] Further, *The Brisbane Courier* reported that the prisoners were better fed than many free labourers in the colony and that 'they have hours of relaxation, holidays, and half-holidays; they enjoy the unrestrained society of each other at stated periods of the day, they have amusements in the shape of games, tuition if they desire it, and music to soothe them. If sick they are tended, and for the time being they are without, care.'[28] In contrast to these positive reports of life in the penal establishment, the prisoners in their 'state of grievances' lamented unjust and tyrannical discipline manifested in disproportionate punishments for arbitrary offences, such as 'leaving a jacket hanging up in the yard', and what they felt was extortion or 'a punishment for being sick' when they had to pay a fee for a surgeon's visit.[29] The prisoners presented their grievances in a petition signed by 239 inmates, which was the majority of the prison population at the time. In his response, the superintendent indicated that the surgeon's fees were set to discourage malingering and said the allegations of mistreatment were 'factually incorrect'.

'A Seasoned Sinner'
On 16 July 1893, 30-year-old Durant was discharged from St Helena after 365 days of incarceration. He arrived back on the streets of Brisbane in the middle of the Australian banking crisis of the 1890s, which has been described as among the most severe in the world during the nineteenth century.[30] According to Timothy A Coghlan, the New South Wales statistician from 1886 to 1904, Brisbane suffered more severely than the rest of the colony and for longer; small manufacturers came to a standstill, 'foundries were deserted, no machinery was made, no ships built or repaired, and no railway construction carried out.' There was little business conducted at the wharves as trade, intercolonial and overseas, had declined, 'and for a while, even local traffic was reduced or suspended'.[31] Increased unemployment and growing hardship made petty crime a way of life for many colonists who were desperate to survive. Between 1888 and 1898 alone, Durant was charged with 20 counts of possession, larceny, drunkenness, obscene language and disorderly conduct. He stole a clock as far afield as Hardgrave Road in West End and tools from Montpelier Road in Bowen Hills. The majority of his criminal activities were restricted to central Brisbane, however, where he was arrested for stealing several pairs of boots, a pawn ticket, a garden syringe, an axe, a rug, a buggy lamp, a saddle, a crowbar, a tent fly and many items of clothing.[32]

In addition to the economic depression, in February 1893, while Durant was at St Helena, Brisbane experienced crippling floods (as described in Chapter 6). Following the floods, Durant disappears from the official record for most of 1894 and early 1895. The depression coupled with the floods and subsequent damage likely encouraged him to look further afield. He was next charged with two counts of larceny in Bundaberg for which he received a sentence of two consecutive three-month terms in Brisbane Gaol (Figure 7.5). Durant was discharged in September 1895 with an extra set of tattoos: an anchor on the back of his left thumb, and a woman's bust and a wreath on his left forearm.[33]

Both official and unofficial records indicate that Durant avoided arrest for all of 1896 and most of 1897. However, on 2 October 1897, he was arrested for larceny at North Quay by Constable Henry Roles, a police officer with only five months' experience, and sentenced to another six months on St Helena. Soon after his release, Durant was in custody again. On 13 April 1898, he was held at the North Brisbane Watchhouse in Adelaide Street on a charge of 'having property for which he could not satisfactorily account'; however, at around 8.45 am, Durant, dressed in a dirty grey-tweed coat, greasy-looking moleskin trousers, a dirty soft-felt or greyish 'Lamington' hat, and a dark-blue shirt, escaped.[34] Following a month on the run, Durant was re-arrested on 17 May by veteran officer Constable Daniel Murrihy in Fortitude Valley.[35] Charles Durant, alias Thomas Evans, appeared at the central police court the same day charged with larceny of a buggy rug and lamps. Durant was also charged with possession of six dessert spoons for which he could not satisfactorily account. Sub-Inspector Nethercote prosecuted the case and stated that:

> [Durant's] notions were not those of an honest man, as after arrest he had 'jumped the watchhouse wall' and had been away nearly a month before being arrested on the second charge. Mr. Pinnock said there were 23 appearances against the defendant. On September 20, 1897, he had been sentenced to six months' imprisonment for larceny, and there were other charges of larceny against him. 'I suppose,' continued the police-magistrate, 'some people would say it

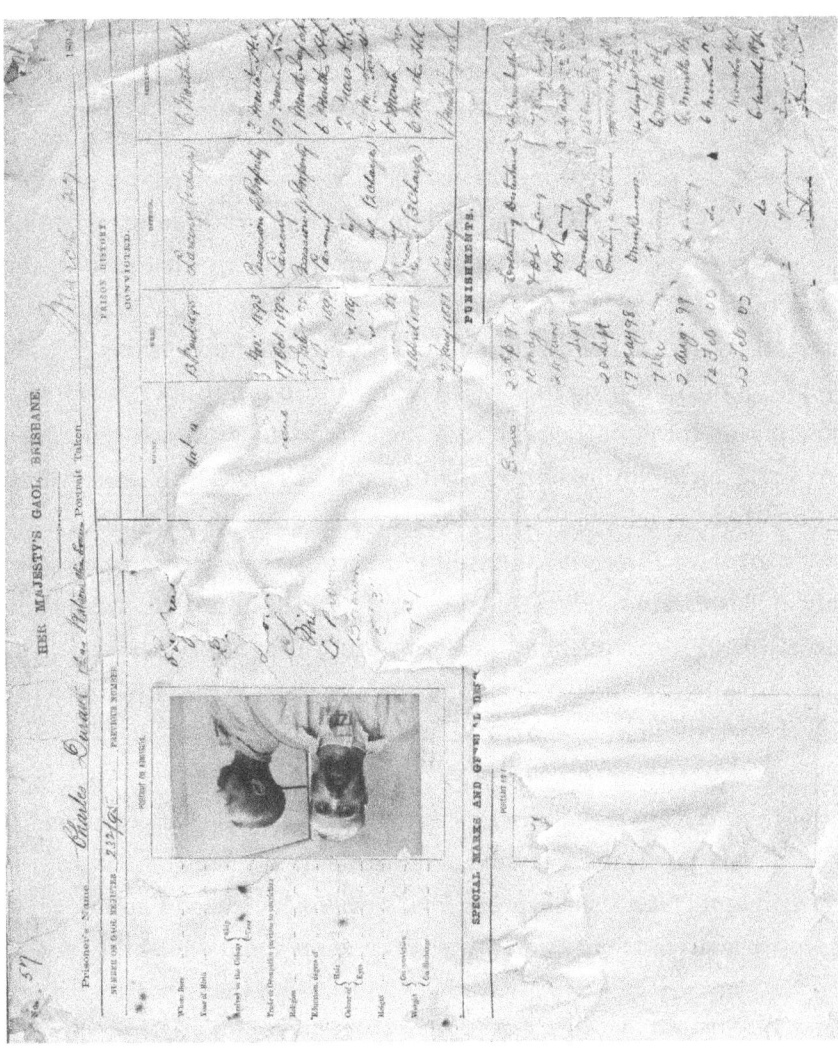

Figure 7.5: Her Majesty's Gaol entry card for Charles Durant, 27 March 1895, including a list of his incarcerations from January 1893 to February 1902. (Queensland State Archives, 18723)

is a disease, and you cannot help it. You are sentenced to six months' imprisonment with hard labour for the first charge, and one month's imprisonment for the second. The sentences to be concurrent.'[36]

Only a fortnight after his release, Durant was arrested for stealing a hammer and plane from a South Brisbane cooperage by newly minted 22-year-old Constable Thomas McLatchey. Durant pleaded guilty at the police court, but, as *The Telegraph* reported, he 'pleaded for another chance, as he had had no food for over 20 hours when he took the things'. However, given his extensive criminal record, the court did not heed his call for mercy: 'Mr. Yaldwyn [the Magistrate] remarked that as the defendant had been in gaol on various charges for 12 months during the last 10 years, he did not think it was much use giving him another chance. The defendant was then sentenced to six months' imprisonment with hard labour.'[37] In August 1899, soon after his release, Durant was arrested again by Sergeant Adam Johnson and Detective Constable First Class Thomas Head from the newly established CIB for stealing a saddle and then attempting to sell it to a second-hand dealer at the Roma Street Markets. The resulting article in *The Telegraph* includes a rare insight into what the police thought of Charles Durant:

> The defendant elected to be dealt with by the bench and pleaded guilty.
> Mr. Murray: Is there anything known about this man?
> Sergeant Denis Shanahan: Yes, your worship. He is a most notorious character. He has served twelve sentences and is one of the very worst characters we have here and is a pest and nuisance to society.[38]

In 1901, Durant managed to spend only two weeks in jail for obscene language; however, the following year he spent 240 days behind bars for a variety of offences, including vagrancy (three months' hard labour), unlawful possession of property (three months' hard labour), obscene language (two weeks) and stealing (three months' hard labour). Overall, between 1888 and 1914, Durant was imprisoned at Her Majesty's Brisbane Gaol at least 42 times and St Helena Island Penal Establishment at least 10 times. Given he accrued over 50 convictions during these 26 years, in Dr James Bruce Thomson's nomenclature, Durant was one of the firm *habitués* who was committed to a life of crime and depravity. In May 1912, at the age of 51, Charles Durant 'pleaded guilty [at the Police Court] to having stolen a pair of boots'. Following this offence, *The Brisbane Courier* reported that 'The police regarded him as an habitual criminal for whose re-formation [sic] they entertained no hope. His Honour [the Police Magistrate] said [the] accused was apparently one of the martyrs to the cause of equal distribution of which he had recently read in a book on sociology but as we had not yet reached that stage, the accused would have to go to gaol for one year.'[39]

Female Prisoners

During Durant's 26 years of criminal activity, Brisbane's population more than doubled from 64,286 in 1888 to 143,510 in 1914. Across this time, vagrancy offences committed by men outnumbered those committed by women 20 to 1. Prior to the introduction of the 1899 *Criminal Code of Queensland*, female prisoners were customarily punished for offending against the social order and their gender (as mentioned in Chapter 5). After the introduction of the code in 1900, a more uniform set of rules was applied across both genders, although women were spared from corporal punishment, such as whipping.[40] As an historical average, women made up approximately 7 per cent of inmates in Queensland prisons, and the majority of these women were petty criminals. Queensland supreme court data for 1888 to 1914 shows an average of five females found guilty on felony charges, which led to lengthier custodial punishment.[41]

The history of female prisons in the Moreton Bay colony began with the establishment of the Female Factory in Queen Street, a seven-room building that was 'initially fenced but subsequently walled to prevent men getting in' where 'the women worked at washing and needlework and picking oakum'. By 1837, there were approximately 70 women at the factory, and they were soon moved to a building in Eagle Farm that was encompassed by a 13-foot fence.[42] The new complex consisted of 'a cookhouse, needle room, punishment cells, a store, school, hospital and wash-house'.[43] The women continued to be similarly employed in washing, needlework and picking oakum, as well as nursing.[44] According to *Pugh's Almanac*, 'the "female factory" proved a grand source of intrigue and vice'.[45] Although a wall was constructed around the building, it did 'not seem to have been proof against the agility and nimbleness of the midnight rovers who had first all secured the blindness of the warders by a liberal use of bucksheesh'.[46]

Fortitude Valley Female Gaol

In 1849, the old Female Factory was repurposed as the Brisbane Gaol, where male and female prisoners were held in separate wards. The new jail was opened at Green Hills, Petrie Terrace in 1859, with Former Chief Constable Samuel Sneyd appointed as jailer and his wife, Margaret, as matron. In 1860, all short-term female prisoners whose sentences did not exceed 30 days were moved to the Toowoomba Gaol due to overcrowding. The Fortitude Valley women's prison was opened in 1863 and became colloquially known as the Fortitude Valley Police Gaol (Figure 7.6).

The Fortitude Valley Police Gaol building was located at the corner of Brook (present-day Brookes) and Church streets and stood in a half-acre paddock immediately adjoining a state school. The one-storey brick jail consisted of a residence fronting Brook Street, and a separate wing containing a jailer's office and two punishment cells, a prisoners' yard, a bath and a kitchen, which was used to prepare meals for the prisoners. Part of the residence was used as a barracks to house three single constables for a time, but, according to the minutes of the report of inquiry into the management of colonial prisons, 'the evil of this was so manifest' that the constables were removed in the early 1880s to another building on the opposite side of Brook Street.[47] The residence was then occupied

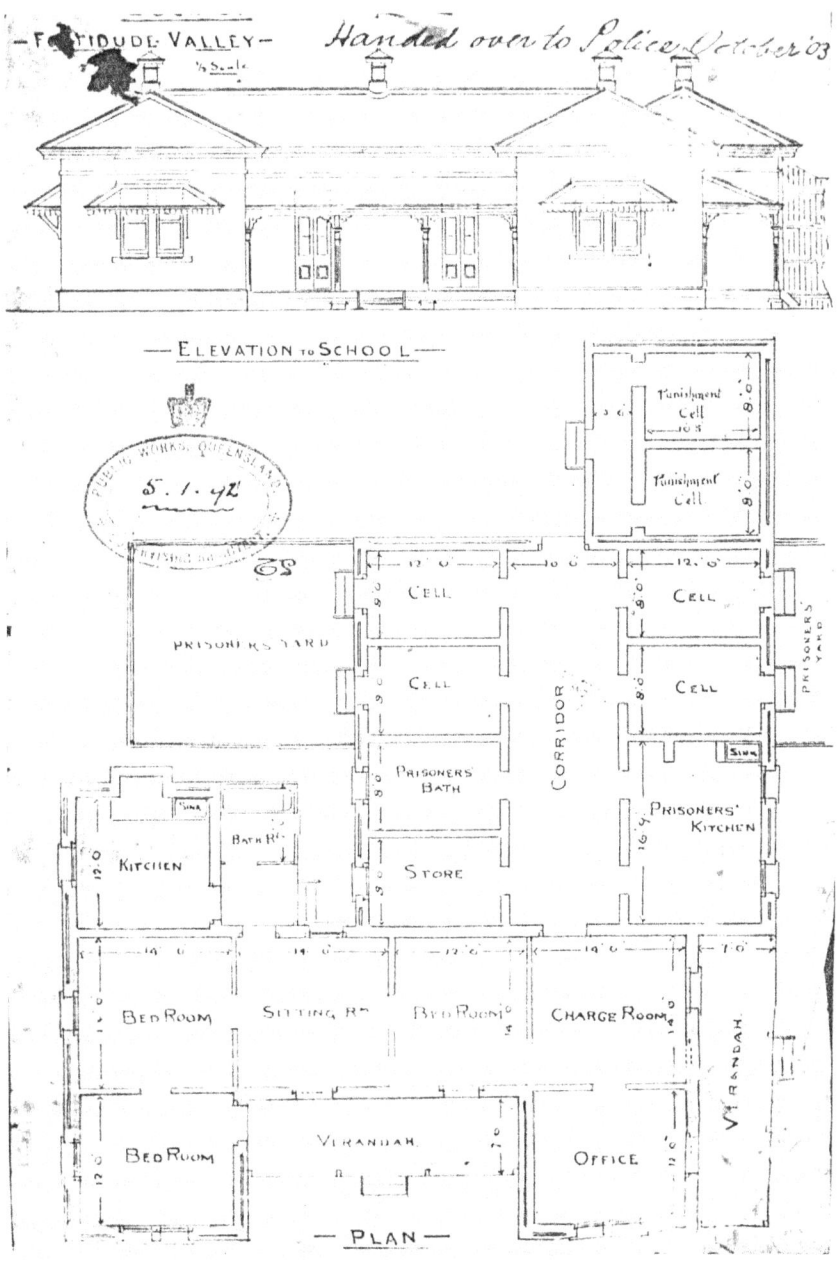

Figure 7.6: Plan of the Fortitude Valley Women's Prison, colloquially known as the Fortitude Valley Police Gaol. In 1904, it became the Fortitude Valley Police Station.
(Queensland Police Museum Collection, PLFV01)

by the jailer, Sergeant Robert Slattery, and his wife, Kate.[48] The building eventually became dilapidated and was replaced in 1889. The inquiry report highlighted the 'very indifferent state of repair', as the building had rotten shingles and roofing, as well as the issue of overcrowding: 'as many as twenty-three women and children have been crowded into the two cells'. On most days, there were around 11 prisoners in the cells, and there were no beds provided.[49] Sanitary conditions were also deficient as 'at night there [were] covered tubs, and in the yard there [were] two earth-closets, neither of them clean'. After cleaning their cells, the women spent their time gossiping, hanging around the verandah, quarrelling or engaging in 'wordy duels' using 'the foulest possible language'.[50] Daily rations within the jail consisted of bread and tea for breakfast, and bread, meat and potatoes for dinner.

All female offenders apprehended and on remand in Brisbane were detained at the Fortitude Valley prison. Further, all women committed to trial were sent to the prison until a sufficient number was assembled to justify an escort to the Toowoomba Gaol. According to the inquiry report, 'Children, young girls, and criminals who have served ten, twenty and thirty terms of imprisonment in gaol [were] herded together.'[51] Neglected children were also sent to the Fortitude Valley Police Gaol. As *The Brisbane Courier* reported in 1887, this lack of classification and separation of prisoners in turn prevented 'the possibility of reformation on the part of the convicts' because 'it contaminate[d] prisoners not wholly bad; it, in short – as was tersely put by a shrewd observer – manufacture[d] criminals'.[52]

Prior to the late-nineteenth-century penal reforms, juvenile offenders were often housed with adult criminals, as reformation was not the primary purpose of incarceration. However, due to the work of social reformers such as Mary Carpenter, in the second half of the nineteenth century, reformatories and industrial schools became a preferable alternative to imprisonment for juvenile offenders. The old Toowoomba courthouse was converted into the Industrial and Reformatory School for Women and Girls in 1882 to house juvenile female offenders. However, the reformatory did not have the anticipated effect as it was essentially a part of the Toowoomba Gaol. In the Ministers' Association of Toowoomba evidence submitted to the inquiry board in 1887, reverends from across a variety of Protestant denominations advised that the reformatory in its state at the time was 'a school of vice' and said the children were 'educated in the career of criminals'.[53] In his testimony, Police Commissioner Seymour, 'a great believer in lash', stated that in his opinion 'the youngsters' should not be imprisoned at all but given 'a few lashes and let go to their work again, instead of putting them with older criminals, where they learn to do worse'.[54]

The *Prisons Act of 1890*, which was passed following the 1887 inquiry, placed a comptroller general in charge of all prisons and provided him with authority to visit and inspect the prisons of the colony, hear all applications and inquire into all complaints, employ all prisoners at industrial labour or on public works, and submit annual reports to the minister.[55] A visiting justice was tasked with similar duties, along with the revision of sanitation, classification of prisoners and inflicting corporal punishment. The Act also prescribed total segregation of men and women by imprisonment in separate buildings or wards to prevent inmates of the opposite sex from seeing each other or conversing. In 1903, the State Prison for Women was opened at Boggo Road. The same year, the police moved into the Church Street building and it became the new Fortitude Valley Police Station. Along with the expansion of Brisbane's penal establishments, in 1905 the organisation of Brisbane's police force also grew in complexity. The Brisbane Police Sub-District was established, which included 24 stations in addition to the Petrie Terrace Police Depot. Police numbers increased to a total of 221, including 174 constables, with the majority stationed at the Roma Street (92), Fortitude Valley (19), South Brisbane (20) and Woolloongabba (14) police stations. Each police station district was separated into a series of beats with at least one police officer allocated to each beat for an eight-hour shift every day.

Maria Ellis alias Durant

Despite the reforms to segregate male and female offenders, and the expansion of the force to identify and prevent crime, a number of criminal relationships flourished in the early 1900s. One such relationship recorded in the police reports and newspapers of the time was between Charles Durant and Maria Ellis, alias Durant. Ellis, a slightly built 50-year-old woman who was 5 feet 2 inches tall, appears in the police record in June 1901 after being discharged from the women's prison in Fortitude Valley following 48 hours' imprisonment for obscene language (her third conviction). Maria Ellis must have met Charles Durant on the streets between their respective prison stints as, from 1902 onwards, she began to use his aliases of Wilson, Durant and Cannon as her own. In 1905, Maria Ellis (alias Durant) and Charles Durant were arrested for the theft of £6 13s 6d and a steel-wire purse from Alexander Davidson of Ann Street, but only Ellis was charged. This was her seventh conviction and she was sentenced to three months with hard labour at the newly constructed State Prison for Women.[56]

'54 for 54th'

By 1907, Durant and his extensive list of crimes and convictions began to garner notoriety within the justice system. In July, he was arrested by Constable Hugh Donnelly for breaking and entering a counting house in Montpelier Road, Bowen Hills, and for the theft of a set of tools. Given his astounding number of previous convictions, Durant was committed to stand trial at the next supreme court sessions. On 26 August, Durant was found guilty and sentenced to four years with hard labour by Chief Justice Cooper and a jury of 12 people. Durant's explanation for the offence was drink: 'he said he had been drinking, and he found the tools by the roadside and took them away to his camp. All his misfortunes, he said, had come from drink.'[57] During the trial, the prosecutor, Mr Kingsbury, indicated the police did not regard the prisoner as a dangerous class of criminal. There were 15 previous convictions against him for stealing and five small convictions for having property in his possession of which he could not account. There were also 26 convictions against him for bad language and vagrancy. *The Brisbane Courier* reported Mr Kingsbury's account of Durant's previous crimes and the prisoner's response:

> The Chief Justice: How many is that altogether?
> Mr. Kingsbury: Forty-six. The longest term of imprisonment he has suffered was two years for stealing.
> The Chief Justice (to the prisoner): You seem to be a habitual thief as well as what you call yourself – a drunkard.
> The Prisoner: If you will give me a light sentence I will leave the colony.
> The Chief Justice: But they won't have you in any other.
> The Prisoner: I will take a ship and go home.
> The Chief Justice: Steal one, I suppose – I don't know how you are to get one otherwise. It is really a hard thing to know what to do with you. Can you do any work?
> The Prisoner: Fencing, cane-cutting, and bush work.
> The Chief Justice: They will make some use of [you] in gaol.[58]

Charles Durant alias Wilkinson, Watson, Williams, Wilson, Evans, Cannon and 'The Tool Stealer' found petty crime profitable and that incarceration provided a roof, bed and regular meals. He rarely lost any weight while imprisoned and even gained a stone during his longest jail term of four years. Durant disappears from the official record after 23 January 1915 at the age of 54 with his 54th conviction. In the 26 years between 1888 and 1914 in which Charles Durant appeared in at least 67 official records and 65 newspaper articles, he spent 15 years (5,583 days) either in the Brisbane Gaol or St Helena Island Penal Establishment. While incarcerated, Charles missed almost every major Brisbane event: the 1889 and 1893 floods, the 1892 Brisbane cyclone, the 1893 Commercial Bank of Australia suspension, the exhibition building opening in 1891, the Queensland National Art Gallery opening in 1895 and the 1912 General Strike.

During the last 10 years of Durant's criminal career, alcoholism increasingly beleaguered his life. Between 1905 and 1914, he was arrested 12 times for drunkenness, an offence for which he was imprisoned for a total of four months and nine days. From January 1915 onwards, neither a death notice nor other official paperwork indicate what happened to him after his release from a week in prison for drunkenness in December 1914. It is unsurprising that an individual such as Durant could so easily disappear from the historical record. Considering the strains of his 54-year felonious career and his alcoholism, this recidivist offender probably did not enjoy a rich and rewarding dotage.

Habitual Criminals

Charles Durant's life as a habitual criminal was not unique. In its January 1915 issue alone, the *Queensland Police Gazette* listed Samuel Barrie, alias Douglas or Thompson, as being imprisoned for drunkenness on his 13th charge; Leonard Millett for drunkenness and obscene language on his 27th charge; Wriothesley B. Noel, alias William Neil, Roy O'Hara or Mortimer, for drunkenness on his 25th charge; and Mary Healy, alias Green, for drunkenness on her 108th charge.[59] From January 1915 to 30 June 1916, 12,931 males and 2,166 females were taken into custody. In the Brisbane district alone, 8,496 men and 1,521 women were convicted of drunkenness; 1,099 men and 205 women were convicted of obscene, profane, indecent or insulting language; 634 men and 65 women were convicted of stealing; and 39 men and 11 women were convicted of vagrancy.[60] Durant's alias 'The Tool Stealer' was a criminal trajectory applicable to around one-fifth of the Queensland colonial prison population of the time as penal records show that larceny was the most commonly committed property offence in the colony. It is likely the growing complexity of the city topography coupled with the increasing rates of production of cheaper ready-made goods that made larceny the preferred crime of opportunity.

Between 1875 and 1886, the percentage of prisoners to population stood at under 1 per cent, and half of the colonial prisoner population was aged between 20 and 30 years. The ever-increasing number of prisoners in the colony demanded an increase in police organisation and administration, as well as prison establishments. In 1887, *The Brisbane Courier* reported that 'An analysis of statistics collected by the board and the evidence of police-magistrates, heads of the police force, and the Sheriff show that crime in the colony has not increased in the same ratio as the population, though a saving clause appears to indicate that crime is on the increase in and around Brisbane.'[61] This increase in crime in Brisbane mirrors crime statistics across other post-industrial urban centres as the increasing population offered anonymity to offenders.

Charles Durant was one of Queensland's hardened recidivists and spent a considerable part of his life in prison. Given their numerous and repeated convictions, Mr and 'Mrs' Durant frequented all the major penal establishments, police jails and lock-ups of the colony during the late 1800s and early 1900s. The Durants' recidivist records and time in prison were not unique. In the second half of the nineteenth century, recidivism rates in the colony oscillated between 1 in 4.7 to 1 in 6.4 at its peak in 1876. This coincided with new scientific methods that allowed for better identification of offenders, such as fingerprinting and photography, with criminals' unique physical features regularly published in the police gazettes. Alongside these scientific advances, humanitarian reforms underpinned by the progressive ideas of the Enlightenment led to penal reforms across Britain and its dominions. Concurrently, phrenology and theories of moral deficiency replaced the previous medicalised view of deviancy, and criminality came to be seen as a choice. More so, Social Darwinism fostered the new science of eugenics, which, in extreme cases, advocated for lifetime incarceration in an effort to reduce the propagation of the criminal class or *habitués*. Despite the scientific advances in criminal identification and evolving theories of policing deviancy, criminal numbers in the colony continued to grow. This ever-expanding prisoner population demanded an increase in penal establishments and their administration. The proposed solution for both was panopticon-styled buildings, which maximised the number of cells to house prisoners while minimising carceral supervision. The panopticon served as a blueprint for many key penal establishments, including Boggo Road Gaol in Brisbane, which further standardised and professionalised the policing of prisoners in the colony.

Conclusion

> It is by the general influence of good Laws, aided by the regulations of an energetic Police, that the blessings of true Liberty, and the undisturbed enjoyment of Property, are secured.
>
> Patrick Colquhoun, *A Treatise on the Police of the Metropolis*[1]

IN 1904, FIVE years after the Royal Commission into the Constitution, Administration and Working of the Criminal Investigation Branch of the Police Force of Queensland, Sergeant Michael O'Sullivan was transferred from his regional posting to Brisbane and assigned with reorganising the much-criticised detective department.[2] He was an outsider, and his promotion caused a minor strike in the Criminal Investigation Branch (CIB). When O'Sullivan joined the CIB, he found that the men 'were utterly unsuited for detective work'.[3] Major William Cahill, who served as police commissioner from 1905 to 1916, directed O'Sullivan to select and try out the men he deemed talented for detective work. 'It was on those lines that the staff was built up', O'Sullivan wrote in his memoir, *Cameos of Crime*, 'but even then there were disappointments, as some men who were brought up on six months' trial failed to live up to the required standard, and had to go back into uniform.'[4] Following a lengthy trial process, O'Sullivan's group of men, who were chosen for talent rather than internal connections, delivered long-awaited success to the department. The Queensland Police Commissioner's annual report for 1914 shows a remarkable increase in arrests, prosecutions and successful convictions across all levels of the judiciary between 1906 and 1914. Conviction rates in the courts also rose from 26 to 44 in the supreme court, 16 to 80 in the district court and 105 to 275 in the police court.[5] As O'Sullivan described, 'Queensland finally fared favourably within an annual interchange of statistical returns between various police departments [within Australia], showing the percentage of successes and failures in the investigation of all crimes reported.'[6] O'Sullivan did not 'lay claim to any special genius in elucidating crime', but instead stated that because the CIB's 'body of men, usually numbering twenty-five, combined and working as a team' were 'determined to keep the criminal element under', they were able to identify and prosecute criminals more successfully.[7] According to Harry C Perry in *A Son of Australia: Memories of W. E. Parry-Okeden, ISO, 1840–1926* (Parry-Okeden preceded Cahill as the police commissioner), the CIB 'stood the test of time and with some minor alteration it still remain[ed] the Criminal Investigation Branch as [Parry-Okeden] drafted it'.[8] O'Sullivan went on to have a fruitful career within the Queensland Police, which saw him receive 19 transfers across Queensland, including to the 'disturbed districts' in the west during the Shearers' Strike of 1894. O'Sullivan retired at the rank of acting deputy commissioner in 1923.

As policing bodies shifted from a group of fragmented and decentralised units to centralised professional organisations, police forces within the Australian colonies and across the British Empire came to embody the ideological principles of humanism, rationalism and utilitarianism. Italian philosopher Cesare di Beccaria's treatise examining legislative governance, *An Essay on Crimes and Punishments* (1764), stipulated that punishment must be proportionate to the crime, so that it functions as a deterrent rather than retribution.[9] His work crystallised much of the progressive thinking prevalent in the eighteenth and nineteenth centuries, which has persisted into the legal system in place today. Di Beccaria's treatise emphasised that an effective system of policing ensured the certainty of an offender's apprehension and thus the inevitability of punishment. The principle of utilitarianism, advocated by English Enlightenment thinker Jeremy Bentham, underpinned further critical developments in the legal system, such as preventative policing, penitentiary reform, and discipline and labour in prisons. The practice of rewarding good behaviour and offering prisoners the opportunity for reform through labour became the first attempts at rehabilitating criminals. These changes led to transportation for life substituting hanging as the maximum punishment for several offences that had previously been punishable by death.

During the nineteenth century, a police force founded on these ideological principles became integral to a well-functioning colonial society. Further, as societal understanding of criminality and law enforcement was constantly changing to align with new philosophical and scientific concepts, the colonial police forces were ever changing. Being part of the evolving police force afforded colonial officers many opportunities: for Peter 'Duff' Murphy it was a chance for resocialisation, for Samuel Sneyd it provided a secure civic career, and for Samuel Lloyd, Thomas Tyrrell and James Nethercote it offered an upward social trajectory. The organisation was responsible for enforcing accepted social behaviours and norms, protecting and preserving life and property, and preventing, detecting and prosecuting crime. It also engaged in suppressing behaviours deemed anti-social, immoral and deviant, thereby assuming the role of morality police. Offences that disrupted public peace and idyllic notions of orderly society, such as using obscene language and drunkenness, dominated police court proceedings. The biographies of colonial recidivist offenders Susan McGowan and Charles Durant reveal the proliferation of gendered and classist justice. Men outnumbered, and continue to outnumber, women in the judicial and penal systems. The life trajectory of many female defendants at this time followed a common pattern of unwanted pregnancy, unemployment and/or desertion by a spouse, which led to petty crime and prostitution. In comparison, male offenders regularly turned to crime in absence or scarcity of employment, or due to financial or behavioural issues often linked to excessive drinking. The colonial prisons and lock-ups lacked provisions for prisoners' segregation, particularly the segregation of adult and juvenile offenders, which led to future recidivism. Most women and men alike who were trapped in the cycle of criminality came from the lower socio-economic classes, and the frequent short-term imprisonment they experienced resulted in a blurring between their life inside and outside of penal establishments.

As the century progressed, the attention of colonial law enforcers turned to the new science of policing and uniform codification of the judiciary, with the latter culminating in the development of the 1899 *Criminal Code*, which is still in use today. This new science of policing, which was grounded in educational developments, incentivised diligent training and study, as well as individual merit, positioning these as the pathway for promotions. Further, as the population increased and became more mobile, transportation systems diversified and new methods of communication emerged. These structural changes coupled with scientific innovations and technological advances, such as the use of forensics and wireless communication, resulted in improved crime-fighting methods and influenced policing practices.

At the turn of the twentieth century, the Queensland Police Force began rapidly evolving into a professional and centrally organised institution. Compulsory first-aid training and classes were introduced in police depots, and, from 1896 onwards, officers were expected to be able to ride, care for and repair their bicycles. In 1904, the fingerprint bureau was established and produced a centralised reference database, which made interstate criminal identification more efficient. By 1910, nearly every station within a 5-mile radius of the centre of Brisbane was connected by telephone. In 1935, following the approval of a wireless station with the call sign 'VKR', three patrol cars were equipped with one-way radio communication. A permanent two-way radio transmission station was established six years later and allowed two-way communication between the station and patrol cars. The same year, 1941, the scientific section of the Queensland Police started implementing forensic chemistry, scientific photography and chirography (the study of handwriting), which transformed evidence collection and processing. These advances remodelled the police into a professional scientific enterprise and elevated the police service as an occupation.

Despite the scientific advances to crime prevention and detection across the nineteenth and twentieth centuries, the bobby-on-the-beat approach to policing has persevered. Many modern urban police organisations initially moved away from the beat model, but have reintroduced systems and duties, including regular foot patrols and community integration, that have brought the force back to its roots.[10] In fact, the uniformed police beat and emphasis on preventative policing has 'remained the bedrock of police work'.[11] The *Rules for the General Government and Discipline of Members of the Police Force of Queensland* (1869) advised that 'It is indispensably necessary that [a police constable] should be perfectly acquainted with all the parts of the [assigned] beat or section, with the streets, thoroughfares, courts, and houses. [It is] expected, [a constable] possess such a knowledge of the inhabitants of each house as to enable [them] to recognize their persons, and thus prevent mistakes, and be enabled to render assistance to the inhabitants when called for.'[12] These directives are equally appropriate today, a century and a half later. The political and social concepts might have changed but the ideological principles of the organisation and the basic police duties have remained consistent into the twenty-first century.

While the modern-day Queensland Police Service is far more technologically advanced than their colonial counterparts, and are equipped with training, knowledge and instruments that allow for greater crime prevention and criminal apprehension, the oath officers take upon joining the force is relatively unchanged. The men and women who join the ranks of Peter 'Duff' Murphy, Samuel Sneyd, Samuel Lloyd, Thomas Tyrrell and James Nethercote, and all those who came before and will come after them, still swear to keep and preserve peace and prevent all offences against the same.

Acknowledgements

I WOULD LIKE to express my sincerest gratitude to Lisa Jones, the curator of the Queensland Police Museum, Virginia Gordon, assistant curator, and Georgia Grier, museum assistant, for facilitating this research by granting access to the museum's collections – their support, knowledge and assistance were instrumental for the successful completion of this book. I am forever in debt to Lisa for her expertise, readiness to help and her contribution to this book as an author. Lisa authored Chapter 2, which traces the service career of Samuel Sneyd, and co-authored Chapter 7, which examines the life of criminal *habitué* Charles Durant.

I am grateful to Dr Bill Metcalf for his encouragement, Dr Ray Kerkhove and Dr Jonathan Richards for their specialist inputs, as well as associate professors Bruce Buchan and David Barrie for their invaluable feedback on the draft manuscript. I would also like to extend my gratitude to my wonderful editor, Felicity Dunning, as well as Madonna Duffy, Publishing Director, at the University of Queensland Press.

I am especially grateful to my family for their support throughout this project: my mother, Natalia Talnikova, for always nudging me onwards, my mother-in-law, Kirsten Marion, for the indefatigable edits, my husband, K Sean Jenkins, for love and forbearance, and my son, Ciaran, (born after the project began) for being the greatest helper and hinderer one could ever hope for.

The research for this book has been made possible through the Lord Mayor's Helen Taylor Research Award for Local History, Brisbane City Council.

Appendix A

Queensland Police Officers – 1828 to 1863 (Moreton Bay Penal Colony, Brisbane Town, Fortitude Valley, South Brisbane, Kangaroo Point and Ipswich)

Listed alphabetically by surname with the year their service started and police section (if known) in brackets.

Allone, Daniel (1852)
Alone/Allone, Daniel (1856)
Anderson, William (1853)
Apjohn, William (1860)
Askew, Edward Stephen (1862)
Atkins, Provincial Police Inspector Heyward (1851)

Balfrey, John (pre-1864)
Barry, Richard (1862)
Barry, Thomas (pre-1864)
Bayley, Wallace Paget (pre-1864)
Beardsmore, Thomas (1848)
Beggs/Biggs, HW (1848)
Biggs/Beggs, John (1848)
Bigley, C (pre-1864)
Bishop, John (1843; Moreton Bay Penal Colony)
Black, Francis (pre-1864)
Bloomfield, [Unknown] (1858)
Bodel, John (pre-1864)
Bol, John (pre-1864)
Booth, John (1850)
Bordmore, Henry (1853)
Bottington/Bettingten/Bellington, Chief Constable Richard (1833)
Bourne, R (1858)
Bow/Boe, John (1854)
Brady, Peter (1859)
Bragg, Charles (1856)
Brennan, Denis (pre-1864)

Brian, [Unknown] (1851)
Broderick, John (1859)
Brookes, [Unknown] (1857)
Brophy, John (pre-1864)
Brown, George (1840; Moreton Bay Penal Colony)
Brown, Joseph (pre-1864)
Browne, Henry (pre-1864)
Buckley, [Unknown] (pre-1864)
Burke, James P (pre-1864)
Burke, Michael (pre-1864)
Burke, [Unknown] (1849)
Burton, George (pre-1864)

Cahill, Patrick (1859)
Canner, [Unknown] (1856)
Canning, John Harvey / John Henry (1861)
Cannot, Samuel (1857)
Carmody, Bartholomew (1859)
Carson, William (1854)
Carton/Carten, Joseph (pre-1864)
Cassles, John (pre-1864)
Clarke, Arthur T (pre-1864)
Coffey, John (pre-1864)
Connell, John (pre-1864)
Connolly, Matthew (1853)
Connor, James (1856)
Connor, Chief Constable Michael (1854)
Connor, Samuel (1858)
Conroy, John (1849)

Conroy, John (1851)
Cooper, Charles (1853)
Corby, F (pre-1864)
Cosgrove, Michael (1858)
Costigan, Patrick (1863)
Cottrell, Edward (pre-1864)
Crawford, Wiliam H (pre-1864)
Cronk, [Unknown] (1853)
Cross, B (pre-1864)
Cross, James (pre-1864)
Curry/Currie, Jackson (1856)

Davis, [Unknown] (1857)
Delany, [Unknown] (pre-1864)
Devine, George (pre-1864)
Devine, William (1857)
Dillane, Thomas (pre-1864)
Doane, [Unknown] (1855)
Doherty, W (pre-1864)
Donaldson, Frederick (pre-1864)
Dowle, James (1857)
Dowling, Lawrence (pre-1864)
Dowling, Martin (1853)
Downes/Downs, John (1852)
Doyle, James (1855)
Doyle, William (pre-1864)
Dunn, James (pre-1864)
Dunn, [Unknown] (1855)
Dunn, [Unknown] (1855)
Dunn, [Unknown] (1857)
Dunne, [Unknown] (1858)

Edwards, James (1857)
Egan/Eagan, Charles (pre-1864)
Egan, John (1840; Moreton Bay Penal Colony)
Eggilston, [Unknown] (1855)
Elliget/Allicott/Elleget, John (1858)
Elliott, George (pre-1864)

Farrelly/Farelly, Andrew (pre-1864)
Finlay, Henry (1846)
Fitzpatrick, Chief Constable William (1843)
Flaherty, Michael (1861)
Flannery, Denis (pre-1864)
Fogarty, Thomas (1857)
Foran, Jeremiah (pre-1864)

Gallagher, John (pre-1864)
Gallwey, Daniel (pre-1864)
Giles, Robert (1840; Moreton Bay Penal Colony)
Ginivan, Lawrence/Laurence (pre-1864)
Ginna, James (pre-1864)
Gorman, [Unknown] (pre-1864)
Graham, Edward (pre-1864)
Gratton/Grattan, Henry (1847)
Greenaway, William (pre-1864)
Griffin, Chief Constable Thomas John (1860)
Gronow, HL (pre-1864)
Gunn, William (1858)

Hanrahan, Andrew (pre-1864)
Harris, William (1856)
Hart, Chief Constable William (1849)
Henniker, Frederick (pre-1864)
Higgins, Martin (1843)
Hildrew/Hildrews, John (pre-1864)
Hill, George (pre-1864)
Hingston, [Unknown] (1850)
Hitches, WF (pre-1864)
Hoar, [Unknown] (1856)
Hoey, James (1857)
Hogan, P (pre-1864)
Holy, James (1844)
Honston/Houston, James (1845)
Hore, Robert (1848)

Johnson, Ralph Cholmondeley Godschall (pre-1864)
Jones, Thomas (pre-1864)

Kenna, [Unknown] (1859)
Kennedy, Patrick (pre-1864)
Kerr, Robert (pre-1864)
Keys, Henry (1856)
King, Walter Stewart (1862)

Laidler, [Unknown] (1855)
Laing, Owen (pre-1864)
Laing/Lang, Thadeus/Thaddeus (pre-1864)
Lang, J (pre-1864)
Laurenson, Henry (pre-1864)
Lewis, John Armstrong (1863)
Love, Paul (1863)
Lynch, T (pre-1864)

Macalister, [Unknown] (1847)
Mahon, P (pre-1864)
Maloney/Moloney, Stephen (pre-1864)
Malony, Martin (pre-1864)
Manly, Chief Constable Edward Mayne (1850)
Manson, W (pre-1864)
Marshall, Michael (pre-1864)
McBride, [Unknown] (1848)
McCarthy, Denis (pre-1864)
McCrohon, William Henry (1846)
McDonough, Peter (pre-1864)
McFadden, [Unknown] (1849)
McFadden, [Unknown] (pre-1864)
McGrath, John (1843)
McGrath, Patrick (pre-1864)
McGuire, James (pre-1864)
McGuire, Thomas (1848)
McGuirk, [Unknown] (1858)
McIntosh, Chief Constable John (1828)
McMahon, John (pre-1864)
McMartin, AR (pre-1864)
McMullan, Ewan (1858)
Meadows, JP (1846)
Merrick, John (1850)
Mitchell, Joseph (1850)
Monsell, [Unknown] (1851)
Moore, John (pre-1864)
Moore, William (1847)
Moroney, John (pre-1864)
Morris, [Unknown] (1859)
Mulholland, L (pre-1864)
Mullally, John (pre-1864)
Mullane, Michael (pre-1864)
Mullane, Patrick (pre-1864)
Murphy, Chief Constable Peter 'Duff' (1842)

Neale, Henry (1858)
Neil, Patrick (1853)
Neil, Patrick (1858)
Nihill, Patrick (pre-1864)
Nutting, John Bligh (pre-1864)

O'Brien, Darby (pre-1864)
O'Connor, Jeremiah (pre-1864)
O'Connor, John (1856)
O'Connor, [Unknown] (1855)

O'Donnell, John (pre-1864)
O'Hara, Michael (pre-1864)
O'Regan, Daniel (pre-1864)
Orr, R (1856)
Owen, Bedell Stamford (pre-1864)
Owens, Jospeh (1863)

Paschen, Otto Oscar (pre-1864)
Pegg, [Unknown] (pre-1864)
Phillips, John (1850)
Powell, Walter David Taylor (1855)
Power, Michael (pre-1864)
Price, George F (pre-1864)

Quigley, [Unknown] (1850)
Quinn, Chief Constable Edward (1853)
Quirk, Chief Constable Thomas Francis (1859)

Rainbow, William Watson (1857)
Rampling, Henry (1856)
Ramsay, James (1846)
Ramsay/Ramsey, James (1843)
Reid, Archibald (pre-1864)
Reilly, John (pre-1864)
Reilly, Owen (pre-1864)
Rice, Thomas (pre-1864)
Rich, Barry (1862)
Riley/Reilly, John (1849)
Roche, Thomas (pre-1864)
Rochfort, John J (pre-1864)
Rocks, Terence (1856)
Rooke, GJ (pre-1864)
Roy, John (1855)

Scanlon/Scanlan, Jeremiah (1843)
Shephard, Benjamin (1855)
Sherman, Robert (1863)
Smith, David (pre-1864)
Sneyd, Chief Constable Samuel (1850)
Sparkes, [Unknown] (1849)
Spence, Thomas (1855)
Spencer, Richard (1858)
Stevens, Jesse Edward Martin (1861)
Stevenson, John (1863)
Storey, William (1857)
Stretton, William (pre-1864)
Swinburne, [Unknown] (1852)

Thompson, William (1840; Moreton Bay Penal Colony)
Timmony, [Unknown] (1855)
Tredennick/Tredenicke/Tredenneck/Tredenick, James (1850)

Uhr, Reginald Charles Heber (pre-1864)

Walker, Frederick (pre-1864)
Walker, John (1848)
Walker, John (pre-1864)
Walsh, William (1863)
Ward, JA (pre-1864)
Ward, Richard R (1855)

Watters, William (pre-1864)
Watts, William G (1853)
Wheeler, Edward (pre-1864)
White, John (1863)
Whyte, Commandant's Clerk & Chief Constable William (pre-1864; Moreton Bay Penal Colony)
Williams, Thomas Spence (pre-1864)
Woods, Frederick Newton (pre-1864)
Wright, Alfred Samuel (1850)

Young, Daniel (1843)

Appendix B

Queensland Police Officers – 1864 to 1900 (Brisbane and Ipswich)

Listed alphabetically by surname with sworn-in date in brackets.
Information current as of December 2019.

Acton, John (19.10.1876)
Acton, Robert (10.03.1871)
Adams, James (29.03.1864)
Adams, William (8.06.1898)
Ahern, Dennis (18.10.1864)
Ahern, James Keogh (3.11.1884)
Ahern, Thomas (16.12.1875)
Ahern, William (27.03.1871)
Aherne, Philip (3.12.1887)
Aikens, Patrick (6.05.1868)
Aird, William James (24.10.1898)
Aldridge/Alldridge, Walter (23.10.1873)
Allen, John Maxwell (28.01.1874)
Allen, John Patrick (12.02.1890)
Allen, Robert S (10.07.1867)
Allison, Robert (18.10.1882)
Allison, Samuel (22.05.1883)
Amies, Samuel Lowell (19.09.1883 & 6.03.1889)
Amies, Thomas Lowell (3.04.1872)
Anderson, Anders Henning (25.02.1874)
Anderson, Thomas Kerr (29.05.1872)
Apjohn, Michael (7.12.1870)
Apjohn/Lloyd-Apjohn, Charles Caleb Lloyd (1.12.1885 & 18.12.1886)
Argue, William (4.08.1887)
Arlott, Henry George (16.02.1876)
Arlott, William (1.07.1874)
Armitage, William (26.03.1886)
Armstrong, Frank Ayerst (14.07.1899)
Armstrong, Robert (6.09.1871)
Armstrong, Robert (5.08.1874)

Armstrong, William (15.02.1865)
Ashton, George (11.09.1865)
Ashton, John (23.01.1878)
Aspinall, Edward (9.08.1887)
Aspinall, George Charles (11.08.1896)
Astleford, James (11.09.1878)
Atkinson, James (29.08.1874)
Atkinson, Thomas (2.06.1869)
Atteridge, John (10.01.1877)
Atterige, Philip (6.06.1877)
Aubin, Myrtil (11.04.1865)
Auld, Thomas (1.12.1885 & 1.08.1894)

Bagget, William (24.12.1897)
Bailey, John (2.08.1884)
Bailey, William (18.06.1868)
Bailey, William John (16.01.1890)
Bain, Donald (23.09.1884)
Bain, George (25.07.1877)
Bain, Walter (3.08.1891)
Baines, John (14.11.1872)
Baker, Thomas (24.04.1875)
Balaam, William Patrick (16.01.1890)
Ball, Joseph (12.12.1884)
Ballantine, Thomas (8.01.1867)
Balle, Francis (23.08.1878)
Banfiel, James (18.07.1872)
Banks, Edmond (7.07.1893)
Barclay, Lindsay (5.08.1880)
Barfoot, William (27.05.1868)
Barnardo/Bernardo, Augustus (3.01.1866)
Barrett, Edmund (21.12.1889)

Barrett, Michael (3.08.1891)
Barrett, Richard (4.04.1866)
Barron, Alexander D (17.05.1882)
Barry, Edward (11.03.1885)
Barry, John Elliott (19.02.1868)
Barry, Patrick (18.05.1891)
Barry, Richard (21.12.1889)
Barton, Dunbar H (12.03.1881)
Barton, William (18.11.1877)
Basford, John (31.12.1883)
Bateman, Stanley Howard (20.04.1896)
Baumann/Beaumann, Joseph (21.11.1877)
Bayley, William Henry, ([Unknown] 1864)
Beale, Percy (24.10.1865)
Beary, Patrick (10.01.1891)
Beasley, John (1.05.1865)
Beatty, Frederick (25.02.1874)
Beatty, Joseph Alexander (8.11.1876)
Becher, Michael Alleyn Richard (28.02.1889)
Beggan, Bernard (25.11.1867)
Behan, James (17.12.1874)
Behan, John (9.04.1891)
Behan, Michael (8.02.1872)
Behan, Patrick Joseph (23.08.1888 & 20.02.1891)
Belford, Richard (6.05.1874)
Bell, Henry (10.06.1889)
Bell, Robert Talon (7.09.1894)
Bell, Thomas (16.07.1873)
Bendon, John (9.04.1884)
Bennett, Francis (7.09.1870)
Bennett, Michael (21.12.1889)
Benson, Edward Lalice (27.06.1886)
Benzies, Alexander (1.07.1884)
Bergin, James (16.05.1877)
Bestmann, John (23.08.1894)
Billam, William (1.11.1875)
Blackmore, Edward James (25.11.1898)
Blackwell, Thomas (23.10.1878)
Blake, Augustine John (10.08.1870)
Blake, Edward (2.01.1873)
Blake, Edward (11.09.1878)
Blake, John (14.03.1864)
Blake, John Austin (15.12.1890)
Blake, Martin George (5.03.1873)
Blake, Thomas (4.10.1876)

Bleaney, Patrick (19.11.1883)
Blunden, Christopher (7.03.1866)
Bodman, Frank (20.06.1883)
Bolingbroke, Lynch (2.04.1867)
Bolton, Henry Edward (24.12.1896)
Bonis, George (13.08.1866)
Boreham, Charles (14.05.1869)
Boreham, William (20.11.1873)
Bourke, Thomas Henry (1.02.1887)
Bowen, Edward Mostyn Webb (7.08.1873)
Bowen, William (2.09.1875)
Boxhall, Henry (23.10.1878)
Boyle, Terrence (13.02.1873)
Brabazon, R Stafford (18.08.1873)
Brackin, James (1.07.1885)
Bradburn, Patrick (8.06.1885)
Bradburn, Richard (29.04.1886)
Bradfield, James (11.12.1889)
Brady, Edward (11.07.1877)
Brady, John (6.06.1877)
Brady, Martin (10.06.1868)
Brady, Peter (1.01.1864)
Brady, William (17.01.1871)
Brannelly, John (14.09.1871)
Brassell, John (8.04.1876)
Breen, David (30.11.1888)
Breene/Breen, Thomas (12.06.1878)
Brennan, Edward (22.01.1873)
Brennan, Kyran (1.10.1873)
Brennan, Martin Joseph (1.11.1890)
Brennan, Nicholas Peter (7.09.1894)
Bretherton, Charles (12.11.1872)
Brett, George (26.11.1883)
Brett, Robert (26.11.1883)
Brett, Thomas (29.04.1886)
Brimstone, Bernard Barton (19.04.1899)
Brinkley, George (30.06.1868)
Brinkley, George (1.06.1869)
Briody, Myles (19.04.1876)
Broderick, Daniel (4.08.1886)
Broderick, Michael (23.12.1885)
Brolan, Dennis (13.05.1886)
Brooks, Charles Henry (19.09.1878)
Brophy, John William (17.01.1881 & 28.10.1886)
Brosnan, Michael (19.04.1886)
Brown/Browne, Charles Frederick ([Unknown] 1874)

Browne, Henry (1.05.1872)
Browne, James (20.03.1891)
Browne, John (12.02.1890)
Browne, Leonard (1.01.1866)
Browne, William (21.01.1874)
Bruce, John (13.01.1870)
Brumfield, Austin (6.11.1872)
Bryan, Wilmont (29.07.1874)
Buchan, Alexander (24.12.1896)
Buchanan, David (17.05.1867)
Buckley, Daniel (3.12.1889)
Buckley, Michael (1.01.1864)
Buckmaster, George (14.01.1871)
Bulger, Thomas (20.04.1864)
Burke, James Henry (10.08.1865)
Burke, James P (1.01.1864)
Burke, John (10.06.1864)
Burke, John (3.12.1887)
Burke, John (4.03.1890)
Burke, Michael (4.01.1867)
Burke, Patrick (15.06.1886)
Burke, Robert H (17.09.1873)
Burke, Thomas (2.03.1864 & 24.05.1869)
Burns, Malcolm Stewart (1.11.1897)
Burton, George R (28.06.1876)
Bushnell, John (4.11.1889)
Butler, Edmond (10.01.1877)
Butler, Martin (20.12.1876)
Butler, Thomas (13.05.1874)
Butler, William Thomas (31.10.1888)
Butterworth, Archibald William (28.05.1887)
Butze, Gustave (1.05.1884)
Buxton, Henry (25.02.1874)
Byrne, Andrew (4.11.1868)
Byrne, George (18.07.1872)
Byrne, John (1.12.1875)
Byrne, Michael (9.07.1873)
Byrne, Patrick (22.05.1883)
Byrne, Thomas (30.09.1886 & 30.05.1896)
Byron, Michael (11.04.1882)

Cadden, William (1.05.1884)
Cafferty, Austin (31.12.1883)
Cahill, Andrew (12.09.1866)
Cahill, Daniel (13.05.1867)
Cahill, Daniel (9.09.1867)

Cahill, John (17.05.1887)
Cahill, Malachy (20.04.1864)
Cahill, Michael (10.05.1876)
Cahill, Patrick (5.11.1867)
Cahill, Patrick (10.06.1872)
Cahill, Patrick (23.08.1894)
Callaghan, Aeneas/Æneas (8.06.1885)
Callinan, Patrick (8.04.1874)
Callinan, Patrick (12.10.1876)
Callinan, Thomas (1.07.1884)
Cameron, John (26.01.1874)
Cameron, John Kenneth (23.08.1894)
Cameron, Thomas (6.05.1868)
Campbell, Donald (1.11.1866)
Campbell, John Joseph (16.12.1898)
Campbell, Louis (7.02.1877)
Campbell, Peter (8.11.1873)
Campbell, Samuel (23.09.1882)
Canning, John (28.06.1876)
Canning, John (8.06.1885)
Canning, Owen (4.03.1874)
Canning, William Thomas (29.06.1880)
Cannon, Michael (21.12.1881)
Cantwell, John (21.09.1886)
Cantwell, Patrick (22.03.1876)
Caplis, F (20.06.1868)
Caraher, Thomas (11.01.1886)
Cardwell, Francis S (22.03.1866)
Carew, Michael (15.08.1889)
Carfoot, Thomas (19.11.1883)
Carmody, Michael (14.12.1876)
Carmody, Michael Joseph (1.05.1885)
Carpenter, Hugh (28.10.1886)
Carr, John (3.12.1887)
Carr, John Henry (21.09.1886)
Carroll, Denis (20.06.1877)
Carroll, Francis (27.10.1864)
Carroll, James (3.01.1866)
Carroll, James/Patrick (26.04.1876)
Carroll, John (18.05.1882)
Carroll, John William (5.02.1873)
Carroll, Patrick (2.05.1881)
Carter, Gustave (19.05.1875)
Carver, John (31.12.1884)
Case, Ernest William (31.07.1895)
Casey, David (17.05.1887)
Casey, John (21.06.1899)
Cassidy, Alexander (1.08.1877)
Cassidy, John (27.08.1890)

Cassles, John (1.01.1864)
Casson, Thomas (27.05.1868)
Caulfield, Henry Patrick (19.03.1892)
Caulfield, Michael (10.07.1889)
Cavanagh, Michael (1.05.1883 & 16.07.1886)
Chalmers, Archibald (20.03.1891 & 9.02.1893)
Chardon, Francis George Henry (20.02.1891)
Charters, James (1.09.1884)
Chase, WDM (1.03.1864)
Chearnley, Walter (27.04.1881)
Cheeke, Walter F (7.10.1876)
Christie, Robert George (23.08.1894)
Claffey, John (26.05.1870)
Claire, Thomas (11.03.1885)
Clampett, Michael (20.03.1878)
Clancey, Patrick (9.01.1878)
Clancy, Charles (12.10.1883)
Clancy, Henry Alfred (16.05.1899 & 21.08.1901)
Clancy, Hugh (27.09.1876)
Clancy, Patrick (4.05.1867)
Clancy, Thomas (4.03.1890)
Clare, Lawrence James (1.09.1885 & 1.09.1887)
Clare/Clair, John (25.04.1874)
Clark, Arthur (9.04.1879)
Clarke, Arthur T (1.01.1864)
Clarke, James (1.04.1868)
Clarke, William Archer (3.08.1885)
Clayton, Dowell Pelham (20.03.1891)
Cleary, Cornelius (10.09.1890)
Cleary, Henry (11.07.1891)
Cleary, Joseph (9.01.1878)
Cleary, Patrick (12.02.1873)
Clements, William ([Unknown] 05.1868)
Clibborn, Thomas G (1.09.1873)
Clinch, Luke (13.01.1864)
Clines, Thomas (1.07.1891)
Clinton, Patrick (9.10.1878)
Clohesy, James (16.07.1880)
Clulow, William John (6.09.1883)
Clutterbuck, John Austin (10.07.1878 & 31.03.1881)
Coakley, Daniel (12.01.1870)
Cochrane, John Albert (19.09.1898)
Cochrane, William (5.06.1869)

Cockle, John (12.01.1870)
Coffey, John (1.01.1864)
Colclough, Edward (20.09.1865)
Coleman, Henry (7.02.1871)
Colerin/Colvin, William (23.07.1873)
Coles, Octavius (1.02.1887)
Coll, Denis (22.05.1878)
Collins, Daniel (4.08.1890)
Collins, John (29.10.1873)
Collins, Martin (3.08.1865)
Collins, Patrick (2.04.1887)
Collis, Thomas (24.02.1897)
Collopy, Matthew (10.08.1865)
Collopy/Callopy, Joseph M (31.05.1877)
Colman, Michael (1.09.1887)
Colohan, Thomas (1.01.1866)
Coman, Joseph (26.02.1896)
Compigne, Walter (27.06.1865)
Concannon, Thomas (13.11.1885)
Concannon, William (23.09.1885)
Condrin, Thomas (2.12.1870)
Connell, John (1.01.1864)
Connell, Patrick (1.07.1874)
Connolly, Michael (28.12.1881)
Connolly, Richard (1.11.1890)
Connolly, Thomas John (28.05.1887)
Connor, James (1.01.1864)
Conroy, William (31.12.1883)
Conry, James (4.01.1888)
Considine, William (20.09.1877)
Conway, Benjamin (20.06.1883)
Conway, Edward (31.10.1887)
Conway, Joseph (1.05.1891)
Cook, James (1.12.1864)
Cook, Thomas (2.10.1873)
Coomb, Edward Henry (1.09.1872)
Cooper, Henry (14.08.1869)
Corbett, John (24.11.1875)
Corcoran, Michael (1.05.1885)
Corkery, John (10.02.1892)
Corkran, Thomas Knight (30.07.1874)
Corney, William Ellis (16.05.1899)
Cosgrove, Jeremiah (1.06.1869)
Cosgrove, Michael (1.01.1864)
Costello, Daniel (16.07.1890)
Costello, James (1.11.1883)
Costello, John (3.01.1866)
Costigan, Patrick (1.01.1864)
Coughlan, James (22.09.1875)

Coughlan, Patrick (21.01.1874)
Courtney, Isaac J (9.01.1878)
Courtney, John (1.08.1889)
Covell, Henry Horton (7.04.1896)
Cowan, Joseph (28.07.1875)
Cowley, John (20.08.1883)
Cowley, Philip Webster (21.06.1899)
Cox, George Thomas (6.09.1889)
Coyle, James (23.09.1885)
Craig, Edward (11.03.1874)
Crampton, Edward (20.02.1891)
Craven, William (1.01.1865)
Crawford, Charles Edward (13.02.1882)
Crawford, William H (1.01.1864)
Cremins, Patrick (3.05.1887)
Cresswell/Creswell, Henry (2.10.1874)
Cronau, John (17.10.1894)
Cronin, Lawrence (17.02.1875)
Cronin, William (2.11.1875)
Croom, Joseph Francis (28.11.1874)
Cross, James (1.01.1864)
Crummy, James (12.01.1870)
Crystall/Cristall, Charles H (12.10.1878)
Cuddihy, John (17.09.1894)
Cuddihy, Michael (1.06.1889)
Cuffe, George (16.03.1897)
Cuffe, Thomas (17.08.1866)
Culhane, Thomas Joseph (17.10.1894)
Cull, Denis (27.08.1890)
Cull, John (16.06.1887)
Cullen, John (17.08.1894)
Culliney, Patrick (7.04.1885)
Cummins, James (1.07.1885)
Cummins, Patrick James (10.10.1872)
Cunningham, Francis Bernard (3.08.1891)
Curran, Patrick (21.01.1887)
Curran, Peter (20.09.1869)
Currie, Alexander E (1.08.1877)
Currie, Thomas (30.04.1897)
Curry, Robert (5.06.1890)
Curtayne, Clive (2.07.1885)
Curtis, Cecil Reginald (19.01.1883)
Curtis, Robyn Gayle (9.10.1878)
Cusack, Laurence (20.04.1882)
Cusack, Michael (1.[Unknown].1865)
Cuthbert, Robert (28.08.1878)

Daley, Mathias (23.12.1884)
Dalglish/Dagleish, RD (29.08.1877)
Daly, Hugh (15.05.1878)
Daly, James (15.07.1875)
Daly, John (30.01.1889)
Daly, Michael (15.12.1890)
Daly, Patrick (2.06.1882)
Dandy, James (1.12.1864)
Daniel, James (7.06.1886)
Dargan, Thomas (23.12.1885)
Dargan/Dargon, John Joseph (3.06.1875)
Davidson, Alex B (1.03.1884)
Davidson, Charles Weston (7.09.1882)
Davidson, John (1.12.1897)
Davies, Netterville R (2.01.1878)
Davies, Thomas Whelam (2.02.1876)
Davis, Frederick (29.04.1875)
Davis, Mathias (8.04.1874)
Davis, NR (2.01.1878)
Davis, Patrick (14.11.1896)
Davis, William (6.11.1872)
Davis, William (23.04.1873)
Davoren, Peter (1.11.1883)
Dawes, Thomas Wightman (29.07.1880 & 5.04.1884)
Day, Maitland Tyrrell (23.03.1873)
de Verdon, Nevil (20.02.1899)
Deasy, John (6.02.1885)
Deevy, John (10.01.1891)
Deevy, Michael (7.04.1898)
Degnam, Patrick (16.01.1879)
Delamer, Michael (21.03.1866)
Delaney, Patrick (21.10.1873)
Delany/Delaney, Edmund (27.04.1881)
Dempsey, John (27.06.1865)
Dempster, Thomas (21.09.1886)
Devaney, Patrick (20.03.1891)
Devaney, Thomas (21.12.1889)
Deverell, Thomas (23.10.1878)
Devine, Charles (18.01.1867)
Devine, Charles (7.10.1870)
Devine, John (19.03.1881)
Devitt, Joseph (7.02.1899)
Dewhurst, Robert (3.12.1889)
Diamond, William (26.06.1878)
Dickinson, Joseph (16.05.1888)
Dickmann, Christian (7.02.1874)
Dickson, John (23.05.1865)

Dillon, George (16.07.1890)
Dillon, James (25.06.1866)
Dillon, Lawrence (6.06.1872)
Dingwall, Roderick (1.05.1891 & 1.08.1894)
Dobbyn, Samuel Wilson (25.02.1885)
Dodsworth, John James (10.07.1878 & 31.01.1883)
Doherty, Cornelius (29.08.1877)
Doherty, Thomas (6.05.1868)
Doherty, Thomas (26.11.1883)
Dolan, Eugene Hugh (14.10.1899)
Dolan, John (23.10.1878)
Dolan, John (15.11.1882)
Donnollan, Patrick (14.10.1889)
Donoghue, Patrick (4.09.1878)
Donoghue, Thomas (2.05.1881)
Donohue, James (9.04.1891)
Doolan, James (23.08.1871)
Dooly, John (25.11.1898)
Doonan, Philip (5.09.1865)
Dore, Robert John (1.08.1881)
Dorsey, Alexander (1.10.1866)
Douglas, Alexander Douglas (9.06.1872)
Dowd, Patrick (8.08.1899)
Dowding, Edward James (13.11.1878 & 9.12.1887)
Dowling, James (1.04.1874)
Dowling, Lawrence (1.01.1864)
Dowling, Michael (3.04.1883)
Dowling, Robert (25.03.1874)
Downes, Harry Edward (29.10.1873)
Downes, John Crichton (6.11.1885)
Downey, Joseph (1.03.1884)
Downey, Patrick (4.03.1874)
Downey, William (12.07.1877)
Downie, James (9.09.1871)
Downie, William (6.08.1866)
Downing, Daniel ([Unknown].10.1866)
Downing, Martin Luther (20.03.1878)
Doyle, Joseph (23.08.1894)
Doyle, Michael (11.02.1867)
Doyle, Patrick (23.08.1894)
Doyle, Thomas (27.09.1876)
Doyle, Timothy Herbert (22.07.1898)
Drescher, William Henry (1.09.1887)
Driscoll, William (16.07.1886)
Driscoll/O'Driscoll, Andrew (12.01.1867)
Drumm, James (1.07.1882)

Drummond, JE (20.06.1864)
Drummond, William (25.01.1888)
Duff, Thomas (14.05.1874)
Duffin, Isaac (6.01.1875)
Duffy, John P (6.04.1877)
Duffy, Patrick (16.10.1890)
Duffy, Patrick VRK (24.06.1874)
Duggan, Cornelius (10.07.1883)
Duke, George Herbert (30.04.1897)
Dundass, William (27.05.1868)
Dunlea, James (23.08.1894)
Dunleavie/Dunlevie, Daniel (20.11.1873)
Dunlop, John Richardson (15.11.1889)
Dunn, James (1.01.1864)
Dunn, John Bowen (16.12.1881)
Dunne, Michael (23.08.1894)
Dunne, Patrick (19.01.1870)
Durham, Hubert Roland Pasley (23.04.1884)
Durham, John (16.05.1877)
Durham, Thomas (5.09.1877)
Dwyer, Edmond (1.12.1875)
Dyas, George (2.06.1864)
Dyer, Richard (28.06.1870)

Eagleden, Henry J (23.11.1876)
Eames, George Gore (7.08.1873)
Eames, William W (20.05.1865 & 23.06.1869)
Earls, William (27.01.1875)
Ebbitt, Benjamin (24.10.1888)
Ede, William (7.01.1876)
Edwards, George (24.10.1865)
Edwards, Herbert Henry (16.09.1889)
Edwards, Percy Joseph (25.07.1894)
Egan, James (27.04.1881)
Egan, John (15.04.1874)
Egan, Michael (14.07.1870)
Egan, Michael (1.10.1885)
Ellegett, John (3.05.1867)
Ellen, Alfred (25.10.1871)
Elligett, John (1.01.1864)
Elliott, George (1.01.1864)
Elliott, George (29.01.1879)
Esplin, Peter (10.01.1891)
Evans, Cecil William (29.04.1875)
Evans, George (7.04.1885)
Evans, Thomas George (15.11.1882)

Fadden, William Arthur (1.05.1891)
Fagan, Laurence (6.04.1867)
Fagan, Patrick (10.11.1876)
Fagg, Edward Arthur (6.11.1885)
Fahey, Bartley (1.05.1885)
Fahey, John (11.01.1886)
Fahey, Peter (1.06.1881)
Fairbrother, George Vaughan (18.07.1888)
Fairnsworth, Festus J (21.09.1869)
Fairweather, Robert (15.02.1886)
Fallon, Joseph (18.05.1881)
Faris/Farris, John David (5.08.1868 & 24.05.1869)
Farmer, CF (30.06.1868)
Farquharson, John (6.09.1871)
Farrell, James (4.03.1867)
Farrell, William (15.01.1879)
Fay, George (25.01.1879)
Feely, Patrick (26.07.1866)
Feenaghty, Patrick (1.09.1868)
Feltham, Thomas (16.05.1877)
Fenwick, Robert (7.04.1896)
Ferguson, Adam (17.07.1885)
Ferguson, John (15.09.1875)
Ferguson, John (28.10.1886)
Ferguson, Richard (17.10.1877)
Ferguson, William (19.03.1874)
Ferguson, William (30.06.1886)
Ferris, Patrick (6.05.1868)
Ferry, Manes/Manus (6.04.1864)
Fields, Thomas (5.08.1874)
Fife, John (19.12.1872)
Finnucan/Finnucane, George Benjamin (17.04.1873)
Fischer, August (9.03.1898)
Fisher, Luke (26.11.1883)
Fitzgerald, David (19.01.1886)
Fitzgerald, James (1.08.1888)
Fitzgerald, James (18.05.1891)
Fitzgerald, James O'Byrne (1.07.1890)
Fitzgerald, John (3.08.1883)
Fitzgerald, John (3.01.1887)
Fitzgerald, Maurice E (6.11.1878)
Fitzgerald, Patrick (16.01.1878)
Fitzgibbon, Daniel Joseph (1.11.1894)
Fitzgibbon, Edward Francis (1.05.1885)
Fitzmaurice, Thomas (28.06.1876)
Fitzpatrick, Daniel (8.08.1877)

Fitzpatrick, Edwin (12.08.1880)
Fitzpatrick, John (24.12.1897)
Fitzpatrick, Joseph (6.02.1884)
Fitzpatrick, Michael (20.12.1882)
Fitzsimmons, Charles (14.06.1876)
Flaherty, Michael (1.01.1864)
Flanigan, Charles (17.09.1894)
Flatrey, Patrick (14.02.1890)
Fleming, Patrick Finnigan (18.02.1875)
Fletcher, Charles Banister (18.05.1891)
Fogarty, James (26.11.1883)
Foley, John (18.09.1877)
Foley, Michael (20.02.1891)
Ford, Thomas (17.10.1877)
Ford/Forde, Bernard (15.03.1875)
Forrest, George (16.11.1886)
Forsyth, Edward James (15.02.1886)
Foster, Martin Blake (13.01.1876)
Fowler, Duncan (29.05.1890)
Fox, Alexander (23.08.1894)
Fox, Edward (15.12.1887)
Francis, William ([Unknown] 1864)
Francklyn, Henry C (11.08.1871)
Franzen, Seth (3.11.1873)
Fraser, Angus (15.11.1882 & 19.07.1884)
Fraser, WM (6.03.1867)
Fraser, William (23.12.1885)
Frederick, Edward (5.04.1876)
Freestone, Charles George Frederick (29.11.1899)
Freestone, Joseph Richard Earl (14.07.1899)
French, James Washington (29.05.1890)
French, John (7.09.1894)
French, W (13.01.1864)
Fryday, Richard (3.08.1891)
Fuller, Stephen (26.03.1886)
Furey, John Patrick (10.08.1865)
Furlong, John (14.03.1877)
Fury, James (8.05.1896)

Gaffney, John (3.10.1898)
Gaffney, Martin (14.12.1882)
Galbraith, Percy Dumas Fead (16.01.1884)
Gallagher, Dominic J (30.05.1877)
Gallagher, John (1.01.1864)
Gallagher/Gallaher, Patrick (13.03.1874)
Galligan, James (1.09.1868 & 1.05.1869)

Galligan, John (13.02.1882)
Galligan/Gilligan, Patrick (21.11.1877)
Gallwey, Daniel (1.01.1864)
Galvin, Patrick (8.03.1886)
Gardiner, John (14.06.1869)
Gardiner, Robert Michael (1.11.1883)
Garlick, Henry (17.06.1876)
Garraway, Roland Walter (9.06.1885 & 5.04.1897)
Gavagan, John (23.09.1885 & 2.07.1887)
Gavagan, Patrick (6.02.1885)
Gaven, William (18.12.1888)
George, John W (2.09.1872)
George, Stephen (9.04.1884)
Geraghty, James Francis (13.12.1877)
Gerhardt, Henry (23.12.1889)
Gibson, Hamilton (1.01.1873)
Gibson, John (11.08.1875)
Gibson, Michael (31.12.1883)
Gilliece/Gilliell, Patrick (1.08.1872)
Gilligan, Morgan Francis (30.06.1886)
Ginivan, Lawrence/Laurence (1.01.1864)
Ginnane/Gennane/Gurnane, Patrick James (16.03.1876)
Glackin, Hugh (29.06.1870)
Glancy, John Thomas (20.06.1878)
Glancy, Peter (3.01.1887)
Gleason, Patrick (16.01.1878)
Gleeson, Timothy (6.05.1868)
Glindemann, John (1.05.1891)
Glover, George J (2.06.1875)
Godwin/Goodwin, Thomas (29.04.1886)
Gooch, Thomas Walter (18.12.1869)
Goodall, Thomas (15.09.1875)
Gorman, Charles Joseph (30.04.1897)
Gorman, Gerald T/GJT (18.08.1875)
Gorman, [Unknown] (1.01.1864)
Gormelly, Patrick Bernard (14.10.1889)
Gough, Henry Bloomfield (1.07.1866)
Goulding, John (16.07.1872)
Gowran, Peter (30.01.1889)
Graham, David (12.01.1866)
Graham, David (25.06.1866)
Graham, Edward (1.01.1864)
Graham, Michael Henry (29.09.1865)
Graham, Robert (1.11.1890)
Graham, William (10.02.1881)
Grant, Alexander (6.09.1877)
Graves, William Henry (1.03.1884)

Gray, CG (1.01.1864)
Gray, Thomas (8.06.1885)
Greaney, John (14.03.1877)
Greavey, Patrick (7.03.1867)
Green, Joseph Donnelly (7.04.1896)
Greenaway, William (1.01.1864)
Greene, Arthur (19.03.1881)
Greene, Robert (14.07.1880)
Greenfield, Henry (13.05.1886)
Greevy/Grevy, Patrick (8.01.1879)
Gregg, Patrick (18.07.1872)
Grey, John (14.09.1870)
Grier, Samuel J (24.10.1877)
Griffin, Daniel Andrew (13.09.1899)
Griffin, James (25.02.1874)
Griffin, James (22.06.1895)
Griffin, John (5.10.1868)
Griffin, Michael (15.03.1877)
Griffin, Michael (23.01.1891)
Griffin, Patrick (9.01.1882)
Griffin, Patrick (15.08.1887)
Griffiths, Israel (26.01.1867)
Grimes, Samuel (19.01.1870 & 16.02.1883)
Grimley, Arthur Edward (30.07.1889)
Grimshaw, Henry James (4.10.1876)
Grimshaw, Joseph (21.10.1875)
Grocock, Charles (16.11.1886)
Groundwater, Harold (1.09.1868)
Growcock, Michael (4.04.1888)
Grugeon, Harry (27.01.1875)
Gunn, John (31.12.1884 & 15.10.1896)
Gunn, William Morrison (1.10.1885 & 11.02.1888)
Guthrie, Thomas (15.03.1887)
Guy, Thomas (25.01.1888)

Hackett, Michael (29.04.1867)
Hagan, John Charles (27.07.1896)
Haimes, William (5.08.1874)
Haines, John (27.09.1876)
Haire, Michael (17.10.1877)
Hall, John Travers (10.07.1878)
Ham, Robert (11.09.1873)
Hamill, William (20.11.1891 & 23.08.1894)
Hamilton, Alexander (21.05.1891)
Hamilton, Hugh (1.12.1897)
Hamilton, John (13.06.1878)

Hamilton, Robert Fitzgerald (6.11.1872)
Hamilton, William James (30.06.1886)
Hamley, Richard Ernest (12.02.1890)
Handlin, Peter (1.11.1894)
Hanley, Henry (23.03.1867)
Hanley, John (1.12.1882)
Hanlon, George Grant Clinton (5.12.1877)
Hanlon, James (4.11.1889)
Hannah/Hanna, John (23.03.1876)
Hannan/Hannon, Robert (2.05.1874)
Hannigan/Hanigan, Michael (23.05.1877)
Hanrahan, Andrew (1.01.1864)
Hanrahan, Timothy (30.04.1897)
Hansen, Charles (23.08.1888)
Harbert, Edwin (1.01.1865)
Harden, Henry (23.06.1875)
Hardie, David (2.01.1895)
Harding, John Fletcher (14.09.1881)
Hardy, John (8.01.1867)
Hargrave, James (12.01.1871)
Harlan, John (12.12.1884)
Harland, William (3.07.1878)
Harrington, Daniel (5.02.1884)
Harrington, Thomas C / Thomas E (21.07.1880)
Harrington, Timothy (6.11.1885)
Hart, Richard (14.05.1884)
Harte, Hugh (6.02.1864)
Hartmann, Jacob (13.09.1872)
Harty, John (6.11.1878)
Harty, Patrick (3.05.1883 & 31.12.1884)
Harvey, William Luck (14.03.1891)
Haslet, William (5.10.1868)
Haughtey, Frederick Vincent (29.05.1890)
Hawe, Edward (30.08.1888)
Hawe, John (10.04.1885)
Hawkes, George (21.02.1887)
Hawkins, John (23.01.1872)
Haydon, Thomas (24.09.1888)
Hayes, James (7.09.1894)
Hayes, John (4.01.1888)
Hayes, John (14.03.1888)
Hayes, Martin (4.03.1890)
Hayes, Patrick (4.03.1899 & 6.12.1900)
Hayes, Thomas (25.06.1873)
Head, Thomas (17.05.1887)

Healy, John (1.02.1867)
Healy, Maurice Mckenna (15.12.1890)
Healy, William Edward (22.07.1898)
Healy/Healey, Michael (13.01.1875)
Heaney, Samuel George (1.09.1891)
Heaney, Thomas James (18.12.1888)
Heaslip, George (6.05.1868)
Heaslip, George (13.11.1885)
Heathcote, Joseph (25.03.1884)
Heather, John (17.01.1877)
Heenan, James (21.12.1886)
Hefferan, James (6.09.1883)
Hegarty, William (2.04.1887)
Hegarty/Hagarty, Thomas (14.05.1869)
Hely, Edmond F / Edward F (10.09.1874)
Hempenstall, Thomas (19.08.1868)
Henders, John (1.09.1883)
Henderson, Richard William (14.05.1886)
Henderson, Thomas (29.05.1874)
Hennessey, Thomas (23.08.1894)
Hennessy, Martin (30.04.1897)
Hennessy, Thomas (1.03.1881)
Henry, James (3.08.1891)
Henry, John (1.09.1884)
Henry, Patrick (1.05.1867)
Henry, Peter (19.02.1887)
Herbert, Thomas (1.01.1864)
Herbert, Thomas Cuffe (1.03.1872)
Hewetson, William F (29.11.1876)
Hickey, John (2.01.1878)
Hickey, Patrick (8.03.1877)
Hickey, Thomas (22.06.1870)
Hickson, William John (17.10.1877)
Higgins, John Joseph (25.07.1894)
Higgins, Patrick (19.02.1864)
Higgins, William (11.08.1894)
Higgins, William A (14.10.1871)
Higgins, William Archibald (10.05.1871)
Higginson, James (20.03.1891)
Higman, John Charles Frederick (13.12.1883)
Hill, Cecil Fulford (28.02.1865)
Hill, George (1.01.1864)
Hill, James (4.06.1877)
Hill, John (20.04.1885)
Hill, Richard (3.12.1887)

Hill, Thomas (22.05.1884)
Hilliard, George (22.09.1875)
Hilton, James Joseph (5.08.1880)
Hinch, John (19.01.1870)
Hinch, Thomas (14.01.1881)
Hinchy, Michael (20.06.1868)
Hobday, James Mayall (9.12.1874)
Hodgson, James (1.04.1867)
Hoelscher, Louis Albert (25.07.1894)
Hofland, Herbert Thomas (4.03.1897)
Hogan, John Patrick (19.03.1881)
Hogg, James (4.05.1868)
Holden, James Edward (13.09.1899)
Holdway, George (25.01.1888)
Holmes, Francis (1.04.1868)
Holmes, William Robert (24.12.1896)
Holohan, James (23.05.1889)
Holohan, Patrick (6.11.1885)
Holt, Joseph (4.11.1874)
Hooker, Francis (10.11.1876)
Hopper, James (23.12.1885)
Horan, Edmond (2.11.1886)
Horan, William (2.11.1886)
Hosford, William (19.11.1883)
Houlahan, John (9.07.1873)
Hourigan, Edmond (1.05.1891)
Hourigan, Patrick (1.11.1876)
Howden, William (2.06.1875)
Howe, Patrick/Frederick (24.02.1875)
Hudson, Matthew (6.11.1885)
Hughes, Hugh (3.05.1883)
Hughes, Matthew (6.10.1871)
Humby, Charles Clarence (28.07.1884)
Hunt, Edmund (23.05.1865)
Hunter, George (29.04.1867)
Hurd, Alfred (19.11.1883)
Hurley, Simon (24.04.1873)
Hurley, Thomas (26.09.1877)
Hurst, Henry (16.07.1890)
Hussey, George Forbes (4.03.1897)
Huston, William (28.04.1881)
Huston, William (16.02.1888)
Hutchinson, Thomas (19.03.1867)
Hyland, James (23.12.1885)
Hynes, James (1.09.1897)
Hynes, Joseph (1.07.1874)

Ingram, John (26.08.1868)
Irwin, Francis (25.03.1874)

Irwin, James (14.03.1893)
Irwin, John M (26.08.1868)
Irwin, Stephen (13.05.1867)
Irwin, Thomas (24.11.1881 & 8.03.1886)

Jackson, Cornelius (30.06.1886)
Jackson, John (10.04.1885)
James, Frank (10.02.1875)
James, Harry (4.07.1871)
James, John (13.12.1873)
James, John (11.03.1875)
Jardine, Frank Lascalles ([Unknown] 1868)
Jeffers, George (7.04.1888)
Jenings, Charles Campbell (21.09.1886)
Jenkins, Walter H (22.01.1870)
Jesse, Thomas (1.04.1868)
Jessop, Edward (14.01.1881)
Jessop, Samuel (9.10.1878)
John, George DT (18.05.1882)
Johns, Jonathan (10.07.1878)
Johnson, Adam (24.01.1881)
Johnson, Edward (5.08.1870)
Johnson, George William (3.05.1878)
Johnston, David (7.09.1882)
Johnston, James (14.09.1871)
Johnston, James (20.08.1886)
Johnston, William John (1.11.1894)
Johnston/Johnstone, Henry (4.10.1876)
Johnstone, Edward (14.03.1877)
Jones, George (23.09.1884)
Jones, George Edward (5.03.1884 & 17.05.1887)
Jones, Patrick (21.01.1874)
Jones, William John (18.06.1889)
Josey, Benjamin George (24.12.1896)
Joyce, Patrick (1.05.1891)
Joyce, Pierce (1.08.1889)
Joyner, Benjamin (8.05.1873)
Judge, Joseph (22.06.1875)

Kay, James Edmond (23.12.1885)
Kean, Patrick (15.12.1887)
Keane, Denis (17.07.1878)
Keane, James (5.09.1877)
Keane, James (4.01.1888)
Keane, John (30.01.1889)
Keane, Michael (1.05.1885)
Keane, Patrick (19.08.1864)
Keane, Patrick (18.05.1885)

Keane, Patrick Jeremiah (3.01.1887)
Keane, Robert (29.10.1872)
Keating, Michael (14.10.1889)
Keeffe, Matthew (5.09.1877)
Keenan, Patrick (28.01.1874)
Keene, Charles (17.01.1895)
Kefford, Joseph (8.06.1885)
Kelleher, John (20.05.1864)
Kelly, Alfred (13.03.1893)
Kelly, Dalton (6.09.1871)
Kelly, Daniel (2.02.1867)
Kelly, George (1.09.1897)
Kelly, John (4.02.1864)
Kelly, John (14.07.1871)
Kelly, John (21.12.1881)
Kelly, John Arthur (4.04.1899)
Kelly, Joseph (11.03.1876)
Kelly, Martin (19.04.1886)
Kelly, Michael (27.08.1866)
Kelly, Michael (26.09.1877)
Kelly, Michael (23.08.1888)
Kelly, Michael (4.03.1890)
Kelly, Mortimer (1.04.1868)
Kelly, Patrick (12.01.1882)
Kelly, Patrick John (27.08.1890)
Kelly, Peter (25.07.1877)
Kelly, Thomas (17.10.1894)
Kelly, William (15.01.1883)
Kelly, William J (11.07.1877)
Kennedy, Arthur John (12.06.1899)
Kennedy, Bernard (31.07.1888)
Kennedy, Edward Briggs (28.02.1865)
Kennedy, James (25.08.1875)
Kennedy, Michael (24.11.1871)
Kenny, Bernard (11.09.1878)
Kenny, Henry Butler (12.06.1899)
Kenny, James (15.08.1877)
Kenny, James (4.03.1890)
Kenny, John (12.10.1870)
Kenny, Peter (6.09.1871)
Kent, William H (1.01.1876)
Keogh, Patrick (14.03.1877)
Kerr, Robert (1.01.1864)
Kerr, William (24.10.1877)
Kidney, Henry (8.09.1875)
Kiely, John (16.01.1882)
Kiely, William (20.08.1886)
Kiernan, Edward (28.02.1883)
Kiernan, James (1.05.1888)
Kilfeder/Kilfedder, Robert (3.01.1866)
Kilkeary, Edward (23.07.1873)
Kilkeary, Thomas (16.07.1874)
Kilpatrick, Alexander (14.08.1872)
Kilpatrick, James (1.05.1884)
Kilpatrick, Robert (3.11.1884)
Kindregan, Patrick (10.08.1865)
Kineavey/Kineary, John (10.02.1874)
King, Herbert (5.05.1866)
King, James (1.12.1882)
King, Michael (16.02.1888)
King, Samuel (1.03.1877)
King, Walter Stewart (Junior) (14.09.1871)
King, William John (19.10.1894)
Kippen, James M (25.07.1877)
Kirkpatrick, Gordon (27.03.1875)
Kirwan, James (27.02.1878)
Kittson, Michael (1.04.1868 & 4.02.1870)
Klibbe, Henry George (1.06.1897)
Knight, James (14.05.1878)
Kunkel, Thomas (1.07.1889)

Lacey, WH (1.01.1872)
Lambert, Roland John (29.11.1899)
Lamont, Duncan (12.02.1874)
Lane, Timothy (9.01.1878)
Lang, J (1.01.1864)
Langford, M (12.05.1864)
Langusch, William Henry (24.12.1897)
Larkin, John (27.08.1866)
Latimer, Thomas (12.01.1867)
Law, Robert (16.01.1877)
Lawler, John Robert (17.05.1882)
Lawlor, Michael (14.02.1890)
Lawrence, John (7.04.1888)
Lawrence, Samuel (8.03.1886)
Lawton, Patrick (20.03.1889)
Laxton, William Henry (1.05.1884)
Leacy, George Hugh (7.09.1894)
Leahy, Denis (28.05.1887)
Leary, Arthur (3.08.1885)
Lee, JJ (21.01.1864)
Lee, Morgan (3.04.1878)
Lee, William (21.01.1864)
Leech, Thomas (3.08.1885)
Leitch, David (20.03.1878)
Lenham, William (30.03.1893)

Lester, Leonard Thomas (19.04.1899)
Leyden, James Stephen (23.08.1888)
Lidstone, Andrew (23.02.1876)
Linnane, Peter James (14.12.1882)
Linton, Robert (27.09.1875)
Little, Robert (30.12.1892)
Llewellyn, Trevor (1.05.1873)
Lloyd, Charles Richard (1.09.1884)
Lloyd, Samuel John Collis (1.12.1864)
Loch, Adam Peel (7.05.1895)
Loch, George Edmond (1.12.1897)
Lonergan, John (4.05.1868)
Lonergan, Matthew (22.07.1864)
Lonergan, Thomas (27.05.1868)
Long, Alexander (12.02.1876)
Long, Daniel (8.04.1874)
Long, John (23.06.1875)
Long, Michael (3.08.1891)
Longrigg, WR (5.08.1868)
Loretzin/Lorentzin, Nicholay (19.03.1873)
Lough, Willliam (1.07.1885)
Loughnane, Thomas (25.02.1885)
Louth, Stephen (12.04.1877)
Love, Robert (16.11.1886)
Lowman, Michael (21.05.1889)
Lowth/Louth, Thomas (24.10.1878)
Luck, Sidney Charles (1.06.1897)
Ludgate, Henry (3.08.1865)
Ludwig, Joseph T (16.03.1881)
Luttrell, Patrick (6.02.1868)
Lyall, George John (25.06.1873)
Lynch, Henry H (22.03.1876)
Lynch, John (25.02.1890)
Lynch, Michael Thomas (5.06.1890)
Lynch, Patrick (28.07.1875)
Lynch, Patrick (15.03.1887)
Lynch, Peter (4.02.1891)
Lynch, Phillip (22.07.1875)
Lynden, Robert (9.09.1868)
Lynn, William L (28.01.1881)
Lynott, James Henry (11.10.1889)
Lyons, Thomas (23.02.1883)

Macaulay, James (23.09.1897)
Mackay, Alexander (22.03.1876)
Mackay, Patrick (14.06.1872)
Mackereth, William Henry (1.09.1884)
Maclellan/McLellan, Alexander (4.02.1875)
Macmahon, Charles James (20.11.1873)
Macvicar, John HY (10.10.1877)
Madigan, Patrick (1.09.1891)
Magee, William (26.02.1896)
Maginnis, Frederick George (31.12.1883)
Maguire, Abraham (18.06.1868)
Maguire, Charles (8.08.1877)
Maguire, Francis (5.07.1872)
Maguire, John (17.10.1877)
Maguire, William (7.04.1888)
Maher, John (30.11.1888)
Maher, Patrick (30.03.1864)
Maher/Meaher, Jeremiah (17.05.1887)
Mahon, James (20.05.1864)
Mahon, John (1.09.1868)
Mahon, Joseph (16.02.1887)
Mahon, Michael (28.10.1886)
Mahoney, Michael (2.10.1896)
Mahony, James (8.03.1871)
Maitland, Edward A (3.01.1874)
Mallon, John (7.06.1886)
Malone, Hugh (15.07.1881)
Malone, Richard (3.08.1874)
Maloney, M (1.01.1864)
Maloney/Moloney, Stephen (1.01.1864)
Maloney/Moloney, Thomas (7.06.1886)
Manning, James (30.03.1875)
Mannion, John (23.08.1871)
Manton, James (1.01.1864)
Mardall, JA (1.04.1868)
Marshall, Augustus (11.01.1886)
Marshall, Edward (23.05.1877)
Marshall, Michael (1.01.1864)
Martin, Edward (4.03.1867)
Martin, Henry (4.11.1889)
Martin, James (8.02.1872)
Martin, Owen (19.05.1885)
Martin, William (1.10.1885)
Masterson, Michael (30.08.1878)
Matheson, Donald (6.11.1872)
Matthews, GWA (5.08.1874)
Matthews, Peter (14.10.1872)
Matthews, William James (30.12.1885)
Maxwell, Robert (10.05.1881)
Mazlin, John (9.01.1878)
McAndrew, William (22.05.1869)
McArthur, Thomas Archibald (26.06.1885)
McBride, Thomas (7.02.1877)

McBrien, Edward (14.03.1888)
McBrine, James (20.03.1891)
McCabe, James (26.11.1867)
McCabe, Myles (18.12.1888)
McCabe, Neal (22.07.1875)
McCabe, Patrick Joseph (11.08.1896)
McCann, Henry (2.06.1875)
McCann, Henry (1.01.1877)
McCann, James Henry (19.04.1875)
McCann, Michael (28.07.1875)
McCann, Stephen (26.10.1872)
McCarthy, Austin (1.09.1884)
McCarthy, Christopher (24.09.1888)
McCarthy, Daniel (1.04.1868)
McCarthy, Denis (1.01.1864)
McCarthy, James (2.07.1887)
McCarthy, John (27.08.1873)
McCarthy, John (22.01.1891)
McCarthy, John (11.09.1894)
McCarthy, Michael (12.05.1864)
McCarthy, Michael (3.01.1866)
McCarthy, Michael (10.02.1881)
McCarthy, Michael (18.10.1887)
McCarthy, Michael (4.11.1889)
McCarthy, William John (16.06.1886)
McCartney, William (1.10.1885)
McConechy, Alexander Haig (8.03.1883)
McConnell, William (22.03.1866)
McCormack, Martin (14.03.1877)
McCormack, Michael (27.03.1875)
McCormack, Patrick (16.11.1886)
McCormack, William (16.01.1884)
McCoy, James (1.08.1889)
McCreery, Michael John (28.07.1875)
McCulkin, Thomas (31.12.1883)
McCulla, Douglas (29.04.1875)
McCullagh, Samuel (8.01.1879 &
    31.12.1883)
McCullogh/Mccullough, Daniel
    (27.05.1868)
McDermott, Michael Coleman
    (8.08.1873)
McDevitt, James (27.08.1870)
McDonagh, Peter (12.09.1866)
McDonald, Allan (7.11.1866)
McDonald, Arthur (25.08.1875)
McDonald, John (7.10.1870)
McDonald, Robert D (8.08.1877)
McDonald, Thomas (2.01.1879)

McDonnell, John (3.02.1865)
McDonogh, Patrick Henry (1.07.1885)
McDonough, Patrick (6.05.1868)
McDonough, Peter (1.01.1864)
McElhinney, Samuel (1.11.1894)
McElligott, Maurice (30.06.1868)
McElroy, Felix (1.06.1869)
McErlane, James (1.02.1887 &
    25.07.1894)
McEvoy, James Joseph (23.05.1899)
McFarlane, Angus (22.11.1871)
McFarquhar, Henry R (23.03.1875)
McGann, Michael (30.10.1888)
McGinley, Michael (1.02.1876)
McGinley/McGinlay, Edward
    (30.07.1864)
McGovern, Edward (29.06.1870)
McGrath, James (10.01.1878)
McGrath, James (23.09.1882)
McGrath, John (29.07.1874)
McGrath, John (9.12.1880)
McGrath, John (21.12.1889)
McGrath, Patrick (1.01.1864)
McGrath, Thomas (11.09.1878)
McGregor, Robert (8.11.1876)
McGuinness, Arthur (5.09.1877)
McGuinness, James (24.07.1878)
McGuire, James (14.10.1875)
McHugh, Patrick (23.09.1885)
McIlwraith, John (1.01.1864)
McInerney/McInerny, James (16.02.1888)
McIntosh, George Fraser (5.01.1883)
McIntyre, Thomas (1.09.1868)
McJannett, George (27.06.1865)
McKay, William (19.11.1883)
McKay, William Henry (6.11.1885)
McKay/Mackay, John Robert
    (20.08.1886)
McKellar, John James (24.10.1898)
McKenna, Christopher (1.12.1885)
McKenna, Michael (19.05.1875)
McKenzie, John (22.05.1869)
McKenzie, John (1.05.1883)
McKiernan, Francis James (23.12.1884)
McKiernan, Michael (13.01.1864)
McKinlay/McKinley, Joseph (2.02.1886)
McKowne, John (10.11.1876)
McLatchey, Thomas (7.01.1898)
McLean, Hector (1.03.1884)

McLean, James (19.04.1886)
McLean, Murdo (15.03.1887)
McLean, William (10.02.1886)
McLellan, George (7.10.1874)
McManus, Hugh (27.06.1865)
McMillan, James Edward (7.06.1886)
McMullan/McMullen/McMullin, John (31.10.1865)
McNally/McNalley, Peter (4.10.1876)
McNalty, Neason (11.11.1875)
McNamara, Denis (18.05.1891)
McNamara, James (1.11.1876)
McNamara, Richard (19.03.1892)
McNamara/Macnamara, John (1.09.1885)
McNamee, John (20.03.1891)
McNeill, Alexander (23.02.1874)
McNeill, Duncan Alexander (27.12.1889)
McNeill, James (1.05.1885)
McNeill, Robert (11.04.1882)
McNevin, Hugh (27.02.1878)
McNulty, Thomas (23.05.1865)
McNulty, Thomas (26.01.1870)
McNulty, William (1.07.1890)
McOnigly/McOingley, Stephen Dorian (15.08.1889)
McPhee, Edward (28.06.1876)
McRae, Hugh (14.03.1888)
McSharry, James (23.12.1886)
McSharry, Matthew (1.06.1874)
McSweeney, John (29.05.1872)
McSweeney, Patrick (25.01.1871)
McSweeney, Patrick (7.08.1872)
Mead, Albert Hallard (8.05.1891)
Meade, Henry (10.06.1871)
Meade, Patrick (11.07.1887)
Meara, John (20.06.1877)
Medley, Joseph (13.11.1885)
Mee, Patrick (21.01.1874)
Mee, Thomas (1.02.1887)
Meegan, James (14.04.1871)
Meenaghan, John (22.03.1876)
Melville, Timothy (27.01.1875)
Melville, William James (11.08.1896)
Merchant, Alexander (12.02.1883)
Merry, John T (31.05.1876)
Meston, William (4.03.1899)
Meyer, Hermann William Henry (1.08.1877)

Miers, Thomas AC (25.02.1874)
Miles, Robert (27.05.1868)
Millar, James (20.08.1889 & 3.11.1899)
Miller, Alexander (23.08.1894)
Miller, George (12.10.1876)
Miller, John (30.09.1874)
Miller, John Emeric Vidal (5.01.1892)
Miller, Patrick (15.12.1890)
Miller, Peter (20.07.1876)
Miller, Peter (24.12.1896)
Millett, Thomas S (7.10.1876)
Millett/Millet, Solomon (24.07.1872)
Mills, WG (15.06.1864)
Minogue, William (5.08.1868)
Mitchell, Alexander (27.08.1890)
Mitchell, John (29.06.1876)
Molloy, John Joseph (16.05.1899)
Molloy, Michael (1.07.1868)
Molloy, Patrick (5.06.1884)
Molloy, Robert (29.07.1874)
Molloy, Thomas (16.01.1890)
Moloney, Stephen (19.04.1886)
Moloney, Thomas (7.06.1886)
Moloney/Molloney, John (21.01.1868)
Monaghan, Patrick (27.08.1866)
Moneykyrle, William LE (24.01.1873)
Montgomery, Thomas (8.06.1872)
Montgomery/Montgomerry, James (21.12.1881)
Mooney, John (1.02.1870)
Mooney, Thomas (30.09.1886)
Moore, George Augustus (4.08.1890)
Moore, Henry (28.05.1887)
Moore, Hugh Charles (16.12.1875)
Moore, John (1.01.1864)
Moore, John (20.03.1891)
Moran, Darby (26.03.1886)
Moran, Martin (21.12.1889)
Moran, Thomas (21.11.1877)
Morandi, Charles (24.10.1865)
Morgan, Thomas Ernest (1.02.1872)
Morley, Daniel Charles (5.07.1880)
Moroney, Bartholomew (6.05.1868)
Moroney, Patrick (24.10.1888)
Moroney, Patrick James (5.02.1897)
Morrin/Marrin, John (8.08.1877)
Morris, Alfred (1.12.1885)
Morris, Charles (8.03.1886)
Morris, Thomas (15.09.1875)

Morrison, Alexander (6.08.1872)
Morrissey/Morissey, Richard (11.07.1882)
Morse, William (19.10.1876)
Mosse, Stanley (18.04.1871)
Mulcahy, Hugh (15.02.1886)
Muldoon, John (29.05.1872)
Mullan, Patrick (22.03.1866)
Mullane, Patrick (1.01.1864)
Mullen, Patrick (8.08.1899)
Mullin, Robert (9.04.1866)
Mullins, Patrick (8.05.1896)
Mulqueeney, Patrick (12.12.1873)
Mulvena, Robert (21.09.1886)
Munns, John (3.04.1883)
Murch, Alfred Code (1.12.1883)
Murdock, Robert C (16.06.1875)
Murnan, Patrick (9.01.1878)
Murphy, Daniel (7.04.1898)
Murphy, David (4.07.1872)
Murphy, Denis (6.01.1875)
Murphy, James (2.10.1872)
Murphy, James (1.12.1875)
Murphy, James (4.08.1887)
Murphy, James Alexander (31.07.1888)
Murphy, John (12.09.1866)
Murphy, John (1.10.1885)
Murphy, John Robert (21.12.1889)
Murphy, Joseph Vincent (1.09.1897)
Murphy, Peter (29.05.1872)
Murphy, Timothy (1.05.1891)
Murphy, William (3.12.1889)
Murphy, WJ (25.08.1868)
Murray, Frederick Johnstone (2.03.1865)
Murray, James (16.11.1886)
Murrihy, Austin (5.02.1897)
Murrihy, Daniel (18.05.1891)

Nalty, Valentine FA (23.01.1865)
Napier, George (29.01.1879)
Nash, William James (14.03.1893)
Naughton, James (17.01.1871)
Neller, Joseph John (19.09.1898)
Nethercote, James (5.07.1876)
Netterfield, Nathaniel (18.01.1867)
Newey, Samuel P (21.11.1877)
Newman, Bernard (18.05.1891)
Newman, James Patrick (30.04.1897)
Nicholson, Henry John (1.10.1869)
Nixon, James (26.03.1884)

Nobbs, Daniel/David (1.06.1869)
Noble, Francis Mowbray (1.03.1884)
Nolan, Patrick (12.03.1891)
Nolan, Peter (28.11.1868)
Nolan, Peter (1.02.1875)
Noone, Patrick (10.05.1881)
Norman, Connolly (4.01.1888)
Norris, James H (7.02.1877)
Norris, MJ (12.05.1865)
Nott, William (12.06.1864)
Nowlan, George Denis B (20.06.1868)
Nugent, Owen Eugene (26.11.1883)
Nursey, Charles JF (1.01.1874)
Nutting, Charles Marshall (4.09.1872)
Nutting, William Bligh (1.12.1873)

O'Brien, Daniel Patrick (7.09.1894)
O'Brien, Darby (1.01.1864)
O'Brien, Denis (24.01.1872)
O'Brien, Edmond (1.12.1884)
O'Brien, Frank (14.05.1875)
O'Brien, Hugh (23.02.1881)
O'Brien, James (17.01.1881)
O'Brien, James (1.07.1891)
O'Brien, Jeremiah (2.02.1886)
O'Brien, John (13.06.1864)
O'Brien, John Patrick (29.05.1890)
O'Brien, Maurice (8.07.1874)
O'Brien, Patrick (1.05.1891)
O'Bryen, Myles (2.08.1884)
O'Callaghan, Crosbie (3.10.1883)
O'Callaghan, Denis (2.06.1870)
O'Callaghan, James (1.05.1865)
O'Callaghan, John (3.12.1887)
O'Callaghan, Patrick (16.11.1886)
O'Connelly, Richard (12.11.1875)
O'Connor, Bartholomew (9.12.1874)
O'Connor, Daniel (30.10.1888)
O'Connor, Eugene (1.01.1879)
O'Connor, John (7.04.1888)
O'Connor, Maurice Roche (30.06.1886)
O'Connor, Michael (16.05.1888)
O'Connor, Michael (8.07.1896)
O'Connor, Patrick John (27.01.1897)
O'Connor, Stanhope (1.01.1875)
O'Day, Patrick (16.07.1874)
O'Dea, John (7.02.1899)
O'Dea, Thomas (8.08.1877)
O'Doherty, James (18.07.1877)

O'Donnell, John (19.12.1877)
O'Donnell, John (9.10.1878)
O'Donnell, Thomas (14.05.1869)
O'Donohue/O'Donohoe, John (19.03.1873)
O'Donovan, Daniel (24.09.1888)
O'Dwyer, John Taylor (1.12.1883)
Oelrichs, Edward (15.05.1895)
O'Flynne, John James (11.03.1876)
O'Grady, Jeremiah (30.04.1897)
O'Grady, John (1.05.1885)
O'Grady, Michael John (12.06.1899)
O'Hara, Michael (1.01.1864)
O'Hara, Patrick (16.12.1898)
O'Hehir, Thomas Joseph (23.04.1874)
O'Kearney, Charles (1.05.1891)
O'Kearney, James (2.07.1887)
O'Keefe, Joseph (23.12.1885)
O'Keiffe/O'Keeffe, Patrick (23.10.1869)
Old, James Robert Ernest (1.02.1887)
O'Leary, James (4.11.1867)
O'Leary, James (20.11.1869)
O'Leary, John (5.06.1890)
O'Loan, Hugh (1.09.1868)
O'Loghlin, John (12.06.1883)
O'Malley, Peter (29.12.1868)
O'Meara, Patrick (3.08.1891)
O'Neill, Cornelius (6.11.1878)
O'Neill, Eugene (28.01.1870)
O'Neill, James Eugene (3.10.1877)
O'Neill, John (27.04.1881)
O'Neill, Thomas (1.06.1881)
O'Neill, William (24.02.1875)
O'Neill, William (10.05.1878)
O'Neill, William (11.08.1896)
Ordish, Lionel William Charles (27.11.1890)
O'Regan, Daniel (1.01.1864)
O'Regan, Daniel Thomas (1.05.1891)
O'Regan, John (4.09.1878)
O'Reilly, Patrick (17.01.1872)
O'Rourke, Hugh (1.09.1887)
O'Rourke, James (1.01.1870)
Orr, R (1.01.1864)
Orr, William Christopher (2.01.1883)
Orton, Robert (6.11.1885)
O'Shea, James (3.05.1887)
O'Shea, John Thomas (10.02.1892)
O'Sullivan, Denis (13.08.1873)

O'Sullivan, James Francis (31.05.1876)
O'Sullivan, John (1.01.1880)
O'Sullivan, John (24.07.1890)
O'Sullivan, John Edward (1.11.1894)
O'Sullivan, Michael (20.08.1883)
O'Sullivan, Patrick (14.09.1866)
O'Sullivan, Patrick (3.07.1878)
O'Sullivan, Timothy (8.08.1899)
Owens, Joseph (2.01.1867)

Paine, John Jones (22.09.1870)
Palmer, John (1.07.1884)
Palmer, Joseph Henry (5.07.1873)
Palmer, Peter Robert (9.07.1873)
Park, John (8.04.1867)
Parke, Patrick Halkett (11.03.1891)
Parker, Joseph (18.08.1875)
Parkes, John Kinahan (2.05.1885 & 2.08.1887)
Parry-Okeden, Police Commissioner William Edward (1.07.1895)
Parsons, David (9.12.1882)
Patterson, Charles (3.05.1872)
Peevor, Thomas George (1.07.1874)
Pendock, William (13.05.1886)
Percey, Alfred James (1.12.1883)
Perkins, George Henry (11.12.1889)
Perry, Edward (24.09.1873)
Perry, George (26.07.1881)
Perry, John (1.12.1878)
Peters, George Edward John (11.11.1899)
Peters, Harry Leonard (14.04.1891)
Peters, Michael James (25.07.1894)
Pharr, Henry Hero (1.02.1884)
Phelan, Patrick (31.12.1883)
Phillips, John (23.09.1884)
Phillips, John (27.05.1896)
Phillips, Sydney Edwin (1.05.1885)
Pickering, Walter (27.05.1868)
Picket/Pickett, Henry (28.01.1874)
Pierce, Ernest Henry (3.08.1885 & 26.04.1889)
Pigg, Joseph (16.07.1890)
Pike, James MC (8.09.1875)
Pointon, George (5.08.1868)
Pollard, George Thomas (11.01.1886)
Polmeer, John Henry (1.05.1884)
Pope, Daniel (22.07.1898)
Pope, Edwin (16.05.1877)

Porter, Robert (4.04.1872)
Porter, Thomas Ogilvie (25.02.1890)
Portley, Michael (27.04.1881)
Poulsen, James (4.11.1875)
Power, Patrick (11.03.1874)
Power, Patrick (1.12.1882)
Power, Thomas (5.12.1887)
Power, William Edward (17.03.1873)
Price, Alfred (11.08.1896)
Price, Frank (3.05.1887)
Priday, Samuel S (2.10.1865)
Priestley, Charles (25.03.1874)
Primrose, Henry Charles (26.08.1868 & 19.09.1877)
Pringle, William Cother (18.12.1888)
Pritchard, William Henry (7.02.1899)
Proctor, Edward Acton Gibbon (1.12.1883)
Proctor, John (23.08.1877)
Proud, James (19.09.1898)
Purvis, Thomas (6.02.1885)

Quain, Richard (27.05.1868)
Quillinan, Charles (25.03.1884)
Quilter, William (20.08.1886)
Quinlan, Martin (1.04.1868)
Quinn, John (31.07.1878)
Quinn, John (9.12.1880)
Quinn, John W (1.06.1869)
Quinn, Michael (19.03.1881)
Quinn, Patrick (16.02.1888)
Quinn, William (30.04.1872)

Rafter, James (3.02.1874)
Raftery, Michael (3.08.1865)
Raleigh, James (16.09.1868)
Raleigh, John (20.11.1869)
Raleigh, Patrick (14.04.1871)
Ralph, Charles (2.01.1878)
Rayner, Herbert Ezra (26.02.1896)
Rayner, John (8.12.1884)
Reardon, Daniel Peter (15.12.1890)
Redmond, Malcolm (1.05.1891)
Reed, John (30.04.1897)
Reid, William (1.12.1897)
Reilly, Bernard (6.11.1878)
Reilly, Michael (1.05.1885)
Rennison, John (12.09.1866)
Rennison, Thomas (11.03.1876)

Reville, James (4.11.1896)
Reynolds, John (12.12.1877)
Reynolds, Peter (9.02.1889)
Rice, Herbert (20.10.1876)
Rice, John (2.02.1886)
Richards, John / Solomon John (10.10.1899)
Richards, John B (24.05.1871)
Richardson, Amos Edward (24.10.1888)
Richardson, Frederick William (23.08.1871)
Richardson, George Horsman (25.03.1874)
Ridge, Thomas/Joseph (13.08.1872)
Riley, R (1.01.1868)
Riley, Richard (3.01.1866)
Riley, Terence (8.05.1877)
Riordan, Charles (29.10.1875)
Riordan, John (8.03.1886)
Roberts, John (6.06.1877)
Roberts, John (18.07.1877)
Roberts, Nathaniel (1.12.1882)
Robinson, Edward (23.10.1869 & 30.12.1874)
Robinson, Frederick (21.10.1872)
Robinson, Thomas (15.08.1872)
Robson, John Matthew (4.03.1885)
Roche, John (1.12.1883)
Roche, Thomas (4.02.1891)
Rockett, John (8.06.1898)
Roe, John Morris (15.02.1865)
Rogan, John (24.02.1874)
Rohde, Engelbricht/Engelbrecht (21.01.1874)
Roles, Henry (30.04.1897)
Ronaldson, William (20.06.1877)
Rooke, GJ (1.01.1864)
Rooney, Mark (19.12.1877)
Roots, George (25.11.1898)
Roper, Thomas (4.09.1878)
Ross, Henry (22.11.1889)
Ross, Robert (18.05.1868)
Rourke, Francis (6.11.1885)
Ruddle, Denis (17.09.1894)
Runge, Henry (1.07.1898)
Rutledge, Robert (3.08.1891)
Rutledge, Thomas (12.01.1867)
Ryan, Andrew (14.10.1889)
Ryan, Christopher (29.08.1889)

Ryan, Denis (15.05.1878)
Ryan, Denis ([Unknown] 1880)
Ryan, Denis (3.04.1883)
Ryan, James (24.10.1877)
Ryan, John (12.03.1877)
Ryan, John (12.06.1885)
Ryan, John (16.11.1886)
Ryan, John (7.07.1893)
Ryan, Martin (4.02.1891)
Ryan, Michael (3.08.1891)
Ryan, Michael J (6.06.1872)
Ryan, Morgan (5.06.1878)
Ryan, Patrick (1.02.1877)
Ryan, Patrick (5.09.1877)
Ryan, Patrick (25.04.1878)
Ryan, Thomas (25.02.1875)
Ryland, Joseph (20.03.1878)

Sadleir, R (1.04.1868)
Salm, William Henry (24.02.1897)
Sands/Sandes, James (18.06.1868)
Sangster, James (4.08.1890)
Sargint, Harry (14.05.1890)
Satchwell, Hubert (31.08.1883)
Savage, Charles Douglas (19.10.1876)
Scale, William (5.08.1874)
Scanlan, Arthur James (24.02.1897)
Scanlan, Charles (1.08.1889)
Scanlon, Thomas (22.11.1871)
Scott, Alexander Matthew Clarendon (3.06.1872)
Scott, James (3.12.1887 & 12.05.1890)
Scott, James Hamilton (1.08.1868)
Scott, Joseph William (16.05.1888)
Scullin, P (20.05.1864)
Seaton, Joseph (10.09.1890)
Seery, Joseph Michael (1.09.1897)
Sewell, Thomas (8.07.1896)
Seymour, Police Commissioner David Thompson (1.01.1864)
Seymour, Thomas Henry Louis (16.02.1888 & 25.06.1900)
Shanahan, Denis (15.12.1887)
Shanahan, Maurice (29.04.1886)
Shann, John (8.05.1890 & 11.08.1898)
Shannon, James (3.06.1874)
Shaw, Benjamin (6.11.1878)
Sheehan, James (23.08.1894)
Sheridan, Martin (15.12.1890)

Sheridan, Michael (7.12.1864)
Sherlock, Arthur (18.06.1897)
Sherrin, Arthur Herbert (1.05.1891)
Shields, Francis (25.01.1871)
Shields, Joseph (23.12.1885)
Shine, William (25.07.1894)
Siddins, Henry Alfred (23.08.1894)
Siebert, William (25.02.1882)
Simpson, Alexander (10.07.1889)
Simpson, William (1.11.1876)
Sinclair, Donald S (17.05.1876)
Size, John (28.12.1876)
Skehan, Cornelius (23.05.1865)
Skerman, Herbert William (1.06.1897)
Slattery, Daniel (18.05.1881)
Slattery, Martin (13.12.1886)
Slattery, Robert (28.11.1871)
Slattery, Thomas (3.05.1866)
Sleator, William/James (25.08.1875)
Sloan, William (5.05.1899)
Small, James William (1.04.1874)
Small, Walter (29.08.1877)
Smart, Alfred (25.08.1873)
Smith, Charles James (29.06.1891)
Smith, David (1.01.1864)
Smith, David (29.02.1872)
Smith, David (8.07.1896)
Smith, George (15.10.1873)
Smith, George (9.02.1876)
Smith, George (1.01.1879)
Smith, George (17.10.1894)
Smith, Howell (1.01.1878)
Smith, Jacob (21.06.1876)
Smith, James (4.08.1890)
Smith, James Alexander (20.02.1899 & 5.11.1900)
Smith, John (1.06.1869)
Smith, John (15.03.1887)
Smith, John (24.12.1896)
Smith, Reuben (15.12.1890)
Smith, Thomas (6.11.1872)
Smith, Thomas (9.04.1890)
Smith, William (13.11.1873)
Smith, William (24.09.1874)
Smyth, David (1.05.1891)
Smyth, Patrick (10.07.1883)
Smyth, Robert (15.07.1874)
Smyth, Samuel (6.06.1866)
Smyth, Thomas (31.07.1873)

Smyth, Thomas (5.12.1874)
Sorley, Peter (12.12.1884)
Spann, Carl August Gottlieb (1.06.1897)
Sparks/Sparkes, Thomas (13.01.1876)
Spence, Percy David (2.10.1896)
Spink, Frederick William (2.04.1891)
Stacey, Samuel (4.12.1873)
Stack, Garrett (22.06.1871)
Staley, John (5.07.1865)
Stapleton, Michael (15.01.1879)
Staveley, George (28.05.1887)
Steedman, William (7.02.1877)
Stenson, Patrick (9.01.1878)
Sterne, George (11.08.1896)
Stevens, Jesse (1.01.1864)
Stevens, Robert (10.05.1876)
Stewart, David (16.03.1881 & 27.10.1885)
Stewart, John (29.07.1880)
Stinson, Samuel (3.08.1885)
Stirling/Sterling, John (31.05.1876)
Stockley, Samuel (22.05.1871)
Stokes, Richard W (20.06.1865)
Stonebridge, Frederick W (16.07.1873)
Stratton, Richard (21.11.1877)
Strong, Stephen (16.02.1876)
Stuart, John (9.06.1869)
Stubbs, John (23.10.1878)
Sullivan, Daniel (27.11.1878)
Sullivan, Denis (21.12.1889)
Sullivan, Hugh (18.05.1882)
Sullivan, John (2.02.1886)
Sullivan, Patrick (8.04.1874)
Sullivan, Robert (29.07.1874)
Sullivan, Timothy (7.06.1886)
Sullivan, William (26.02.1874)
Sutcliffe, Charles William (26.03.1890)
Sutherland, Donald S (1.01.1877)
Sutton, George (23.09.1885)
Swainson, James (27.05.1870)
Swann/Swan, John (5.08.1878)
Swanson, George Joseph (3.04.1875)
Swanton, George (16.01.1890)
Sweeney, Francis (31.12.1883)
Sweeney, John (23.12.1881)
Sweeney, Patrick (4.05.1869)
Sweeney, William (24.09.1888)
Swiney, John (8.03.1886)

Talbot, John (14.12.1882)
Tansey, John (6.11.1878)
Tate, Edward J (22.07.1875)
Tatton, John (1.07.1885)
Tatton, William (17.11.1882)
Taylor, Alfred (13.05.1874)
Taylor, Alfred (29.07.1880)
Taylor, James (3.04.1883)
Taylor, William Elphinstone (5.10.1872)
Teasdale, Thomas Walmsley (1.06.1897)
Thiele, Joseph Terran (11.11.1899)
Thomas, John (25.03.1875)
Thompson, Benjamin William (2.06.1875)
Thompson, James William (4.12.1872)
Thompson, John (6.01.1875)
Thompson, John (4.08.1890)
Thompson, John Raphael (6.02.1885)
Thomson, John (3.03.1885)
Thornton, Thomas Isaac (29.05.1865)
Thorpe, William (28.08.1878)
Tiernan, Thomas (6.04.1881)
Tierney, John (24.09.1891)
Tighe, Matthew (26.03.1886)
Tighe, Sydney Vincent (2.02.1898)
Timmins, Francis (1.03.1872 & 8.12.1881)
Tipping, William John (18.02.1875)
Tobin, Edward (10.06.1874)
Tobin, George (1.12.1866)
Tom, William (23.05.1877)
Toohill, Daniel (4.05.1882 & 31.07.1894)
Toomey, Michael Francis (25.01.1888)
Torpy, Luke (31.08.1869)
Towner, Lionel Edward Dyne (1.09.1873)
Townsen, Warren (6.12.1869)
Townsend, Edwin J (21.08.1874)
Townsend, William (11.02.1878)
Tracey, James Bernard (25.07.1894)
Trevelyan, Edmund James Willoughby (6.02.1885)
Troy, Michael (14.10.1889)
Trunks, John (7.04.1888)
Tubman, Robert (2.07.1887)
Turke/Turk, Andrew (27.03.1875)
Turkington/Torkington, Robert James (12.06.1883)

Turner, Gerald (14.03.1877)
Turner, Peter (6.02.1873)
Twinem, George (21.01.1887)
Tyrrell, Thomas (7.03.1866)

Urquhart, Frederick C (25.04.1882)

Vaux, Walter R (12.08.1880)
Veith, Russell Harris (16.03.1876)

Wade, Charles E (3.04.1883)
Wade, William Henry (4.02.1875)
Waldron, John (17.06.1874)
Waldron, John (16.01.1878)
Walker, Gilbert Ramsey (8.08.1899)
Walker, John (1.05.1869)
Walker, John Edward (8.03.1872)
Walker, Samuel (27.11.1878)
Wallace, William (26.08.1868)
Waller, John Thomas (25.03.1874)
Walsh, Charles (13.11.1873)
Walsh, Charles (12.08.1878)
Walsh, David (6.04.1864)
Walsh, Edward (23.09.1872)
Walsh, Francis (28.01.1874)
Walsh, James (1.12.1875)
Walsh, John (22.03.1865)
Walsh, John (1.07.1891)
Walsh, John (7.09.1894)
Walsh, John Patrick (15.12.1890)
Walsh, Martin (6.02.1885)
Walsh, Michael (4.11.1868)
Walsh, Michael (1.09.1897)
Walsh, Michael (4.04.1899)
Walsh, Patrick (6.06.1895)
Walsh, Richard (15.12.1890)
Walsh, Thomas (6.06.1866)
Ward, John (7.04.1896 & 10.01.1899)
Ward, John C (11.07.1877)
Ward, Martin (23.08.1894)
Wareham, Daniel (11.09.1878)
Warren, John (7.04.1874)
Waters, Benjamin (16.03.1876)
Watson, Thomas (23.12.1885)
Watson, Thomas James (1.09.1897)
Watters, William (1.01.1864)
Waugh, William (17.10.1877)
Wayman, William Joseph (6.03.1879)
Weale, William A (5.05.1877)

Webb, Frederick (17.10.1894)
Welding, Thomas Frederick (15.02.1886)
Welsh, Patrick (1.11.1894)
West, Thomas George (6.09.1889)
Whelan, John (19.04.1876)
White, Henry Edwin (12.06.1883)
White, John (1.01.1864)
White, Robert (22.01.1865)
White, Samuel James (1.09.1891)
White, Thomas (1.03.1872)
White, William N (15.07.1875)
Whiteside, Robert (1.11.1897)
Wiffen/Wiffin, Frederick Ernest
  (19.04.1886)
Williams, David Ludgate (28.07.1884)
Williams, Henry (23.02.1881)
Williams, James Watkin (24.10.1898)
Williams, William Charles (7.04.1896)
Williamson, David (18.12.1888)
Williamson, James (26.09.1877 &
  1.11.1883)
Willis, Frederick (8.08.1864)
Willis, Robert (24.10.1872)
Wilmot/Wilmott, Edward Eardly
  (5.02.1864)
Wilson, Alexander Moses (1.11.1894)
Wilson, James (1.09.1897)
Wilson, John (6.09.1871)
Wilson, John (24.09.1873)
Wilson, John (7.07.1893)
Wilson, Robert (28.06.1883)
Wilson, Thomas Joseph (1.11.1890)
Wilson, William (24.10.1888)
Wilson, William (11.08.1896)
Wilson, William James (26.10.1882)
Winks, Randolph (27.05.1896)
Wolfe, John (23.06.1868)
Wood, Abraham (9.09.1871)
Woodcraft, Richard Francis
  (30.01.1872)
Woodhouse, Joseph (1.05.1888)
Woodhouse, Robert (20.12.1882)
Woodhouse, Thomas (1.12.1882)
Woodlands, George (29.09.1899)
Woods, James (2.04.1887)
Woods, John (7.12.1867)
Woods, Thomas (4.01.1867)
Woods, William (27.12.1876)
Woodside, William (3.12.1889)

Wright, Charles (27.03.1875)
Wright, George William (10.04.1883)
Wycliffe, George (30.03.1870)
Wyer, Joseph (13.12.1883)
Wyer, Joseph Patrick / Patrick Joseph (20.02.1891)
Wyer, William (1.12.1885)

Young, Huston (4.04.1899)
Young, John (1.10.1885)

Zillman, William (1.06.1897)

Appendix C

Brisbane Night Duty Beats

Number 1 Section
Number 1: Commencing at the corner of Edward and Queen streets, thence by the right along Queen Street to Eagle Street, thence by the right along Eagle Street to Mary Street, thence by the right along Edward Street to the point of starting.

Number 2: Commencing at the corner of Queen and Albert streets, thence by the right along Queen Street to Edward Street, thence by the right along Edward Street to Alice Street, thence by the right along Alice Street to Albert Street, thence by the right along Albert Street to the point of starting.

Number 3: Commencing at the corner of Queen and George streets, thence by the right along Queen Street to Albert Street, thence by the right along Albert Street to Alice Street, thence by the right along Alice Street to George Street, thence by the right along George Street to the point of starting.

Number 4: Commencing at the corner of George Street and Queen Street, thence by the right along George Street to Alice Street, thence by the right along Alice Street to William Street, thence by the right along William Street to Turbot Street, thence by the right along

Turbot Street to George Street, thence by the right along George Street to the point of starting.

Number 2 Section
Number 5: Commencing at the corner of Adelaide and George streets, thence by the right along Adelaide Street to Edward Street, thence by the right along Edward Street to Queen Street, thence by the right along Queen Street to George Street, thence by the right along George Street to the point of starting.

Number 6: Commencing at the corner of Little Edward Street, thence by the right along Wickham Terrace to Leichhardt Street, thence by the right along Leichhardt Street to Wharf Street, thence by the right along Wharf Street to Wickham Terrace, thence by the right along Wickham Terrace to the point of starting.

Number 7: Commencing at the corner of Edward and Queen streets, thence by the right along Edward Street to Little Edward Street and Wickham Terrace, thence by the right along Wickham Terrace to Wharf Street, thence by the right along Wharf Street to Queen Street, thence by the right along Queen Street to the point of starting.

Number 8: Commencing at the corner of Queen and Wharf streets, thence by the right along Wharf Street to Leichhardt Street, thence by the right along Leichhardt Street to Boundary Street, thence by the right along Boundary Street to Petrie's Bight, thence by the right along Petrie's Bight to the point of starting.

Number 3 Section (Fortitude Valley)
Number 9: Commencing at the corner of Ann and Brunswick streets, thence by the right along Ann Street to Wickham Street, thence by the right along Wickham Street to Brunswick Street, thence by the right along Brunswick Street to the point of starting.

Number 10: Commencing at the corner of Ann and Brunswick streets, thence by the right along Ann Street to James Street, thence by the right along James Street to Harcourt Street, thence by the right along Harcourt Street to Brunswick Street, thence by the right along Brunswick Street to the point of starting.

Number 4 Section (South Brisbane)
Number 11: Commencing at the Brisbane Bridge in Stanley Street, thence along Stanley Street to Vulture Street, and back the same street to the point of starting.

Notes

INTRODUCTION

1 Government Printer, Brisbane, 1869, p. 9.
2 Brisbane was eventually chosen over Edenglassie as the name of the colonial settlement; John McIntosh, a watch and clock maker by trade, arrived in New South Wales in February 1814 on *General Hewitt*. He was a short man (5 feet 5 inches tall), of pale complexion with light brown hair and hazel eyes, and had a scar under his left ear. McIntosh eventually moved to the Moreton Bay penal settlement and married Christiana Ferris, also a transportee, who was born in England in 1800.
3 'Government Notice', *Sydney Gazette and New South Wales Advertiser*, 16 January 1826, p. 1.
4 Wright Mills, C 1959, *The Sociological Imagination*, Oxford University Press, Oxford, p. 6.
5 Ibid.
6 'Governor Brisbane's Instructions to Lt Miller', quoted in Steele, JG 1975, *Brisbane Town in Convict Days 1824–42*, University of Queensland Press, Brisbane, p. 2.
7 Ibid, p. 25.
8 'The Brisbane River: 100 Years Ago; by an Old Brisbanite', *The Brisbane Courier*, 22 March 1930, p. 10.
9 For more on the history of Brisbane as a convict settlement, see Steele, JG, *Brisbane Town in Convict Days 1824–1824*, and Johnston, R 1988, *Brisbane: The first thirty years*, Boolarong Press, Brisbane.
10 Quoted in Reece, B 1991, *Exiles from Erin: Convict lives in Ireland and Australia*, Palgrave Macmillan, United Kingdom, pp. 171–72.
11 Steele, JG, *Brisbane Town in Convict Days 1824–1842*, p. 71.
12 Months before McIntosh's death, his wife, Christiana, was imprisoned for drunkenness at New Castle Gaol (annual gaol no. 82, *New Castle Gaol Entrance Book*, <ancestry.com.au>). A year later, she petitioned for permission to marry Joseph Nicholson (aka Nicholls), a free man, which was denied as she was still recorded as being married to John McIntosh. In 1844, she petitioned again and the permission was granted. However, on 31 January, Christiana married fellow convict James Broad in East Maitland (*New South Wales Registers of Convicts' Applications to Marry, 1826–1851*, pp. 84–5).
13 Steele, JG, *Brisbane Town in Convict Days 1824–1842*, p. 200.
14 In one such case, a few goats became a serious nuisance in South Brisbane, 'in consequence of their congregating under the verandah of Mr Orr's house, especially

at night time, during the wet weather'. On one occasion, Mr Orr was ascending the steps of his house when a huge billy goat knocked him head over heels. The owners of the goats were fined 5s; 'Local Intelligence', *The Moreton Bay Courier*, 5 December 1846, p. 2, viewed on 26 August 2019, <nla.gov.au/nla.news-article3715808>.

15 Coote, W 1882, *History of the Colony of Queensland*, William Thorne, Brisbane, pp. 29–30.
16 'News from the Interior. Moreton Bay', *The Sydney Morning Herald*, 12 December 1842, p. 2.
17 O'Keeffe, M 1978, The Convict Element in Pre-Separation Queensland', *Settlement of the Colony of Queensland: A seminar by the John Oxley Library*, Library Board of Queensland, Brisbane, p. 1.
18 'Correspondence from Wickham to CS, January–February 1843', *Letters Relating to Moreton Bay and Queensland Received 1822–1869*, State Library of Queensland, reel A2.13, pp. 273, 480–84.
19 'Volunteer Force, Government Departments', *Pugh's Almanac and Queensland Directory* 1860–61, Brisbane, p. 57.
20 Until 1893 the Water Police were under the command of the Marine Department; Chesterton, BM, *New South Wales Police: A brief guide to historical resources*, Queensland Police Museum, Brisbane, p. 16; Lindsay, P 2012, *True Blue: 150 years of service and sacrifice of the NSW Police Force*, HarperCollins, Sydney, p. 43.
21 Patrick Colquhoun first popularised the new science of policing in his *Treatise on Police of the Metropolis* in 1796; See Connors, L 1990, 'The "Birth of the Prison" and the Death of Convictivism: The operation of the law in pre-separation Queensland, 1839–1859', PhD thesis, University of Queensland, Brisbane; Connors, L 2015, *Warrior: A legendary leader's dramatic life and violent death on the colonial frontier*, Allen & Unwin, Sydney.
22 Nettlebeck, A et al. 2016, *Fragile Settlements: Aboriginal peoples, law & resistance in southwest Australia and prairie Canada*, University of British Columbia Press, Vancouver.
23 Kerkhove, R 2018, 'Aboriginal Camps as Urban Foundations? Evidence from Southern Queensland', *Aboriginal History*, vol. 42, pp. 147, 164.
24 For more information on the force and its constituents (City Police, Water Police, Mounted Border Police, Native Police and Gold Police), as well as its changes, challenges and developments from 1864 to 1992, see Johnston, R 1992, *The Long Blue Line: A history of Queensland Police*, Boolarong Press, Brisbane.
25 Finnane, M 1987, *Policing in Australia: Historical perspectives*, New South Wales University Press, Kensington; Finnane, M 1994, *Police and Government: Histories of policing in Australia*, Oxford University Press, Oxford.
26 Taylor, D 1997, *The New Police in Nineteenth-Century England: Crime, conflict and control*, Manchester University Press, Manchester, p. 137.
27 See Reiner, R 2010, *The Politics of the Police*, Oxford University Press, Oxford.
28 Taylor, D, *The New Police in Nineteenth-Century England*, p. 142.
29 Bartley, N 1892, *Opals and Agates*, Gordon & Gotch, Brisbane, p. 98.
30 Wilson, D 2006, *The Beat*, Circa, Beaconsfield, p. 70.
31 Emsley, C 2009, *The Great British Bobby: A history of British policing from the eighteenth century to the present*, Quercus, London, p. 7.

The leading experts in British policing history – Clive Emsley, Stanley Palmer, VAC Gatrell, David Taylor, Douglas Hay, JM Beattie, Peter King and Robert Storch, along with David Jones, Jennifer S Davis and Francis G Snyder – have leant their expertise to the history of police courts and the police as prosecutors, and been the main reinterpreters of the evolution of law enforcement, penal reform and the history of interpersonal violence. Emsley, an authority on English policing, has contributed immensely to the scholarly discourse in his works, including: *Crime and Society in England 1750–1900* (Longman Group, Harlow, 1987), *The English Police: A political and social history* (Harvester Wheatsheaf, Hemel Hempstead, 1991), *Police Detectives in History, 1750–1950* (Routledge, 2006) and *The Great British Bobby: A history of British policing from the 18th century to the present* (Quercus, London, 2009).

The scholarly Irish policing historiography essentially started with Seamus Breathnach's *The Irish Police from the Earliest Times to the Present Day* (Anvil Books, 1974); Stanley Palmer's *Police and Protest in England and Ireland, 1780–1850* (University of Cambridge Press, Cambridge, 1988); Mary Scanlon's *The DMP* (Minerva Press, London, 1986); Brian Griffin's *The Bulkies: Police and crime in Belfast 1800–1865* (Four Courts, Dublin, 1997); Donal O'Sullivan's *The Irish Constabularies, 1822–1922* (Brandon, Dingle, 1999); Elizabeth Malcolm's *The Irish Policeman, 1822–1922: A life* (Four Courts, Dublin, 2006); Jim Herlihy's *The Dublin Metropolitan Police: A short history* (Four Courts, Dublin, 2001); and Donal P McCracken's *Inspector Mallon: Buying Irish patriotism for a five-pound note* (Irish Academic Press, Dublin, 2009).

Also see Conor Brady's *Guardians of the Peace* (Gill & Macmillan Ltd., Dublin, 1974); Gregory Allen's *The Garda Síochana: Policing independent Ireland, 1922–82* (Gill & Macmillan Ltd., Dublin, 1999); Liam McNiffe's *A History of the Garda Síochána: A social history of the force 1922–52 with an overview for the years 1952–97* (Wolfhound Press, Dublin, 1999); Vicky Conway's *Policing Twentieth Century Ireland: A history of an Garda Síochána* (Routledge, 2014); and Anastasia Dukova's *A History of the Dublin Metropolitan Police and its Colonial Legacy* (Palgrave Macmillan, London, 2016).

Scholarly articles by Nigel Cochrane's 'Public Reaction to the Introduction of a New Police Force: Dublin 1838–45' (1987), Colm Barry's 'The Policeman's Lot is not a Happy One: Duty, discipline, pay and conditions in the DMP, c. 1833–45' (1987) and 'The Police and Protest in Dublin: 1786–1840' (1991), and Brian Griffin's 'Such Vermin: The Dublin Police Force and the public' (1995).

For the history of policing in New South Wales, see Michael Sturma's *Vice in a Vicious Society: Crime and convicts in mid-nineteenth century New South Wales* (University of Queensland Press, Brisbane, 1983); Leslie E Skinner's *Police of the Pastoral Frontier: Native Police 1849–59* (University of Queensland Press, Brisbane, 1975); and Patrick Lindsay's *True Blue: 150 years of service and sacrifice of the NSW Police Force* (HarperCollins, Sydney, 2012).

For the history of policing in South Australia, see Robert Clyne's *Colonial Blue: A history of the South Australian Police Force* (Wakefield Press, Kent Town, 1987); Chas Hopkins's *South Australia Police 1838–1992: A History of the development of operations of the force from its establishment* (self-published, 1995); and Amanda Nettelbeck and Robert Foster's *In the Name of the Law: William Willshire and the policing of the Australian frontier* (Wakefield Press, Kent Town, 2007).

For the history of policing in Western Australia, see AR (Don) Pashley's *Policing Our State: A history of police stations and police officers in Western Australia 1829–1945* (2000); Peter Canole's *Protect and Serve: A history of policing in Western Australia*

(Western Australia Police Service, Perth, 2002); and Chris Owen's *Every Mother's Son is Guilty: Policing the Kimberley frontier of Western Australia 1882–1905* (University of Western Australia Press, Perth, 2016).

For the history of policing in Victoria, see Robert Haldane's *The People's Force: A history of the Victoria Police*, 2nd ed. (Melbourne University Press, Melbourne, 1995); and Marie Hansen Fels's *Good Men and True: The Aboriginal Police of Port Phillip District 1837–1853* (Melbourne University Press, Melbourne, 1988).

For the history of policing in Queensland, see Norman S Pixley's 'An Outline of the History of the Queensland Police Force 1860–1949' (*Journal of the Royal Historical Society of Queensland*, vol. 4, no. 3, 1950, pp. 340–60); Lisa Jones's *150 Years of Policing Queensland, 1864–2014* (Queensland Police Service, Brisbane, 2014); and Jonathan Richards's *The Secret War: A true history of Queensland's Native Police* (University of Queensland Press, Brisbane, 2008).

Also see Duncan Chappell and Paul R Wilson's *The Police and the Public in Australia and New Zealand* (University of Queensland Press, Brisbane, 1969); and GM O'Brien's *The Australian Police Forces* (Oxford University Press, Melbourne, 1960).

32 'An Act to Consolidate and Amend the Laws Relating to the Police Force, 1863', *Supplement to the Queensland Government Gazette of Saturday*, 10 October 1863, no. 100, p. 806.
33 For a more detailed study of the impact of the Scottish Enlightenment on police reform, see Barrie, DG 2012, *Police in the Age of Improvement: Police development and the civic tradition in Scotland, 1775–1865*, Routledge, United Kingdom.

CHAPTER 1

1 Quoted in Russell, HS 1888, *The Genesis of Queensland: An account of the first exploring journeys to and over Darling Downs, the earliest days of their occupation, social life, station seeking, the course of discovery, northward and westward, and a resume of the causes which led to separation from New South Wales*, Turner & Henderson, Sydney, p. 171.
2 Russell, HS, *The Genesis of Queensland*, p. 167.
3 *The Dublin Evening Mail*, 12 August 1826, p. 5.
4 'Conditional Pardon NSW 31 Dec 1847', *Convict Registers of Conditional and Absolute Pardons, 1788–1870*, p. 384, <ancestry.com.au>.
5 In the legislation of 1829, a general Oath of Allegiance that was unexceptionable for Catholics was introduced, and state offices, apart from a few grand exceptions, opened to them.
6 See Dickson, D 2014, *Dublin: The making of a capital city*, Profile Books, London.
7 'The Commission', *The Morning Register* (Dublin), 21 June 1826, p. 3.
8 See Dukova, A 2016, *A History of the Dublin Metropolitan Police and its Colonial Legacy*, Palgrave Macmillan, United Kingdom.
9 Burn, WL, 'Free Trade in Land: An aspect of the Irish question', quoted in Palmer, S 1989, *Police and Protest in England and Ireland, 1780–1850*, Cambridge University Press, Cambridge, p. 25.
10 Dukova, A, *A History of the Dublin Metropolitan Police and its Colonial Legacy*, p. 48.
11 'Police Intelligence', *Saunders's News-Letter*, 28 July 1821, p. 2.
12 'The Commission', *The Morning Register* (Dublin), 24 June 1825, p. 2.
13 'The Commission', *The Morning Register* (Dublin), 21 June 1826, p. 3.

14 Ibid., p. 3.
15 Ibid.
16 Godfrey, B 2013, 'The Convict Stain: Desistance in penal colony', in Rowbotham, J, Muravyeva, M & Nash D (eds), *Shame, Blame and Culpability: Crime and violence in the modern state*, Routledge, United Kingdom, p. 98.
17 Maxwell-Stewart, H 2014, 'Convict Labour Extraction and Transportation from Britain and Ireland, 1615–1870', in De Vito, C & Lichtenstein, A (eds), *Global Convict Labour*, Brill, United Kingdom, p. 169.
18 Costello, C 1987, *Botany Bay: The story of convicts transported from Ireland to Australia, 1791–1853*, Mercier Press, Dublin, p. 107.
19 Bateson, C 1985, *The Convict Ships*, Brown, Son & Ferguson, Glasgow, pp. 346–47.
20 Medical journal of the *Countess of Harcourt* for 12 July to 26 December 1822 by Robert Armstrong, surgeon and superintendent, National Archives United Kingdom, ADM 101/18/2.
21 Reid, R 1823, *Travels in Ireland in the Year 1822: Brief sketches of the moral, physical and political state of the country in the year 1822*, Longman, Hurst, Rees, Orme, and Brown, London, p. 268.
22 Costello, C, *Botany Bay*, p. 12.
23 Reece, B 1991, *Exiles from Erin: Convict lives in Ireland and Australia*, Palgrave Macmillan, United Kingdom, pp. 171–72; also see the description of Captain Logan's approach to commanding the district in the Introduction.
24 A 'lifer' is a transportee convicted for penal servitude for the duration of their natural life.
25 'Conditional Pardon NSW 31 Dec 1847', *Convict Registers of Conditional and Absolute Pardons, 1788–1870*, p. 384, viewed on 20 December 2016, <ancestry.com.au>.
26 'October, 1828', *Gaol Description and Entrance Books, 1818–1930*, viewed on 20 December 2016, <ancestry.com.au>.
27 'Queensland's Half Century', *The Brisbane Courier*, 8 December 1909, p. 24; Waller, KGT 1967, 'Leslie, Patrick (1815–1881)', *Australian Dictionary of Biography*, National Centre of Biography, Australian National University, viewed on 18 January 2017, <adb.anu.edu.au/biography/leslie-patrick-2351/text3073>.
28 Maxwell-Stewart, H, 'Convict Labour Extraction and Transportation from Britain and Ireland, 1615–1870', p. 181.
29 Maxwell-Stewart, H & Kippen, R 2014, '"What is a man that is a bolter to do? I would steal the Governor's axe rather than starve": Old lags and recidivism in the Tasmanian penal colony', in Campbell, J & Miller, V (eds), *Transnational Penal Cultures*, Routledge, United Kingdom, pp. 165–66.
30 Braithwaite, J 2001, 'Crime in the Convict Republic', *The Modern Law Review*, vol. 64, no. 1, pp. 16–17, 19–21.
31 'Patrick Leslie's Diary', quoted in Russell, HS 1888, *The Genesis of Queensland*, p. 166.
32 'In the Early Days. The Birth and Growth of Brisbane and Environs', *The Queenslander*, 20 February 1892, p. 367.
33 'Country News. Port Macquarie Petty Sessions', *The Australian*, 28 May 1842, pp. 2–3.
34 'Law Intelligence, Court of Quarter Sessions, Wednesday July 6', *The New South Wales Examiner*, 8 July 1842, p. 3.
35 'Country News. Port Macquarie Petty Sessions', *The Australian*, 28 May 1842, p. 3.
36 'The Three Bushrangers', *The Sydney Morning Herald*, 21 December 1842, p. 3.
37 'Marriage Certificate 1266/1842 V18421266 91', *Registry of Births, Deaths and Marriages, New South Wales*.

38 'Abstract of the Population on the 2nd March, 1846, in each of the Counties, and Commissioners' Districts, comprised within the Sydney or Middle District, shewing the number of persons of each sex under and above twenty-one years of age respectively who cannot read, can read only, and read and write' 1846, *New South Wales Census*, p. 9; The population of Brisbane county in 1846 was 1,406 persons (936 males and 470 females).

39 Ibid.

40 Peter Murphy Death Certificate C1472, *Registry of Births, Deaths and Marriages, Queensland*.

41 'Correspondence from Moreton Bay William Whyte, Commandants Clerk and Chief Constable to Hon E Deas Thompson, 15 Apr 1840', *Letters Relating to Moreton Bay and Queensland Received 1822–1869*, State Library of Queensland, reel A2.11, pp. 491–92; 'Correspondence from Commandant's Office to Hon CS, 31 Mar 1840', *Letters Relating to Moreton Bay and Queensland Received 1822–1869*, State Library of Queensland, reel A2.11, pp. 174–77; 'Correspondence from Commandant's Office to Hon CS, 18 Feb 1840', *Letters Relating to Moreton Bay and Queensland Received 1822–1869*, State Library of Queensland, reel A2.11, pp. 105–6.

42 'Correspondence from O'Gorman to Hon CS, 27 Aug 1840', *Letters Relating to Moreton Bay and Queensland Received 1822–1869*, State Library of Queensland, reel A2.11, pp. 274, 277.

43 'News from the Interior. Moreton Bay', *The Sydney Morning Herald*, 12 December 1842, p. 2.

44 'Correspondence from Wickham to CS, Nov–Dec 1842', *Letters Relating to Moreton Bay and Queensland Received 1822–1869*, State Library of Queensland, reel A2.13, pp. 003–011.

45 'Correspondence from Wickham to CS, Jan–Feb 1843', *Letters Relating to Moreton Bay and Queensland Received 1822–1869*, State Library of Queensland, reel A2.13, 273, pp. 480–84.

46 'Abstract of the Population on the 2nd March, 1846, in each of the Counties, and Commissioners' Districts, comprised within the Sydney or Middle District, showing the number of persons of each sex and age' 1846, *New South Wales Census*, p. 5.

47 Ibid., p. 6.

48 Ibid., p. 7.

49 Ibid., pp. 8, 12.

50 'Peter Murphy, alias Duff. Conditional Pardon', *New South Wales Convict Registers of Conditional and Absolute Pardons, 1788–1870*, pp. 383–84, viewed on 20 December 2016, <ancestry.com.au>.

51 'Historical Tables, Demography, 1859–2008 (Q150 Release)', *Australian Bureau of Statistics*, viewed on 15 November 2018.

52 Smith, JG 1987, 'The Foundation of Kangaroo Point 1843–1846', in *Brisbane: People, places and pageantry*, Brisbane History Group Papers, no. 6, Brisbane, p. 87.

53 Ibid., p. 95.

54 'Sale by Auction', *The Moreton Bay Courier*, 12 May 1849, p. 2.

55 'Suspicion of Stealing', *The Moreton Bay Courier*, 19 June 1847, p. 2.

56 Ibid.

57 'Indecent Exposure', *The Moreton Bay Courier*, 31 July 1847, p. 3.

58 'Law Intelligence, Central Criminal Court. Monday', *The Sydney Morning Herald*, 8 June 1848, p. 2.

59 Ibid., p. 3.
60 Ibid.
61 'William Fife', *New South Wales Convict Indents, 1788–1842*, viewed on 20 January 2017, <www.ancestry.com>.
62 'The Murder at Kangaroo Point', *Sentinel*, 20 April 1848, p. 2; The Moreton Bay Circuit Court was established two years later in May 1850 and was presided by Justice Therry; Morrison, FW 1888, *The Aldine History of Queensland*, vol. 1, The Aldine Publishing Company, Sydney, pp. 293–94.
63 'Law Intelligence, Central Criminal Court. Monday', *The Sydney Morning Herald*, 8 June 1848, p. 2.
64 'William Fife', *New South Wales Gaol Description and Entrance Books, 1818–1930*, viewed on 2 January 2017, <www.ancestry.com>.
65 'Central Criminal Court', *The Sydney Morning Herald*, 25 August 1848, p. 2.
66 'House Robbery', *The Moreton Bay Courier*, 20 July 1850, p. 2.
67 'Allot 4/ The Crown/ Peter Murphy, Brisbane Ref 48/ 12375. Correspondence from Surveyor General's Office to CS, Dec 1847', *Letters Relating to Moreton Bay and Queensland Received 1822–1869*, State Library of Queensland, reel A2.16, p. 535.
68 'Domestic Intelligence. Investigation Respecting the Affray with the Aborigines', *The Moreton Bay Courier*, 8 December 1849, p. 2.
69 'Brisbane CPS, 19 May 1851' quoted in Connors, L 1990, 'The "Birth of the Prison" and the Death of Convictivism: The operation of the law in pre-separation Queensland, 1839–1859', PhD thesis, University of Queensland, Brisbane, p. 154.
70 'Constables Dismissed. Domestic Intelligence', *The Moreton Bay Courier*, 5 January 1850, p. 2.
71 Ibid.
72 'Charges against Constable', *The Moreton Bay Courier*, 22 January 1853, p. 2.
73 'Domestic Intelligence', *The Moreton Bay Courier*, 25 June 1853, p. 3; the Brisbane Police consisted of one chief constable (with a salary of £125 per annum), one district constable (with a salary of £95 16s 3d per annum) and 11 constables (with a salary of £86 13s 9d per annum each).
74 'Breach of Police Regulations', *The Moreton Bay Courier*, 18 June 1853, p. 2.
75 *Queensland, 1900: A narrative of her past, together with biographies of her leading men*, 1900, Alcazar Press, WH Wendt & Co., Brisbane, p. 21; 'Family Notices', *The Brisbane Courier*, 13 May 1878, p. 2.
76 Godfrey, B & Cox, D 2008, '"The Last Fleet": Crime, reformation, and punishment in Western Australia after 1868', *The Australian and New Zealand Journal of Criminology*, vol. 41.2, pp. 245–46.
77 The research into the early biographical details of Peter 'Duff' Murphy was in part facilitated by a Harry Gentle Resource Centre Visiting Fellowship.

CHAPTER 2

1 *The Brisbane Courier*, 19 March 1864, p. 3.
2 'Classified Advertising', *The Moreton Bay Courier*, 5 January 1850, p. 1.
3 *Act for the Regulation of the Police Force in New South Wales*, 14 Vic., no. 38.
4 'Samuel Sneyd', *Family Pages*, viewed on 15 January 2017, <www.artpages.com.au/sam_sneyd.html>.
5 Holmes, R 2011, *Redcoat: The British soldier in the age of horse and musket*, HarperCollins, London, p. 309.

6 *Manuscript Diary of Capt Geo Mason 1831–1835*, transcribed by Tyson, E, 2005, The Trustees of the King's Own Royal Regiment Museum, Lancaster, viewed on 8 November 2019, <www.kingsownmuseum.com/mason01.htm>.
7 The UK Royal Navy Medical Journals 1817–1857 <ancestry.com> list Samuel Sneyd as travelling on the ship *Asia*, which departed the United Kingdom on 29 September 1831 and arrived in New South Wales on 13 February 1832.
8 *4th Foot Lancaster Kings Own Regiment* & *Manuscript Diary of Capt Geo Mason 1831–1835*, viewed on 15 January 2018, <www.kingsownmuseum.com/mus07-08.htm>.
9 'Samuel Sneyd Obituary', *The Moreton Bay Courier*, 11 July 1885, p. 6; 'List of Staff', *Nominal Return of the Mounted Police in the Sydney or Middle District in 31 December 1848*.
10 'List of Staff', *Nominal Return of the Mounted Police in the Sydney or Middle District in 31 December 1848*.
11 O'Brien, GM 1960, *The Australian Police Forces*, Oxford University Press, Melbourne, p. 20; Prior to his promotion to chief constable, Sneyd moved around the colony to places such as Hartley, Goulburn and Braidwood, and he honoured these placenames by using them as middle names for his first three sons. The family eventually settled in Goulburn. Samuel and Kitty had nine children during their 21-year marriage, seven of them born before they moved to Brisbane; 'Samuel Sneyd Obituary', *The Moreton Bay Courier*, 11 July 1885, p. 6.
12 'Domestic Intelligence – Legislative Council', *The Colonist* (Sydney), 16 November 1839, p. 2.
13 'Vale of Clwyd', *The Australian*, 21 September 1839, p. 3.
14 'Domestic Intelligence', *Sydney Gazette and New South Wales Advertiser*, 5 November 1839, p. 2.
15 'Requesting permission to remain in Sydney, Correspondence from Chief Constable Moreton Bay to Hon Colonial Secretary, Jan 1850', *Letters Relating to Moreton Bay and Queensland Received 1822–1860*, State Library of Queensland, reel A2.20, p. 791.
16 'Police Establishment, Brisbane', *Returns for the Colony of New South Wales for 1850*, p. 354.
17 'An illustrated synopsis of Queensland's history from the earliest days to the present times issued in commemoration of the 50th anniversary of responsible government: A chronology of the state of Queensland', *The Brisbane Courier*, 8 December 1909, p. 23.
18 'Colonial Secretary Notice', *New South Wales Government Gazette*, 1 January 1850, p. 2.
19 Connors, L 1990, 'The "Birth of the Prison" and the Death of Convictism: The operation of the law in pre-separation Queensland 1839 to 1859', PhD thesis, University of Queensland, Brisbane, p. 151.
20 'Inspectors of Distilleries and Inspector of Slaughter Houses', *New South Wales Government Gazette*, 11 January 1850, p. 45.
21 'John Clements Wickham', *Australian Dictionary of Biography*, viewed on 20 January 2017, <adb.anu.edu.au/biography/wickham-john-clements-2790>.
22 'Domestic Intelligence', *The Moreton Bay Courier*, 19 January 1850, p. 3.
23 'Inspectors of Distilleries and Inspector of Slaughter Houses', *Queensland Police Gazette*, 11 January 1850, p. 45.
24 'Queensland Police Officer Service Histories', *Queensland Police Museum Personnel Database*.

25 Advertisement, *New South Wales Government Gazette*, 19 February 1850, p. 277.
26 'Eight Constables Insufficient', *Correspondence from C.A.F to His Excellency Sir Charles Augustus Fitzroy, Colonial Secretary Letters Relating to Moreton Bay and Queensland Received 1822–1860*, State Library of Queensland, reel A2.20, pp. 68–72.
27 Ibid.
28 'In the Early Days', *The Brisbane Courier*, 31 October 1892, p. 2.
29 'In the Early Days', *The Moreton Bay Courier*, 25 January 1851, p. 3.
30 'Letter applying for reward, correspondence from JC Wickham Police Magistrate to Colonial Secretary', *Colonial Secretary Letters Relating to Moreton Bay and Queensland Received 1822–1860*, State Library of Queensland, reel A2.22, pp. 94–96.
31 'Burnett District – From Our Correspondent: The Native Blacks', *The Moreton Bay Courier*, 15 June 1852, p. 1.
32 Ibid.
33 Commissioner of Police, *General Order 596*, 28 Oct 1876, Queensland State Archives, A/36338.
34 A series of Acts passed throughout the eighteenth and nineteenth centuries that were designed to provide better regulations of servants, labourers and work people.
35 'Proceedings of the Central Criminal Court, 3rd February 1851', *Old Bailey Online*, viewed on 13 March 2017, <www.oldbaileyonline.org/browse.jsp?id=def1-485-18510203&div=t18510203-485#highlight>; See 'The Trial of Mr and Mrs Sloane. Central Criminal Court, 5 Feb.', *The Times*, 6 February 1851, p. 7.
36 'Charges of Barbarously Ill-treating a Servant', *The Moreton Bay Courier*, 25 October 1851, p. 2.
37 'Alleged Barbarous Ill Treatment', *The Moreton Bay Courier*, 1 November 1851, p. 2.
38 'Shocking Death of a Constable', *The Moreton Bay Courier*, 15 January 1853, p. 3.
39 'Domestic Intelligence: Charges Against Constable', *The Moreton Bay Courier*, 15 January 1853, p. 2.
40 'Domestic Intelligence', *The Moreton Bay Courier*, 2 April 1853, p. 2.
41 'Bluestone Rum Case', *Truth*, 21 January 1951, p. 21; *The Moreton Bay Courier*, 28 January 1854, p. 2.
42 The members of the police petitioning for a rise in wages included: Chief Constable Samuel Sneyd; District Constable William Anderson; and ordinary constables John Boe, Edward Quinn, Robert Orr, James Tredennick, William Watts, James Holmes, Patrick FitzGibbon, Martin Dowling, Alfred Samuel Wright, Edward Kitchen and Robert Downs.
43 'Petition of Constables and Peace Officers for Town and District of Ipswich', *Colonial Secretary Papers Index*, 29 April 1854, pp. 268–70.
44 'Forwarding Petitions from Constabulary of Brisbane & Ipswich praying for increase of pay, correspondence from JC Wickham, Government Resident to Colonial Secretary', *Letters Relating to Moreton Bay and Queensland Received 1822–1860*, State Library of Queensland, reel A2.29, pp. 806–9.
45 Ibid.
46 'Registry of Deeds Office – Title Deeds', *New South Wales Government Gazette*, 4 February 1853, p. 246.
47 'Reporting on Government Resident Moreton Bay's letter covering Petitions from Brisbane & Ipswich Constabulary, from Office of Inspector General of Police to Colonial Secretary', *Colonial Secretary Papers Index Relating to Moreton Bay and Queensland Received 1822–1860*, State Library of Queensland, reel A2.30, pp. 265–70.

48 'Land Sales', *The Moreton Bay Courier*, 29 November 1856, p. 3.
49 'Died', *The Moreton Bay Courier*, 12 January 1856, p. 3.
50 Brisbane's population grew to 18,544 in 1856.
51 'Supreme Court', *The Moreton Bay Courier*, 10 October 1857, p. 3.
52 'Domestic Intelligence', *The Moreton Bay Courier*, 5 September 1857, p. 2.
53 Ibid.
54 'A Reminiscence of the Fifties', *The Brisbane Courier*, 29 June 1907, p. 12.
55 'Brisbane Criminal Assizes', *The North Australian, Ipswich and General Advertiser*, 27 January 1857, p. 2.
56 'Brisbane River Floods', *The Telegraph* (Brisbane), 5 December 1928, p. 15.
57 'Domestic intelligence', *The Moreton Bay Courier*, 2 May 1857, p. 2.
58 'Brisbane, From our Correspondent', *The Darling Downs Gazette and General Advertiser*, 5 August 1858, p. 4.
59 'Mr Sneyd', *The Moreton Bay Courier*, 11 August 1858, p. 2.
60 'William Hartley Sneyd Marriage', *The Moreton Bay Courier*, 19 November 1859, p. 2; Two weeks later, Queensland separated from its southern neighbours on 10 December 1859, and by the end of the year the population of Queensland was estimated at 23,520.
61 Cadastre Maps Brisbane, 1858 and 1874; 'Deaths. Sneyd', *The South Australian Register*, 9 July 1885, p. 4.
62 'Local Intelligence', *The Moreton Bay Courier*, 26 November 1859, p. 2.
63 'Letter reporting removal from office of Gaoler, Matron & Principal Turnkey Brisbane Gaol, from Colonial Secretary to Government Resident's Office', & 'Letter re temporary appointment of Samuel Sneyd from Government Resident's Office to Colonial Secretary', *Colonial Secretary Letters Relating to Moreton Bay and Queensland Received 1822–1860*, State Library of Queensland, reel A2.43, pp. 4–8.
64 'Local Intelligence', *The Moreton Bay Courier*, 26 November 1859, p. 2.

CHAPTER 3

1 Bowen, G 1889, *Thirty Years of Colonial Government, Vol 1*, Lane-Pool, London, p. 111.
2 Hill, WRO recollections in *Forty-Five Years' Experience in North Queensland, 1861 to 1905*, Queensland Police Museum.
3 *UK Apprentices Indentured in Merchant Navy 1824–1910 for S Lloyd*, p. 78, <ancestry.com.au>.
4 'Samuel Lloyd, No 687', Victoria Police Department, Victoria Police Museum, Melbourne.
5 'Record of Conduct and Service of 2nd Class Det Samuel Lloyd', Victoria Police Department, Victoria Police Museum, Melbourne, p. 2.
6 Ibid., p. 1.
7 Ibid.; 'Miscellaneous Information. Rewards', *Victoria Police Gazette*, 16 June 1864, p. 240.
8 'Miscellaneous Information. Rewards', *Victoria Police Gazette*, 27 October 1864, p. 411.
9 'Cattle Stealing and Prevention Act of 1853 (17 Vic No 3)', in Bain, D 1892, *Queensland Police Guide: Containing an epitome of 184 acts of parliament to 1891, and a supplement of 815 offences, alphabetically arranged, with penalties and punishments*, Watson, Ferguson & Co, Brisbane, pp. 16–17.

10 'Police Regulation Bill', *Legislative Assembly, Record of the Proceedings of the Queensland Parliament*, 20 May 1862.
11 *Mayor's Consultation Budget*, Greater London Authority, viewed on 22 November 2018, <www.london.gov.uk/sites/default/files/mayors_consultation_budget_2018-_2019.pdf>.
12 'Police Regulation Bill', *Legislative Assembly, Record of the Proceedings of the Queensland Parliament*, 20 May 1862.
13 According to the recruitment information in 2017, a Queensland Police constable received $2,700 per fortnight before tax, viewed on 20 February 2019, <www.policerecruit.qld.gov.au/whatWeOffer/Employment-Entitlements.htm>; A London Metropolitan Police constable's starter salary in 2018/19 averaged £500 per week, viewed on 20 February 2019, <www.metfriendly.org.uk/services/police-finance-information/police-pay/>.
14 'Police Regulation Bill', *Legislative Assembly, Record of the Proceedings of the Queensland Parliament*, 20 May 1862.
15 Dukova, A 2016, *A History of the Dublin Metropolitan Police and its Colonial Legacy*, Palgrave Macmillan, United Kingdom, p. 49.
16 'Police Regulation Bill', *Legislative Assembly, Record of the Proceedings of the Queensland Parliament*, 20 May 1862.
17 Ibid.
18 Under the new provisions, the magistrates retained their powers as inspectors, which left the avenues for power abuse open. Anthony William Brown was appointed Brisbane Police Magistrate prior to separation in 1857. At the time, the duty of superintending the police devolved on the Brisbane Police Magistrate, who was also a sheriff.
19 Richards, J 2008, *The Secret War: A true history of Queensland's Native Police*, University of Queensland Press, Brisbane, p. 87.
20 *Manual of Police Regulations for the Guidance of the Constabulary of Queensland* 1876, James C Beal, Government Printer, Brisbane, p. 32.
21 'Table No VIII, Civil Establishment, Police', *Statistics of Queensland, Queensland Votes and Proceedings*, vol. 1, pp. 1, 309 (39); 'Police Commission', *The Brisbane Courier*, 2 September 1899, p. 3.
22 'A Reminiscence of the Fifties', *The Brisbane Courier*, 29 June 1907, quoted in Richards, J, *The Secret War*, p. 68.
23 Artist's impression of the Convict Barracks in Queen Street, Brisbane, neg. no. 31216, JOL.
24 Bartley, N 1897, *Australian Pioneers and Reminiscences*, Gordon & Gotch, Brisbane, p. 271.
25 *The Brisbane Courier*, 21 March 1864, p. 2.
26 'Fire in Edward-Street', *The Brisbane Courier*, 5 September 1864, pp. 2, 8.
27 Ibid.
28 'Another Fire!', *The Brisbane Courier*, 6 September 1864, p. 2.
29 Ibid., pp. 2, 7.
30 'Magisterial Inquiry', *The Brisbane Courier*, 8 September 1864, p. 2.
31 'Terrific and Disastrous Fire. Fifty Tenements Destroyed', *The Brisbane Courier*, 2 December 1864, p. 2.
32 Ibid.
33 Ibid.
34 'Inquest of the Late Fire', *The Brisbane Courier*, 6 December 1864, p. 2.

35 'After the Fire', *The Brisbane Courier*, 3 December 1864, p. 4.
36 'Friday, December 2, 1864', *The Brisbane Courier*, 2 December 1864, p. 2.
37 'Terrific and Disastrous Fire. Fifty Tenements Destroyed', *The Brisbane Courier*, 2 December 1864, p. 2.
38 'After the Fire', *The Brisbane Courier*, 3 December 1864, p. 4.
39 Ibid.
40 'Central Police Court', *The Brisbane Courier*, 5 December 1864, p. 3.
41 Ibid.
42 'Central Police Court, Obscene Language', *The Brisbane Courier*, 28 December 1865, p. 3.
43 'Larceny by a Servant', *The Brisbane Courier*, 24 November 1865, p. 3.
44 'Illegal Conveyance of Spirits', *The Brisbane Courier*, 25 December 1865, p. 3.
45 Dukova, A, *A History of the Dublin Metropolitan Police and its Colonial Legacy*, p. 192.
46 Robert Kilfedder was one of the arresting constables in the murder case of gold escort officer Patrick Cahill (*Robert Kilfedder Personnel File*, Queensland Police Museum).
47 'Suicide of William Ennis', *The Brisbane Courier*, 17 April 1866, p. 3.
48 *Queensland Police Gazette*, vol. III, no. 6, 6 June 1866, p. 49.
49 'Police Obtrusiveness and Defectiveness', *The Brisbane Courier*, 30 July 1867, p. 2.
50 Dukova, A, *A History of the Dublin Metropolitan Police and its Colonial Legacy*, p. 164.
51 'Police Obtrusiveness and Defectiveness', *The Brisbane Courier*, 30 July 1867, p. 2.
52 'Mr. Detective Lloyd', *The Brisbane Courier*, 31 July 1867, p. 2.
53 'Police Obtrusiveness and Defectiveness', *The Brisbane Courier*, 30 July 1867, p. 2.
54 'From the Courier', *Maryborough Chronicle, Wide Bay and Burnett Advertiser*, 11 September 1869, p. 2.
55 Offence Count, Murder, Queensland Supreme Court, 1869–1870 (Finnane, M, et al. 2019, *The Prosecution Project Database*).
56 'Supreme Court', *The Brisbane Courier*, 8 December 1869, p. 2.
57 'Monday, October 18', *The Darling Downs Gazette and General Advertiser*, 27 October 1869, p. 4.
58 'The Trial of Palmer for the murder of Halligan', *Maryborough Chronicle, Wide Bay and Burnett Advertiser*, 16 October 1869, p. 2; 'Palmer's Confession!', *Northern Argus*, 12 June 1869, p. 3.
59 'The Execution of the Murderers', *The Brisbane Courier*, 1 December 1869, p. 3.
60 'General Order No. 493', *Queensland Police Gazette*, 6 April 1870.
61 'Gold Escort', *Police Manual*, 1876, p. 95.
62 The following amount of gold sent by each bank: Queensland National: 3,465 ozs, 18 dwts, 18 grs; Bank of New South Wales: 2,893 ozs 17 dwts 6 grs; AJS Bank: 866 ozs 13 dwts 6 grs; Calculations are based on $1,230.00 US per Troy ounce, December 2018; *Maryborough Chronicle, Wide Bay and Burnett Advertiser*, 23 December 1879, p. 2.
63 'Lloyd, Personnel File, telegram from 1 October 1884, Sr Sgt P Higgins', Queensland State Archives, file no. 1046; 'Lloyd, Personnel File, telegram from 25 November 1884, Sr Sgt P Higgins', Queensland State Archives, file no. 1046.
64 'Dr O'Connor, Police Surgeon, COP correspondence from 7 January 1885', Queensland State Archives, file no. 1046.
65 Dukova, A, *A History of the Dublin Metropolitan Police and its Colonial Legacy*, p. 155.
66 'Police Uniform. General Order No. 678', *Queensland Police Gazette*, vol. XXXIII, no. 22, 16 May 1896, p. 168.
67 *Queensland Police Gazette*, 18 January 1896.

68 Dukova, A, *A History of the Dublin Metropolitan Police and its Colonial Legacy*, p. 155.
69 *Report of the COP for the Year 1897*, Queensland Police Museum Collection.
70 *Queensland Police Gazette*, 16 May 1896, vol. XXXIII, no. 22, p. 168.
71 'Police Commission. Political Influence. Sub-Inspector's Nethercote's Abilities', *The Brisbane Courier*, 1 September 1899, p. 2.
72 *Royal Commission Victoria Police Force*, 1906, p. 113.
73 Wilson, D 2005, 'Traces and Transmissions: Techno-scientific symbolisms in early twentieth-century policing', in Godfrey, B & Dunstall, G (eds), *Crime and Empire, 1840–1940: Criminal justice in local and global context*, Willian Publishing, Devon, p. 112.
74 *Report of the Commissioner of Police for the Year 1897*, Queensland Police Museum Collection, p. 2.
75 Ibid.
76 'The Police Museum, The local Madam Tussaud's, Mementoes of Grave Crimes', *The Brisbane Courier*, 31 May 1895, p. 3.
77 Ibid.
78 Ibid; Jones, L 2018, *The Queensland Police Museum: 125 years of collecting, exhibiting and sharing policing history*, Queensland Police Museum Collection.
79 'Lloyd Personnel File, 02005 COP, 20 February 1896', Queensland State Archives, file no. 1046.
80 Death Reg. B011018, p. 15352; 'Lloyd Personnel File, 08905 COP, 26 May 1909', Queensland State Archives, file no. 1046.

CHAPTER 4

1 1869, James C Beal, Government Printer, Brisbane, p. 30.
2 'January 1838', Maynooth, *Ireland, Catholic Parish Registers, 1655–1915*, viewed on 20 December 2018, <ancestry.com>.
3 'Thomas Tyrrell, 28062', *General Register 1816–1922, RIC* (HO 184), p. 96, viewed on 20 December 2018, <findmypast.com.au>.
4 'COP 06320, 26 May 1897', Queensland State Archives, file no. 1775; 'Thos. Tyrrell (above 14 years)', *Queensland Customs House Shipping 1852–1885: Passengers and crew*, viewed on 20 December 2018, <findmypast.com.au>.
5 'COP 06320, 26 May 1897', Staff File, Queensland State Archives, AF 1775.
6 Wilson, D 2005, 'Traces and Transmissions: Techno-scientific symbolisms in early twentieth-century policing', in Godfrey, B & Dunstall, G (eds), *Crime and Empire, 1840–1940: Criminal justice in local and global context*, Willian Publishing, Devon, p. 109.
7 'Oath', *Manual of Police Regulations for the Guidance of the Constabulary of Queensland* 1869, p. 4.
8 Ibid.; *Instruction Book for Supernumeraries, Kevin Street Depot* (1876) of the Dublin Metropolitan Police was more to the point: when a man was found to be 'bad-tempered, stupid, negligent, or impertinent' he was discharged.
9 *Manual of Police Regulations for the Guidance of the Constabulary of Queensland* 1869, pp. 79–80.
10 'An Act to Consolidate and Amend the Laws Relating to the Police Force, 1863', *Supplement to the Queensland Government Gazette of Saturday, 10th October, 1863*, no. 100, p. 806.
11 *Manual of Police Regulations for the Guidance of the Constabulary of Queensland* 1869, Government Printers, Brisbane, p. 31.

12 Johnston, R 1992, *The Long Blue Line: A history of Queensland Police*, Boolarong Press, Brisbane, p. 33.
13 'Question 79, Evidence by Colonel Henry Atwell Lake', *Civil Service (in Ireland) Enquiry, Dublin Metropolitan Police Report* 1873, Alex Thom, Dublin, p. 5.
14 'Rules to be Observed by Supernumeraries in Kevin-Street Metropolitan Police Depot', *Instruction Book for the Dublin Metropolitan Police Revised by Inspector John Ward* 1865, Alex Thom, Dublin, pp. 100–1.
15 *Queensland Police Gazette*, vol. III, no. 10, 3 October 1866, p. 83; On 1 January 1897, Commissioner of Police (COP) Parry-Okeden issued a new *General Order 681*, after which permission to marry was not to be granted to constables until after they had served four years in the force. COP Cahill further amended the regulations (*General Order 765*) and extended the minimum required service time to five years on 4 October 1906; Marriage Certificate 1868/B/2327, *Registry of Births, Deaths and Marriages, Queensland*.
16 *Registers of Immigrant Ships' Arrivals*, Queensland State Archives, series ID 13086, roll M1696.
17 Caroline Ellen Tyrrell 15 March 1878 (1878/B/23240) – 27 January 1880 (1880/B/13365).
18 *Manual of Police Regulations for the Guidance of the Constabulary of Queensland* 1869, p. 4.
19 *Slater's Pocket Map of Brisbane*, 1865; Cadastre Map of Brisbane, 1874, Brisbane City Council Archives.
20 'Drill', *Manual of Police Regulations for the Guidance of the Constabulary of Queensland* 1869, p. 11.
21 *Register of Members of the Police Force, 1856–1917*, Queensland Police Museum.
22 'Tyrrell Promotion, COP Orders No183, 6 March 1866', Queensland State Archives, file no. 1775.
23 'Barracks, Stables, Etc', *Manual of Police Regulations for the Guidance of the Constabulary of Queensland* 1869, p. 13.
24 *Manual of Police Regulations for the Guidance of the Constabulary of Queensland* 1869, p. 12.
25 Dukova, A, *A History of the Dublin Metropolitan Police and its Colonial Legacy*, Palgrave Macmillan, United Kingdom, p. 57.
26 Riley, Richard (reg. no. 187), Queensland State Archives, AF1525; McArthur, Thomas Archibald (reg. no. 1717), Queensland State Archives, File A/40403, ID 565220.
27 Dukova, A, *A History of the Dublin Metropolitan Police and its Colonial Legacy*, pp. 164–65.
28 Wilson, D, 'Traces and Transmissions', p. 109.
29 *Manual of Police Regulations for the Guidance of the Constabulary of Queensland* 1869, p. 31.
30 'Report of the Commissioner of Police' in *Queensland Votes and Proceedings of 1865*, WC Belbridge, Government Printer, Brisbane, p. 449.
31 'Breach of Town's Police Act', *The Brisbane Courier*, 18 May 1864, p. 4.
32 Hugh Bell was a visiting surgeon at Brisbane Gaol with a salary of £70 p.a., as well as a medical officer for police and Aboriginal Australians, with an additional pay of £75 p.a. ('Statistics of Queensland', *Queensland Votes and Proceedings*, 1867, vol. 1, pp. 1,257, 1,313, 1,317).
33 'Nuisance', *The Brisbane Courier*, 4 December 1869, p. 5; 'Meteorology', *The Brisbane Courier*, 3 December, 1869, p. 2.

34 *Manual of Police Regulations for the Guidance of the Constabulary of Queensland* 1869, p. 10.
35 *Manual of Police Regulations for the Guidance of the Constabulary of Queensland* 1876, Government Printers, Brisbane, p. 6.
36 'Clothing, Rules for the General Government and Discipline of Members of the Police Force of Queensland', *Queensland Votes and Proceedings* 1869, vol. 1, p. 836.
37 *Manual of Police Regulations for the Guidance of the Constabulary of Queensland* 1876, p. 4.
38 'Beats', *Manual of Police Regulations for the Guidance of the Constabulary of Queensland* 1876, p. 20.
39 'Appendix N. Night Duty Beats, Minutes of Evidence Taken Before the Select Committee on the Management and Working of the Police Force', *Queensland Votes and Proceedings* 1869, vol. 1, p. 740 (52).
40 Dukova, A, *A History of the Dublin Metropolitan Police and its Colonial Legacy*, p. 58.
41 *Manual of Police Regulations for the Guidance of the Constabulary of Queensland* 1869, pp. 16, 21.
42 Wilson, D 2006, *The Beat: Policing a Victorian city*, Circa, Beaconsfield, p. 70.
43 Ibid.
44 Dukova, A, *A History of the Dublin Metropolitan Police and its Colonial Legacy*, p. 28.
45 *Report of the Commissioner of Police for the Year 1874*, Government Printers, Brisbane, p. 2.
46 'Population by capital city and rest of state, Queensland, 1823 to 2007', *Australian Bureau of Statistics*, viewed on 20 December 2018.
47 *Report of the Commissioner of Police for the Year 1864*, Government Printers, Brisbane, p. 5.
48 *Town Act 1838, Police Act*, 2 Vic., no. 2; Bain, D 1892, *Queensland Police Guide: Containing an epitome of 184 Acts of Parliament to 1891, and a supplement of 815 offences, alphabetically arranged, with penalties and punishments*, Watson, Ferguson & Co, Brisbane, pp. 99–102.
49 *Police Act of 1855*, p. 103.
50 Harrison, B 1966, 'Philanthropy and the Victorians', *Victorian Studies*, vol. 9, no. 4, pp. 353–74.
51 Wilson, D, *The Beat*, p. 46.
52 'Police Act of 1838', Bain, D, *Queensland Police Guide*, pp. 99–102.
53 See Chapter 7 for more details on local prisons and jails.
54 *Police Act of 1855*, 19 Vic., no. 24; Bain, D, *Queensland Police Guide*, pp. 102–3.
55 'Population by capital city and rest of state, Queensland, 1823 to 2007', *Australian Bureau of Statistics*.
56 *Report of the Commissioner of Police for the Year 1874*, Government Printers, Brisbane.
57 See Richards, J 2008, *The Secret War: A true history of Queensland's Native Police*, University of Queensland Press, Brisbane.
58 Table VI, *Statistical Returns of the Dublin Metropolitan Police for the Year 1875*, 1876, Alex Thom, Dublin.
59 *Annual report of the Board of Police Justices of the City of New York for the year 1875*, Evening Post Steam Presses, New York, p. 17.
60 *Report of the Commissioner of the Metropolitan Police for the year 1875*, The House of Commons, London, p. 1.
61 'Table No. XXXII Return of Persons taken into Custody, Committed for Trial,

Convicted Summarily, and Discharged by the various Courts and Petty Sessions of the Colony, during the Year 1864' in 'Queensland Statistics, Crime', *Queensland Votes and Proceedings* 1865, WC Belbridge, Government Printer, Brisbane, p. 55 (p. 805 of *Queensland Votes and Proceedings*).
62 Dukova, A, *A History of the Dublin Metropolitan Police and its Colonial Legacy*, p. 82.
63 'Queensland Statistics, Crime', *Queensland Votes and Proceedings* 1865–1885.
64 *The Brisbane Courier*, 5 March 1866, p. 2.
65 'Central Police Court', *The Brisbane Courier*, 8 March 1866, p. 2.
66 Wilson, PD 1971, 'The Brisbane Riot of September 1866', in *Queensland Heritage*, vol. 2, no. 4, p. 13.
67 Ibid., p. 14.
68 Quoted in ibid., p. 16.
69 Ibid.
70 'Weekly Epitome', *The Brisbane Courier*, 15 September 1866, p. 5.
71 'The Late Disturbances', *The Brisbane Courier*, 17 September 1866, p. 2.
72 'Police Office Brisbane, 25 January 1875', *Deposition and Minute Books*, Queensland State Archives, item 3726, series ID 11025.
73 'Police Office Brisbane, 26 January 1875', *Deposition and Minute Books*, Queensland State Archives, item 3726, series ID 11025.
74 'Police Office Brisbane, 28 January 1875', *Deposition and Minute Books*, Queensland State Archives, item 3726, series ID 11025.
75 'Report of the Commissioner of Police. Second Report', *Queensland Votes and Proceedings* 1866, p. 749.
76 'Assault Upon a Police Sergeant', *The Brisbane Courier*, 22 June 1880, p. 3.
77 'Assault on a Police Sergeant', *The Brisbane Courier*, 23 June 1880, p. 3.
78 Ibid.
79 Dukova, A, *A History of the Dublin Metropolitan Police and its Colonial Legacy*, p. 189.
80 'Sergeant Tyrell', *The Brisbane Courier*, 7 March 1881, p. 3.
81 'Sweer's Island', *Bailliere's Queensland Gazetteer and Road Guide Compiled by Robt P Whitworth*, 1876, F. F. Bailliere Publisher, Brisbane, p. 180.
82 'Death Certificate 4058385', *Queensland Births, Deaths and Marriages Registry*.

CHAPTER 5

1 *The Telegraph*, 29 December 1880, p. 2.
2 Ibid.
3 Average height (155cm) is based on biometrics provided by the findings of *The Digital Panopticon*, viewed on 20 January 2019, <www.digitalpanopticon.org/Biometrics>; 'Return of Prisoners to be Discharged from Her Majesty's Gaol, Toowoomba, During the Month of July, 1881', *Queensland Police Gazette*, July 1881, vol. 18, no. 14, p. 92.
4 'Minor Offence, City Police Court', *The Telegraph*, 27 July 1880, p. 3.
5 'Minor Offence, City Police Court', *The Telegraph*, 29 January 1880, p. 2.
6 De Souza Whitwell, C & Nicholas, S 1997, 'Height, Health and Economic Growth in Australia, 1860–1940', in Steckel, RH & Flouds, R (eds), *Health and Welfare During Industrialisation*, Chicago University Press, Chicago, p. 403.
7 Zedner, L 1991, *Women, Crime, and Custody in Victorian England*, Clarendon Press, Oxford, p. 2.
8 'Larrikinism. City Police Court, January 21', *The Brisbane Courier*, 22 January 1881, p. 5.

9 'Return of Prisoners to be Discharged from Her Majesty's Gaol, Toowoomba, During the Month of July, 1881', p. 93.
10 'Return of Prisoners to be Discharged from Her Majesty's Gaol, Toowoomba, During the Month of July, 1880', *Queensland Police Gazette*, July 1880, vol. 17, no. 14, p. 105.
11 'Minor Offence, City Police Court', *The Telegraph*, 27 July 1880, p. 3.
12 'Return of Prisoners to be Discharged from Her Majesty's Gaol, Toowoomba, During the Month of July, 1880', p. 105.
13 Zedner, L 1991, *Women, Crime, and Custody in Victorian England*, p. 5.
14 'Lockups. Brisbane', *Report with Minutes of Evidence Taken before the Board of Inquiry Appointed to Inquire into the General Management of the Gaols, Penal Establishments and Lockups of the Colony of Queensland 1887*, p. lxvii.
15 Ibid.
16 'Monday, 5 April, 1880', *Depositions Book No 20* (February 1880 – April 1880), Queensland State Archives, ID 970943.
17 'Monday, 23 August, 1880', *Depositions Book No 22* (July 1880 – October 1880), Queensland State Archives, ID 970944.
18 'Monday, 30 August 1880', *Depositions Book No 22* (July 1880 – October 1880), Queensland State Archives, ID 970944.
19 As evidenced by Hirsch's choice of insults, sectarian tensions were rife in Queensland and had been transplanted onto the colonial soil along with the people, the majority of whom arrived from England, Scotland, Ireland and Wales. There is little recorded evidence of sectarian tensions within the force, but one such example was described by Commissioner Seymour in the *Minutes of Evidence Taken Before the Select Committee of the Management and Working of the Police Force* when a charge against a Roman Catholic constable who 'refused to ring the bell for the Protestant place of worship' was brought by a police magistrate in Gladstone. The place of worship in this case was a courthouse; 'COP Seymour, 18 May 1869, Minutes of Evidence Taken Before the Select Committee of the Management and Working of the Police Force', *Queensland Votes and Proceedings* 1869, p. 696 (8); Commissioner Seymour considered this offence to be 'of very trivial nature' and no action was taken.
20 De Souza Whitwell, C & Nicholas, S, 'Height, Health and Economic Growth in Australia, 1860–1940', p. 389.
21 'Return of Prisoners to be Discharged from Her Majesty's Gaol, Toowoomba, During the Month of May, 1880', *Queensland Police Gazette*, May 1880, vol. 17, no. 10, p. 79.
22 Williams, L 2016, *Wayward Women: Female offending in Victorian England*, Pen & Sword History, United Kingdom, p. 83.
23 'City Police Court', *The Brisbane Courier*, 21 April 1882, p. 3.
24 'City Police Court', *The Brisbane Courier*, 6 December 1882, p. 5; 'Assaults. City Police Court', *The Brisbane Courier*, 9 December 1882, p. 6.
25 'Drunk and Disorderly, City Police Court', *The Brisbane Courier*, 7 December 1883, p. 3.
26 'Summons Cases, City Police Court', *The Brisbane Courier*, 7 December 1883, p. 3.
27 'Return of Prisoners to be Discharged from Her Majesty's Penal Establishment, St Helena, During the Month of March, 1885', *Queensland Police Gazette*, March 1885, vol. 22, no. 6, p. 105.
28 Bellanta, M 2010, 'The Larrikin Girl', *Journal of Australian Studies*, vol. 34, no. 4, p. 499.
29 'Assault, City Police Court', *The Brisbane Courier*, 1 October 1883, p. 3.

30 'City Police Court', *The Brisbane Courier*, 15 January 1884, p. 3.
31 'City Police Court', *The Brisbane Courier*, 13 January, 1885, p. 6.
32 'City Police Court', *The Brisbane Courier*, 17 January 1885, p. 10.
33 'City Police Court', *The Brisbane Courier*, 19 March 1885, p. 3.
34 'City Police Court', *The Brisbane Courier*, 20 March 1885, p. 5; See *Depositions Book No 42* (January 1885 – March 1885), Queensland State Archives, ID 970965, pp. 50, 491; Patrick Brittan was charged with being drunk and disorderly in Albert Street and with destroying police uniform to the value of 21s.
35 Cohen, K, Donoval, V, Kerr, R, et al. 2014, *Lost Brisbane and Surrounding Areas 1860–1960*, Royal Historical Society of Queensland, Brisbane, p. 80.
36 City Police Court', *The Brisbane Courier*, 23 April 1885, p. 6; 'City Police Court', *The Telegraph*, 25 April 1885, p. 9.
37 'Margaret Corkery' and 'Return of Prisoners to be Discharged from Her Majesty's Gaol, Toowoomba, During the Month of July, 1885', *Queensland Police Gazette*, July 1885, vol. 22, no. 15, p. 189.
38 'City Police Court', *The Brisbane Courier*, 8 May 1885, p. 6.
39 'City Police Court', *The Brisbane Courier*, 5 June 1885, p. 6.
40 'City Police Court', *The Brisbane Courier*, 4 July 1885, p. 6.
41 'Return of Prisoners to be Discharged from Her Majesty's Gaol, Brisbane, During the Month of September 1885', *Queensland Police Gazette*, September 1885, vol. 22, no. 19, p. 232.
42 Bellanta, M, 'The Larrikin Girl', pp. 499–512.
43 'Return of Prisoners to be Discharged from Her Majesty's Gaol, Toowoomba, During the Month of March 1886', *Queensland Police Gazette*, March 1886, vol. XXIII, no. 6, p. 97; 'Assault, City Police Court', *The Brisbane Courier*, 31 August 1886, p. 6.
44 'James Feeney', *Queensland Police Gazette*, 22 May 1886, vol. XXIII, no. 11, p. 143.
45 *Report of the Commissioner of Police for the Year 1883*, Government Printers, Brisbane, p. 1.
46 Ibid.
47 'The Christmas Holidays', *The Brisbane Courier*, 24 December 1888, p. 5.
48 'Prostitutes', *Manual of Police Regulations for the Guidance of the Constabulary of Queensland* 1876, James C Beal, Government Printer, Brisbane, p. 180; Clause 47 of *The following Instructions for the guidance of the Members of the Police Force, in the performance of their duty, are published by the Commissioner of Police*: 'Every common prostitute wandering in any street or public highway, or being in any place of public resort, who shall behave in a riotous or indecent manner.'
49 *Report of the Commissioner of Police for the Year 1881*, Government Printer, Brisbane, p. 1.
50 *An Act for the Prevention of Contagious Diseases*, 31 Vic., no. 40; See Levine, P 2003, *Prostitution, Race, and Politics: Policing venereal disease in the British Empire*, Routledge, New York; Evans, R 1984, '"Soiled Doves": Prostitution in colonial Queensland', in Daniels, K (ed.), *So Much Hard Work: Women and prostitution in Australian history*, Fontana Collins, Sydney.
51 'Return of Prisoners to be Discharged from Her Majesty's Gaol, Brisbane, During the Month of March 1884', *Queensland Police Gazette*, July 1884, vol. XXI, no. 15, p. 158; 'Return of Prisoners to be Discharged from Her Majesty's Gaol, Brisbane, During the Month of July 1884', *Queensland Police Gazette*, October 1884, vol. XXI, no. 21, p. 222.
52 *Act for Prevention of Contagious Diseases 1864*, 27 & 28 Vic., no. 85.

53 Zedner, L, *Women, Crime, and Custody in Victorian England*, p. 12.
54 Andrew Garran, quoted in Fisher, R 1989, 'Old Frogs Hollow: Devoid of interest, or a den of iniquity?', in Brisbane History Group Papers, no. 8, pp. 17, 19.
55 Ibid.
56 *Boomerang*, 14 January 1888, p. 8.
57 Fisher, R, 'Old Frogs Hollow', p. 17
58 Fisher, R, 'Old Frogs Hollow', p. 45.
59 'Raid on Gambling Dens', *The Queenslander*, 6 June 1891, p. 1,063.
60 Following police raids and a shop dispute in Albert Street, the physical and social flux of the area coupled with recent elections eventually resulted in a riot in 1888. The anti-Chinese outbreak erupted on 5 May led by a crowd of 'larrikin youths'. The riot commenced near the Exchange Hotel and proceeded to a shop owned by a Chinese immigrant. The crowd knocked down and robbed the shop – 'smashing shop windows, and stealing the goods' (*The Brisbane Courier*, 8 May 1888, p. 4).
61 Fisher, J 2005, *The Brisbane Overseas Chinese Community 1860s to 1970s: Enigma or conformity*, PhD thesis, University of Queensland, Brisbane, p. 428.
62 Ibid., p. 429.
63 *The Brisbane Courier*, 20 October 1887, p. 4.
64 Fisher, R, 'Old Frogs Hollow', p. 40.
65 'Assault, City Police Court', *The Brisbane Courier*, 23 May 1890, p. 6.
66 'The Waters Subsiding. Effects of the Flood', *The Week*, 22 March 1890, p. 5.
67 Ibid.
68 'City Rookeries', *The Telegraph*, 22 February 1890, p. 2.
69 Quoted in Fisher, R, 'Old Frogs Hollow', p. 20.
70 'The Nine Holes', *The Brisbane Courier*, 10 September 1891, p. 3.
71 Ibid.
72 See Luddy, M 2007, *Prostitution and Irish Society, 1800–1940*, Cambridge University Press, Cambridge; and Finnegan, F 2001, *Do Penance or Perish: A study of Magdalene Asylums in Ireland*, Congrave Press in association with Oxford University Press, Kilkenny.
73 'The Nine Holes', *The Brisbane Courier*, 10 September 1891, p. 3.
74 Grave location: 16-4-6 Toowong Cemetery, Brisbane, Queensland.
75 Zedner, L, *Women, Crime, and Custody in Victorian England*, p. 42.

CHAPTER 6

1 *Truth*, 5 July 1914, p. 14.
2 United Kingdom Census 1871, class RG10, piece 2363, folio 82, p. 50, GSU roll 835100.
3 *Register of Immigrants: Western Monarch, 1876*, Queensland State Archives, item ID 18477, p. 1,099.
4 *Registers of Immigrant Ships' Arrivals*, Queensland State Archives, series ID 13086, roll M1697.
5 James Nethercote Personnel File, reg. no. 351, Queensland Police Museum.
6 'MAWDITT Elizth, 20 Earl Derby 20 Jun 1879', Queensland State Archives, item ID M/film 1 Microfilm 2 277 18478 Z1959 M1698; *Australia, Marriage Index, 1788–1950*, B006893, p. 10,915.
7 Birth certificates, *Australian Birth Index, 1788–1922*, viewed on 31 October 2019, <www.ancestry.com.au>.

8   'James Withers, Chief Constable Borough Police Office, Town Hall, Bradford, Yorkshire', Queensland State Archives, file no. 2258.
9   Finnane, M 1994, *Police and Government: Histories of policing in Australia*, Oxford University Press, Melbourne, p. 136.
10 Library and Museum of Freemasonry, London, England, *Freemasonry Membership Registers*; Description: Membership Registers: Colonial and Foreign E 1043–1203 to Colonial and Foreign F 1210–1413, reel no. 25; Membership Registers: Colonial and Foreign M 2277–2461 to Colonial and Foreign N 2465–2643, p. 212.
11 Lane's Masonic Records, version 1.0, viewed on 1 June 2019.
12 'Police Commission. Political Influence. Sub-Inspector Nethercote's Abilities,' *The Brisbane Courier*, 1 September 1899, p. 2.
13 'Commissioner of Police, 21 June 1876', Queensland State Archives, item ID 2258.
14 'Capture of E.B. Holt', *The Western Star and Roma Advertiser*, 10 April 1886, p. 4.
15 Ibid.
16 Ibid.
17 Dukova, A 2016, *A History of the Dublin Metropolitan Police and its Colonial Legacy*, Palgrave Macmillan, United Kingdom, p. 189.
18 See Dukova, A, *A History of the Dublin Metropolitan Police and its Colonial Legacy*.
19 'Daring Burglar', *Maryborough Chronicle, Wide Bay and Burnett Advertiser*, 16 April 1887, p. 4.
20 Ibid.
21 Finnane, M 1991, 'The Varieties of Policing: Colonial Queensland, 1860–1900', in Anderson DM & Killingray D (eds), *Policing the Empire: Government, authority and control, 1830–1940*, Manchester University Press, Manchester, p. 37.
22 Laverty, JR 2009, *The Making of a Metropolis*, Boolarong Press, Brisbane, p. 70.
23 Ibid.
24 Dukova, A 2012, *Crime and Policing in Dublin, Brisbane and London c. 1850–1900*, PhD thesis, University of Dublin, Dublin, p. 177.
25 'City Police Court, Summons Cases', *The Brisbane Courier*, 15 January 1891, p. 3.
26 Perry, HC 1928, *A Son of Australia: Memories of W.E. Parry-Okeden, I.S.O., 1840–1926*, Watson, Ferguson, & Co. Ltd., Brisbane, p. 243.
27 Ibid.
28 Cook, M 2019, *A River with a City Problem: A history of Brisbane floods*, University of Queensland Press, Brisbane, p. 22.
29 'The Floods', *The Brisbane Courier*, 4 February 1893, p. 5.
30 Ibid.
31 'Telegraphic Intelligence', *North Queensland Register*, 1 February 1893, p. 11.
32 *Queensland Police Gazette*, vol. XXIII, no. 25, 25 September 1886, p. 256; *Queensland Police Gazette*, vol. XXVIII no. 27, 4 July 1891, p, 265.
33 Dukova, A, *Crime and Policing in Dublin, Brisbane and London c. 1850–1900*, p. 145.
34 See the Introduction for further discussion of corporal punishment in the Moreton Bay penal settlement.
35 5 Gul IV, no. 22, and 14 Vic., no. 43.
36 Dean, G 2008, *Here Comes the Judge: The Queensland magistrates*, Department of Justice, Brisbane, p. 28.
37 Dukova, A, *Crime and Policing in Dublin, Brisbane and London c. 1850–1900*, p. 156.

38 Handy, JK 1869, *Queensland Magistrate's Guide*, Shepperson, Brisbane.
39 22 Vic., no. 18, and 29 Vic., no. 10.
40 'Assize Intelligence. Brisbane Circuit Court', *The Sydney Morning Herald*, 21 May 1850, p. 2.
41 'Opening of the First Circuit Court in Brisbane', *The Moreton Bay Courier*, 18 May 1850, p. 2.
42 Ibid., pp. 2–4.
43 Little, CB & Sheffield, CP 1948, 'Frontiers and Criminal Justice: English private prosecution societies and American vigilantism in the eighteenth and nineteenth centuries', in *American Sociological Review*, vol. 48, pp. 797–98.
44 Emsley, C 2012, 'The Changes in Policing and Penal Policy in Nineteenth-Century Europe', in Godfrey, B & Dunstall, G (eds), *Crime and Empire 1840–1940: Criminal justice in local and global context*, Routledge, United Kingdom, p. 9.
45 Little, CB & Sheffield, CP, 'Frontiers and Criminal Justice', p. 798.
46 Monkkonen, EH 1981, *Police in Urban America, 1860–1920*, Cambridge University Press, Cambridge, p. 36; As an example of the use of 'blood money': 'In New York, for instance, during the 1850s, the return of a stolen watch could cost a payment of seventy-five dollars to the police.'
47 Ascoli, D 1979, *Queen's Peace: The origins and development of the metropolitan police 1829–1979*, Hamish Hamilton, London, p. 39.
48 Emsley, C, 'The Changes in Policing and Penal Policy in Nineteenth-Century Europe', p. 9.
49 Little, CB & Sheffield, CP, 'Frontiers and Criminal Justice', p. 799.
50 White, M 2004, 'The Development of the Divided Legal Profession in Queensland', *The University of Queensland Law Journal*, vol. 23, p. 313.
51 'Foresters Friendly Society', viewed on 21 July 2019, <www.forestersfriendlysociety.co.uk/about-us/our-history>; 'Foresters' Hall', *Queensland Heritage Register*, no. 601662.
52 'Friendly Society's Funds. Alleged Embezzlement', *The Brisbane Courier*, 19 November 1896, p. 3.
53 ABS cat. no. 3105.0.65.001, Australian Historical Population Statistics.
54 *Report of the Commissioner of Police for the Year 1897*, Government Printer, Brisbane, p. 1.
55 Dukova, A, *Crime and Policing in Dublin, Brisbane and London c. 1850–1900*, p. 182.
56 *Report of the Commissioner of Police for the Year 1897*, p. 1.
57 'Examination of Sub-Inspector Nethercote, 6825', *Minutes of Evidence Taken Before the Royal Commission Appointed to Inquire into the Criminal Investigation Branch and Police Force* 1899, p. 231.
58 *Criminal Investigation Department and Force Inquiry Commissioner* 1898, Government Printers, Brisbane, p. xxix.
59 Ibid.
60 Ibid.
61 Ibid.
62 Ibid., p. xxx.
63 Ibid., p. xxix.
64 'Miscellaneous. Changes in the Force Since Last Publication', *Queensland Police Gazette*, 30 January 1904, p. 307.
65 '"Pink Peter," Pub Prosecutor. Impales an Inspector', *Truth*, 8 October 1905, p. 4.
66 Urquhart was promoted to chief inspector in 1905 and commissioner of police in 1917.

67 'Examination of Sub-Inspector Nethercote, 6825', *Minutes of Evidence Taken Before the Royal Commission Appointed to Inquire into the Criminal Investigation Branch and Police Force*, pp. 230–31.
68 Ibid.
69 'Be Loyal to the Union', *Queensland Police Union Journal*, 1 July 1917, Queensland Police Museum Collection, p. 2.
70 'Examination of Sub-Inspector Nethercote, 6837–6839', *Minutes of Evidence Taken Before the Royal Commission Appointed to Inquire into the Criminal Investigation Branch and Police Force* 1899, p. 232.
71 'Commissioner of Police 15622, 14 September 1907', Queensland State Archives, item ID 2258.
72 'Commissioner of Police 07/25622 R, 26 September 1907', Queensland State Archives, item ID 2258.
73 'Commissioner of Police 08/11017 MB, 10 July 1908', Queensland State Archives, item ID 2258.
74 'Confidential Circular, Commissioner of Police 11238, 1 July 1910', Queensland State Archives, item ID 2258.
75 Ibid.
76 'Medical Certificate of the Cause of Death, Form D', Queensland State Archives, item ID 2258.
77 'Ex-Inspector James Nethercote', Queensland State Archives, item ID 2258.

CHAPTER 7

1 8 October 1911, p. 5.
2 'Charged with larceny', *The Telegraph* (Brisbane), 21 September 1897, p. 2.
3 Harrison, J 1988, 'Queen Street, North Brisbane', *Brisbane in 1888: The historical perspective*, Brisbane History Group Papers, no. 8, p. 7.
4 'Return of Prisoners to be Discharged from Her Majesty's Gaol, Brisbane, during the month of February 1888', *Queensland Police Gazette*, 6 March 1888, p. 77.
5 'Return of Prisoners to be Discharged from Her Majesty's Gaol, Brisbane, during the month of February 1888', *Queensland Police Gazette*, 4 February 1888, p. 77.
6 Emsley, C 2012, 'The Changes in Policing and Penal Policy in Nineteenth-Century Europe', in Godfrey B & Dunstall, G (eds), *Crime and Empire 1840–1940: Criminal justice in local and global context*, Routledge, United Kingdom, p. 20.
7 Bertillon, A 1896, *Signaletic Instructions Including the Theory and Practice of Anthropometrical Identification*, Werner Company, Chicago.
8 'Law report – Alleged breaking and entering', *The Brisbane Courier*, 31 August 1907, p. 10.
9 '1886 census', *Population by capital city and rest of state, Queensland, 1823 to 2007*, Queensland Government Statistician's Office, viewed on 4 April 2019.
10 'Frogs Hollow, Brisbane CBD', viewed on 22 September 2018, <www.yourbrisbanepastandpresent.com/2016/04/frogs-hollow-brisbane-cbd.html>.
11 *Vagrancy Act*, 25 Vic., no. 4, *Vagrant Act Amendment Act 1863*, 27 Vic., no. 10; 'Beggars', *Manual of Police Regulations for the Guidance of the Constabulary of Queensland* 1876, Government Printer, Brisbane, p. 24.
12 'Crime Reports – Their Preparation', *Manual of Police Regulations for the Guidance of the Constabulary of Queensland*, Brisbane, p. 63.
13 28 & 29 Vic., c. 126; 54 Vic., no. 17 c. 39.

14. Morgan, R 2004, 'Howard, John (1726?–1790), philanthropist', *Oxford Dictionary of National Biography*, Oxford University Press, viewed on 4 April 2019, <www.oxforddnb.com/view/10.1093/ref:odnb/9780198614128.001.0001/odnb-9780198614128-e-13922>.
15. Emsley, C, 'The Changes in Policing and Penal Policy in Nineteenth-Century Europe', p. 10.
16. Ibid.
17. Ibid., p. 11.
18. 'Thomson, James (1822–1892)', viewed on 27 October 2019, <en.wikisource.org/wiki/Thomson,_James_Bruce_(DNB00)>; Quoted in Rafter, N 1997, *Creating Born Criminals*, University of Illinois Press, Illinois, p. 82.
19. Emsley, C, 'The Changes in Policing and Penal Policy in Nineteenth-Century Europe', p. 12.
20. John Pratt discussing Michel Foucault's perspective on the penal system in Pratt, J 2005, 'Explaining the History of Punishment', in Godfrey, B & Dunstall, G (eds), *Crime and Empire 1840–1940: Criminal justice in local and global context*, Willan Publishing, Devon, p. 32.
21. Bentham, J 1834, *The Works of Jeremy Bentham, vol. 4, Panopticon, Constitution, Colonies*, published under the Superintendence of his Executor, John Bowring, William Tait, Edinburgh, 39.
22. 'The Gaols Inquiry', *The Brisbane Courier*, 3 September 1887, p. 6.
23. 'No. 5, Return of the Prisoners Received in Brisbane Gaol During 1886, Showing Offences and Nationality of Each', *Report with Minutes of Evidence Taken before the Board of Inquiry Appointed to Inquire into the General Management of the Gaols, Penal Establishments and Lockups of the Colony of Queensland 1887*, p. 283.
24. 217 from England and Wales, 165 from Ireland, 73 from Scotland and 28 from America.
25. 'St. Helena: Gaol Grievances', *Truth* (Brisbane), 23 April 1905, p. 2.
26. 'No 7 Dietary Scales Queensland Gaols', *Report with Minutes of Evidence Taken before the Board of Inquiry Appointed to Inquire into the General Management of the Gaols, Penal Establishments and Lockups of the Colony of Queensland 1887*, p. 284.
27. 'The Gaols Inquiry', *The Brisbane Courier*, 3 September 1887, p. 6.
28. Ibid.
29. 'Appendix – Part 1. St Helena Penal Establishment. No 1. State of Grievances by Prisoners', *Report with Minutes of Evidence Taken before the Board of Inquiry Appointed to Inquire into the General Management of the Gaols, Penal Establishments and Lockups of the Colony of Queensland 1887*, p. 270.
30. Fitz-Gibbon, B & Gizycki, M 2001, 'A History of Last-resort Lending and Other Support for Troubled Financial Institutions in Australia', *Research Discussion Paper*, System Stability Department, Reserve Bank of Australia, p. 1.
31. Hicks, N, 'Coghlan, Sir Timothy Augustine (1855–1926)', *Australian Dictionary of Biography, National Centre of Biography*, Australian National University, published first in hardcopy 1981, viewed on 8 November 2019, <adb.anu.edu.au/biography/coghlan-sir-timothy-augustine-5708/text9651>; Coghlan, TA 1969, *Labour and Industry in Australia from the First Settlement in 1788 to the Establishment of the Commonwealth in 1901*, Macmillan of Australia, Sydney, p. 10.
32. Offences list summarises cases reported in *The Brisbane Courier* and the *Queensland Police Gazette* from 1888 to 1914.
33. 'Return of prisoners to be discharged from her majesty's prison, Brisbane, during the month of September 1895', *Queensland Police Gazette*, 14 September 1895, p. 284.

34 'Supplement to the Queensland Police Gazette', *Queensland Police Gazette*, vol. 35, no. 25, 16 April 1898.
35 Constable Murrihy received a favourable record 'for zeal displayed to extinguish a fire in a barber's shop in Wickham Street, Fortitude Valley on the morning of 23 May 1896 and thereby saving the building from destruction'. ('Favourable Records', *Queensland Police Gazette*, vol. 33, no. 33, 1 August 1896, p. 234.)
36 'Buggy Rug and Lamp', *The Telegraph*, 18 May 1898, p. 2.
37 'South Brisbane Police Court', *The Telegraph*, 8 December 1898, p. 2.
38 'Larceny of a saddle', *The Telegraph*, 3 August 1899, p. 2.
39 'Criminal Sittings', *The Brisbane Courier*, 21 May 1912, p. 4.
40 'Punishments', in *The Criminal Code of Queensland and the Criminal Practice Rules of 1900*, Wilson, WF & Graham, AD (eds), Brisbane, Queensland Government Printer, 1901, p. 39.
41 Finnane, M, et al. 2018, 'Total Indictable Offences by Gender, 1888–1914', *The Prosecution Project Database*.
42 Hendrikson, G & Liston, C 2008, *Women Transported – Life in Australia's Convict Female Factories*, Parramatta Heritage Centre, New South Wales, p. 51.
43 Ibid.
44 Coote, W 1882, *History of Colony of Queensland from 1770 to the Year 1881*, vol. 1, William Thorne, Brisbane, pp. 24–5.
45 'A brief outline of the history of Moreton Bay', *Pugh's Almanac* 1859, p. 65.
46 Ibid.
47 'VI – Fortitude Valley', *Report with Minutes of Evidence Taken before the Board of Inquiry Appointed to Inquire into the General Management of the Gaols, Penal Establishments and Lockups of the Colony of Queensland 1887*, p. lxvi.
48 'QP Service History Robert Slattery (QPPD Record No. 4994)', extracted from the Queensland Police Museum Personnel Database, Queensland Police Museum, Brisbane.
49 'VI – Fortitude Valley', p. lxvi.
50 Ibid.
51 Ibid.
52 'The Gaols Inquiry', *The Brisbane Courier*, 3 September 1887, p. 6.
53 'No 6. Toowoomba Gaol', *Report with Minutes of Evidence Taken before the Board of Inquiry Appointed to Inquire into the General Management of the Gaols, Penal Establishments and Lockups of the Colony of Queensland 1887*, p. 283.
54 '1417. Brisbane. Friday, 25 March 1887. David Thomas Seymour, Esq., Commissioner of Police', *Report with Minutes of Evidence Taken before the Board of Inquiry Appointed to Inquire into the General Management of the Gaols, Penal Establishments and Lockups of the Colony of Queensland 1887*, p. 67.
55 *Prisons Act 1890*, 54 Vic., no. 17.
56 '1417. Brisbane. Friday, 25 March 1887. David Thomas Seymour, Esq., Commissioner of Police', *Report with Minutes of Evidence Taken before the Board of Inquiry Appointed to Inquire into the General Management of the Gaols, Penal Establishments and Lockups of the Colony of Queensland 1887*, p. 67.
57 'Alleged Breaking and Entering, Law Report, Supreme Court-Criminal Sittings', *The Brisbane Courier*, 31 August 1907, p. 10.
58 Ibid.
59 'Magisterial Inquiry: Death of Mary Healy', *The Brisbane Courier*, 26 October 1915, p. 9.

60 'Table B – Criminal statistics return – Brisbane District', *Report of the Commissioner of Police for the Eighteen Months Ended 30th June 1916* 1916, Government Printer, Brisbane, p. 15.
61 'The Gaols Inquiry', *The Brisbane Courier*, 3 September 1887, p. 6.

CONCLUSION

1   Colquhoun, P 1800, *A Treatise on the Police of the Metropolis*, Bye & Law, St John's Square, Clerkenwell, p. 12.
2   Michael O'Sullivan was born in County Cork, Ireland, not far from Blarney Castle. He migrated to Australia to flee potential repercussions for his pranks on tourists intending to kiss the famous Blarney Stone, as he and his nephew amused themselves 'by shying decaying apples at [the stone], thereby making this inspiring piece of granite rather messy'. (O'Sullivan, M 1935, *Cameos of Crime*, Jackson & O'Sullivan Ltd, Sydney, p. 10.)
3   Ibid., p. 162.
4   Ibid.
5   'Criminal Statistics', *Report of the Commissioner of Police for the Year 1914* 1915, Government Printer, Brisbane, p. 5 (503).
6   *Royal Commission into the Constitution, Administration and Working of the Criminal Investigation Branch of the Police Force of Queensland* 1899, Brisbane; O'Sullivan, M, *Cameos of Crime*, pp. 162–65.
7   Ibid., p. 165.
8   Perry, HC 1928, *A Son of Australia: Memories of W. E. Perry-Okeden, I.S.O., 1840–1926*, Watson, Ferguson & Co, Brisbane, p. 261.
9   Di Beccaria, CB 1872, *An Essay on Crimes and Punishment*, WC Little & Co, Albany, viewed on 9 November 2019, <oll.libertyfund.org/titles/2193>.
10 Ainsworth, PB 2002, *Psychology and Policing*, Willan Publishing, Cullompton.
11 Wilson, D 2006, *The Beat: Policing a Victorian city*, Circa, Beaconsfield, p. 270.
12 Section 175–76, 'Constable', *Rules for the General Government and Discipline of Members of the Police Force of Queensland, 1869*, p. 31.

Index

Italicised page numbers within this index refer to references in figures.

Aboriginal Australians
   clashes with 19, 31, 41, 43
   dispossession of 6, 41 43
   General Order 596 *42*, 43
Act for the Better Administration of Justice in New South Wales (1823) 20
Act for the Better Prevention of Cattle Stealing and the Sale of Stolen Cattle, or the *Cattle Stealing and Prevention Act* (1853) 58
Act to Consolidate and Amend the Laws Relating to the Police Force (1863) see *Queensland Police Act* (1863)
Act for Improving the Police of the City of Dublin (1786) 15
Act for Prevention of Contagious Diseases (1868) 113, 114
Act to Regulate Summary Proceedings before Justices of the Peace (1835 and 1850) 129
Act for the Regulation of the Police Force in New South Wales (1850) 34
Act for the Relief of His Majesty's Roman Catholic Subjects (1829) 14
Act for the Union of Great Britain and Ireland (1801) 14
Airey, Peter (or 'Pink Peter') 138
America
   penal regime 18–19
Ancient Order of Foresters 133–4
Anderson, District Constable 47
Anthropometry, *see* bertillonage
Archibald, Alexander 73–4
Armidale 35

arrest, resisting 98
arson 132
Asia 35
assaults 68, 111
   petty 95
   police, on 92, 97–9, 104, 111

Bancroft, Dr Joseph 117
banking crisis 125, 153, 163
Bannister, Chief Constable Bartholomew 38
Bathurst 35
   gold 48
beat duty 8, 9, 89–90, 100–1, 171
   changeover 90
   instructions 89–90
   plain clothes policing 77
   times 89–90
begging 112, 147
Behan, James 70
Bell, Alexander 134
Bell, Dr Hugh 88
Bennett, Senior Constable 58
Bentham, Jeremy 149, 169
Berry, Councillor Alexander 35–6
Bertillon, Alphonse 145
bertillonage 144, 145
bigamy 4, 128, 150
Black, Francis 22
Blake, Constable 63
Bluestone Rum Case 47–8
Booth, Constable John 39
Border Police 6
   establishment 21

Bottington, Chief Constable Richard 4
Bowen
  district court 130
  supreme court 132
Bowen, George 60
Bowen Hills 50
Bowen's Hollow Police 36
Bread or Blood riots 95–7
Breakfast Creek 3, 43
Brennan, Jonathan 15
bribery 132
Brisbane 93
  Adelaide and Edward streets *146*
  Albert Street *110*
  civil disobedience 96–7
  cyclone 163
  district court 130
  expansion of 8–9, 22–3, 33–4, 38, 55, 70–1
  fires 62–8, *65*, *66*, *67*
  flooding 51–2, 61–2, *62*, 116–17, 118, 126–8, *127*, 146, 153–4, 163
  gas street lighting 70
  infrastructure development 70
  lock-up 105–6
  police presence 90–1
  population 23, 38, 41, 56, 58, 62, 90, 125–6, 145, 157
  Queen Street *54*, *98*, *127*
  Slater's pocket map *69*
  Victoria Bridge 126, *127*
Brisbane Detective Office 123–4
Brisbane Gaol 147, 163
  Boggo Road 85, 147–50, *150*, 154, 161, 166
  Petrie Terrace 9, 54, 55, 85, 158
Brisbane General Hospital 83, *85*
Brisbane Police Force 39 see also Queensland Police Force
  districts, division into 38, 40, 56, 161
Brisbane, Sir Thomas 3
Brisbane Volunteers 5
Brown, Bush Constable George 22
Brown, Constable Charles 143
Bryce, General Inspector Lee 117
Bull, Joseph 41
Bundaberg 132
burglary 16
Burke, Sergeant 108

Burton, Tom 47–8
bushrangers 6, 21, 35, 36
Byrnes, Margaret 106

Cahill, Major William 167, 168
Cairns 132
Campbell, Duncan 45
capital offences 131–2
Carisbrook 57, 79
Carpenter, Mary 160
Castle Hill 3
cattle stealing 58
Cawsey, Inspector Henry 77
Central Police Court 98
charge-room 105
Charters Towers 132
chief constable see also by name
  duties 39–43
child desertion 125
Chinese Quarter 115, 116, 117
chirography 171
Clarke, Detective Constable William Archer 76–7, 125
Clermont
  district court 130
Clifford, Samuel 71–2
Clunie, James Oliphant 4
Commission of Inquiry of 1899 into the Criminal Investigation Department and Force 136
Common Law representation system 10
communications technology 170–1
COMputer Facial Identification (COMFIT) 144
Condamine
  district court 130
contagious diseases, see *Act for Prevention of Contagious Diseases* (1868)
conviction rates 168
convicts
  escapees 46, 50–1, 58
  police, as 1–2, 4, 5, 8, 22
  reconviction, rates of 18–19
  tickets of leave 19–20, 22, 23, 39
  transportation 16–19, 169
Cooktown 132
Cooper, Chief Justice 162
Corkery, Margaret 110
corruption 6–7, 12, 56, 59, 139, 142

Countess of Harcourt 17
　Armstrong, Robert (ship surgeon) 17
Court Fortitude 133–4
courts 20–1, 129
　circuit 38, 40, 129, 130–2
　district 129, 130–1
　lock-up 105–6
　petty debts court 129
　petty sessions 20, 23, 33, 94, 129–30
　police court 129
　quarter sessions 20–1
　summons court 129
　supreme 129, 131–2
　traffic court 129
　water police court 129
Cox, Robert 28
crime and punishment 168
crime prevention 7, 10, 60, 87, 88, 92, 131, 169
　failure, allegations of 72–3
Criminal Code of Queensland (1899) 157, 170
Criminal Investigation Branch (CIB) 75–7, 128–9, 156
　conviction rates 168
　establishment 75, 120, 135
　first detectives, list of 76
　Royal Commission into the Constitution, Administration and Working of the Criminal Investigation Branch of the Police Force of Queensland 136–8, 167
　strike 167
criminality, perceptions of 10, 78, 147–9, 169
　female criminality 103–7
　habitual criminals 32, 148–9, 157, 163, 165–6
criminals, identification of 144–5
Cummings, George 27
custodial sentencing 5
Cutbush, Mr 63–4, 66

Dalby
　district court 130
Daly, Constable 104
Darling Downs 13, 19
de Renzy, Sergeant William 38
deceased estates 39

destitution 32
detection of crime 7
detectives *see* Queensland Police Detective Office
deviancy, medicalisation of 10, 148, 165
Devine, Constable 109
di Beccaria, Cesare 147, 168
disorderly conduct 9, 10, 68, 91, 94–7, 109, 134, 153 *see also* riotous conduct
　female criminality 10, 102–3, 104, 107–8
distilleries, inspector of 38–9, 70
District Court Act (1858) 130
'donahs' 111
Donnelly, Constable Hugh 162
Douglas, Chief Inspector Alexander *138*
Drayton 40, 41
drunkenness 28, 31, 68, 91, 94–5, 112, 134, 153, 162, 164, 169
　assaults on police 97, 98
　police recruits 86–7
　women 107, 164
Dubbo 36
Dublin 14–15
　Metropolitan Police 15, 76, 86, 94
Duncan, William 46
Dunn, Tom 47
Durant, Charles 'Dubious' 2, 10–11, 143–7, 169
　alcohol 162–4
　Boggo Road Gaol 149, 157
　Gaol Entry Card *155*
　larceny 147, 153, 154, 162, 164
　mugshot *144*
　Nethercote, prosecution by 154, 156
　recidivist, as 153–7, 162–3, 165–6
　St Helena Island Penal Establishment 150, 153, 154, 157
　'Tool Stealer' 147, 163
Durant, Maria 162, 165
Durundur 31, 45

Eagle Farm 158
Earl Derby 120
economic downturn 125
economic hardship 95, 153, 169
　friendly societies 133–4
Edenglassie 1
education 11

Egan, John 22
electoral gerrymandering 139
Ellis, Jane 44–5
Ellis, Maria *see* Durant, Maria
embezzlement 123, 124, 134
Emu Plains 3
Enoggera 53, 100
equipment 88–9
escort duties 74
eugenics 148, 165
Exmouth 22
expert prosecution witness
   ex-convict as 20
   police officers 128, 156

female criminality *see* women
fingerprinting 144, 165, 170
Fisher, Mary 105, 107
Fitzgerald Inquiry 6
   recommendations 7
Fitzpatrick, Chief Constable William 5, 22, 28, 30, 38
forensics 11, 144, 170, 171
   classification of criminals 144–5
forgery 134
Fortitude Valley Gaol 103, 105, 158
   women's prison 158–60, *159*
fraud 70, 124
Freemasons 122
Fremantle Prison 149
Frogs Hollow (or Old Frog's Hollow) 62, 114–15, 116–7, 146
Fyfe, William 27–8, 32

Galbraith, Sub-Inspector 109
gaming 112
Gatton murder case 136, 137
Gayndah 38, 40
gendered justice 12, 102–11, 114, 157, 169
Geraghty, Sub-Inspector James *138*
Giles, Robert 22
Gipps, Governor Sir George 19
Glancy, Constable 104
Goulburn 35
Graham, John (Dublin watchman) 16
Gray, George 26
Great Dividing Range 19
Grimshaw, Detective 125

Guilford (7) 27
Gympie 74
Gympie Hotel (Brisbane) 110, *110*

habitual criminals *see* criminality
Hadlow 22
Hanley, Jack 47–8
hard labour 18, 21, 41, 97, 104, 109, 111, 147–50, 152, 156–7, 162
   women 104–5, 106, 162
Hayes, Ellen 117–18
Head, Detective Constable Thomas 156
Head, Sir Francis Bond 82
Hegarty, Susan *see* McGowan, Susan
Henders, Detective Sergeant John 76
Herbert, Colonial Secretary Robert 58–9
Higgins, Constable Martin 5, 22
Hill, Frederick John (Oxley Murders) 136
Holt, EB 123–4
Hore, Constable 31
horse stealing 74
Howard, John 147–8
humanism 10, 133, 142, 168
Hunter River 35
Hyland, Margaret *see* Sneyd, Margaret

imprisonment 92
incompetence, allegations of 72
indecency 27
indecent exposure 26, 27, 95
indictable offences 131
Indigenous peoples *see* Aboriginal Australians
and society 2, 11–12
Industrial and Reformatory School for Women and Girls 160
infanticide 131
Innes, William BM (alias Ennis) 71
Ipswich 32, 40, 41, 48, 96
   circuit court 130
   flooding 51
Ireland 8, 14–15
   civil unrest 14–15
   police force 14, 15, 55, 57, 59, 76, 80, 81

Jessop, Constable 104
Jimboomba 50

John Berry (1) 4
Johnson, Sergeant Adam 156
Jones, Councillor Richard 35
judiciary
  courts *see* courts
  professionalisation 133, 142, 170
  standardisation of 10
jury, trial by 131, 162
Justices Act 1886 120
Justices and the Magistracy Act (1886) 129–30
justices of the peace 129
  powers 129–30

Kable, Henry (First Chief Constable of the Sydney Police) 2
Kangaroo Point 13, 23, *25*, 26–7, 63
  Bluestone Rum Case 47–8
  Bowen Terrace *29*
  expansion of police force 30
Kilfedder, Constable Robert 71
Kilmainham Gaol (Dublin) 149
Klumpp, Fredrika 50
Klumpp, Gottlieb 50

labour unrest 125
Lake, Chief Commissioner 82
larceny 21, 125, 134, 147, 149–50, 153, 164–5
  clothes 15, 20, 26, 125
  food 125
  robbery, distinguished 147
  servant, by 68, 70
larrikinism 104, 111–12, 115
  assaults against women 108, 111
  definition 112
  women as 111
Lee, James 95
Leslie, Patrick 13, 18, 23
  Darling Downs expedition 13, 19
Lewis, Inspector 77, 84, 99
lifetime incarceration 148, 165–6
Lightfoot, Ellen 106–7
Lilley, Chief Justice Sir Charles 132
literacy rates 21
Little Wonders shop 63, 64
Lloyd, Eliza Ann (née South) 57, 79
Lloyd, First Class Inspector Samuel 2, 9, 79, 169, 171
  appointment 56–7, 61
  awards 58, 71–2, 74
  background 57
  Brisbane, return to 75
  death 79
  health 74
  Queensland Police Detective Office 61, 68–73, 75
  retirement 79
  Victoria Police 56, 57–8, 79
  Wide Bay District 73–5
Lloyd, Isabella 57
lock-up (city) 105–6
Logan 50
Logan, Captain Patrick 3, 4
loitering 91
London Metropolitan Police 36, 59, 77, 94
Lovett, James 88

McAdam, Sergeant William 38
McAlister, Constable 43
McArthur, Constable Thomas Archibald 87
McDonald, Flora 79
McEvoy, Isabella 44–5
Macfarlane, Magistrate 143
McGowan, Susan 2, 10, 102–3, 169
  assaults against 108–11, 116, 118
  assaults by 107
  disorderly conduct 107–8
  drunkenness 107
  female criminality, and 103–7
  'Nine Holes', in 118
  obscene language 107–8, 109
  prostitution 112–14
  theft 110
McGrath, Constable John 5, 22
McGuire, Constable James 31, 45–6
McIntosh, Chief Constable John 1, 4
Mackay 132
Mackenzie, Evan 26
McLatchey, Constable Thomas 156
McMaster, Alderman 117
Magdalene Asylums (Magdalene Homes or Laundries) 117
magistrates 6, 8–9, 40, 129
  corruption 33, 56, 59
  powers 129–30
  training 130

Mair, Lieutenant 64
Malone, Sub-Inspector Hugh *138*
manslaughter 131, 150
Maranoa 38, 40
Margaret 128 57
marry, permission to 82–3
Maryborough 40, 74
    circuit court 130
Mawditt, Charles Henry 120
Mawditt, Elizabeth Sarah Rose 120
Mawditt, Ellen Elizabeth 120
Mawditt, Ethel Ann 120
Mawditt, John William 120
Mawditt, Lilly Edith 120
Mayne, William (Inspector-General of the Sydney Police) 49
Mercer Tavern 47
Military Mounted Police 3, 35–6
military police 3, 34–5, 55
Miller, Lieutenant Henry 3
Mills, C Wright 2
Molloy, Eleanor 83
Molloy, Maria *see* Tyrrell, Maria
'molls', *see also* 'donahs' 111
Monks, Christopher 15–16, 17, 32
Moore, Sergeant 36
moralising 12, 148–9, 165, 169
morality policing 10, 91–2, 169
    female criminality 103–7, 118
Moreton Bay 1, 2, 20, 38, 46, 91, 157
    circuit assize court 131
    conditions 3–4
    establishment of penal settlement 3
    Female Factory (Queen Street) 157–8
    free settlement 5, 21–3, 33, 48
    penal settlement 129
    regulation of 4–5
Mount Victoria 36
Mounted Border Police 56
Mud Island 14
Mudgee 36
Mulcahy, Catherine *see* Sneyd, Catherine
murder 27–8, 50, 73, 78–9, 131
    Bluestone Rum Case 47–8
    Gatton case 136, 137
    Oxley case 136–7
Murphy, Catherine (née Thompson) 21
Murphy, Edward Joseph 21
Murphy, Elizabeth 21, 26

Murphy, John 21, 30
Murphy, Margaret 21, 26
Murphy, Peter 'Duff' 2, 5, 8, 169, 171
    arrival in Sydney 18
    background 14–16
    Brisbane, move to 22
    character 19, 21
    chief constable 21, 31
    children 21
    conditional pardon 23, *24*
    convictions 15
    Darling Downs expedition 13, 19
    death 32
    district constable 13, 20–1, 26, 39, 43
    Kangaroo Point 26–30
    marriage 21
    resignation 31
    ticket of leave 19–20, 23
    transportation 16–17
Murphy, Peter (son) 21, 30
Murray, William 26
Murrihy, Constable Daniel 154

National Penitentiary (Millbank Prison) 149
National Temperance League 91
Native Police 5, 6, 56, 92–3
Needham, Kate 109
neglect of duty, allegations of 72
Nelson 50–1
Nethercote, Inspector James 2, 10, 125, *138*, 140, *141*, 142, 169, 171
    awards 128, 140
    background 119–20
    Bradford Police 119, 120
    Brisbane Detective Office 123–4
    Charleville 138–40
    CIB 75, 120, 128–9, 134, 138, 142
    death 140
    Durant, prosecution of 154, 156
    expert witness 128
    marriage 120
    police constable 120–2
    private inquiry office 140
    prosecutor, as 128
    retirement 140
    service record *121*
Nethercote, James Philip Mawditt 120

New South Wales
 separation from 40–1, 55, 56
New South Wales Constitution Act (1855) 131
New York
 Board of Police Justices 94
Newcomen Bridge 16
Newgate Prison 15
Nine Holes 114, 115, 117, 118
Norfolk Island 3
 escaped convicts 46
Normanton 132
Northern Districts of New South Wales 5
Number One Fire Brigade 63, 64

oath 1, 60
obscene/offensive language 68, 95, 106, 112, 134, 153, 156, 164, 169
 women 10, 103, 106, 107–8, 109, 164
obstruction of police 98, 104, 111
obtaining money or goods under false pretences 112
O'Carroll, Inspector TF 116
O'Driscoll, Sub-Inspector 117
offences 134 *see also by name*
 statistics 135
One-mile Swamp 41
O'Sullivan, Sergeant Michael 167–8
Oxley 52
Oxley, John 3
Oxley murder case 136–7

Palmer, George Charles Frederick 73–4
panopticon architecture 11, 149, 166
 Boggo Road 149–50, 166
Parramatta 18
 Gaol 45
Parry-Okeden, Commissioner William 75, 77, 85, 135, 138, *138*, 168
pauperism 14, 32
penal reform 10, 147–8, 165, 169
 juvenile offenders 160–1
Pentonville Prison 149
perjury 132
petty theft 27, 95, 125
photography 144, 165, 171
phrenology 10, 145, 148, 165
pickpockets 95
Police Act of 1838 4–5, 92

Police Act of 1855 92
Police Depot (Petrie Terrace) 81, 83–7, 161
police–government relationship 7
police regulations 9, 87–8, 170
 age cut-off 81–2
 entry requirements 82
 marry, permission to 82–3
police pay *see* policing wages
policing *see also* Queensland Police Force
 cost of 35–6, 59
 deaths on duty 31, 45–6
 development of modern 7–8
 disqualifications 81
 duties 87–8
 Freemasons 122
 mistreatment of patrol constables 12
 neutrality and 122
 orthodox theoretical perspectives 7
 plain-clothes 75, 77
 police to population ratio 91
 professionalism 10
 public demand for free constables 22
 reforms 79
 resources, lack of 40, 73
 revisionist theoretical perspectives 7
 strict rules 72
 synthetic theoretical perspectives 7
 turnover rate 72
 wages 36, 48–9, 59, 83
political power abuse 12
 electoral gerrymandering 139
Port Macquarie 3, 20
possession 153, 154, 156
preserving the peace 87, 89
preventative policing 169
prisoner, rescuing or aiding rescue of 98, 104
prisons *see also by name*
 comptroller general 161
 female 157–61, *159*
 life inside 151–3
 mismanagement of 12
 neglected children 160
 populations 150, 152, 165
 rations 152, 160
 segregation of men and women 161, 170
Prisons Act of 1890 161

professional burnout 12
property
  sale of unclaimed 39
  seized from cancelled ticket-of-leave holders 39
prosecutions 134–5
  costs 132
  police as prosecutors 132–4
  private 132–4, 135
  prosecution societies 132–4
  public, shift towards 135, 142
  standardisation of 10
prostitution see also *Act for Prevention of Contagious Diseases* (1868) 112–14, 169
  medical examinations 113–14
Proudfoot, Henry 125
public works 11

Queensland
  population growth 134
Queensland Parliament 56, 59–60
Queensland Police Act (1863) 5, 6, 56, 58–60, 79, 81
Queensland Police Detective Office 79, 123–4
  establishment 61
  General Order 678 75, 77
  reorganisation 75, 135–6
Queensland Police Force 2, 122
  Brisbane *see* Brisbane Police Force
  formal organisation of 6–7
  numbers 90–1, 92–3
  promotion 123, 139, 142, 170
  reorganisation 57
Queensland Police Museum 78–9

railways 124
Ramsay, Constable James 5, 22
rape 131
rationalism 168
Rayner, Constable 136
recidivism 18–19, 32, 143, 144, 170
  Durant 153–7, 162–4, 165–6
  rates 165
recruitment 9, 38, 80–3
  statistics 86–7
Red Cliff Point 3
Register of Members of the Police Force, 1856–1917 72, 86

rehabilitation of criminals 19, 22, 32, 148, 169
Reid, Dr Thomas 17, 18
religion 11, 52–3
Rennie, William 68, 70
restorative justice 19, 22
Riley, Constable Richard 86
riotous conduct *see also* disorderly conduct
  women 103, 104, 105, 107
robbery 16, 17, 28–30
  larceny, distinguished 147
  mail 41
Roche, Jack 139–40
Rockhampton 71
  district court 130
Rocks, Constable Terence 50
Roles, Constable Henry 154
Roma
  circuit court 132
  district court 130
Ross, Sub-Inspector Henry *138*
'rowdies' 111
royal commission 77, 135–8, 142, 167
Royal Foresters 134
Rules for the General Government and Discipline of Members of the Police Force of Queensland (1869) 60, 171

Sacred Heart 91–2
St Helena Island Penal Establishment 109, 147, 149, 150–2, 154, 157
  life in 151–3
  tailoring workshop *151*
Savage, Sub-Inspector Charles *138*
Scanlon, Constable Jeremiah 5, 22
scientific developments 10–11
sentencing
  courts of petty sessions 129
servants, ill treatment of 43–5
Servants and Masters Acts 43
Seymour, Commissioner David Thompson 43, 60, 75, 78, 111–12, 161
  General Order 212 83
Shanahan, Sergeant Denis 136, 156
Sheridan, Richard 46
signalment
  anthropometrical 145

descriptive 145
  peculiar marks, by 145
Sketland, WH 22
Slater, George 68, 70
Slattery, Kate 160
Slattery, Sergeant Robert 160
slaughter houses, inspector of 39
Sloane, George 44
Sloane, Theresa 44
Small, Acting Sergeant 136
Sneyd, Catherine 'Kitty' (née Mulcahy) 35, 37, 45
  death 52–3
Sneyd, Chief Constable Samuel 2, 8–9, 30–1, 34, *37*, 169, 171
  appointment 36, 38–9
  Bluestone Rum Case 47–8
  death 54
  deployment to Australia 34–7
  duties 39–43, 50–3
  Ellis Case 43–4
  escaped convicts, capturing 46, 50–1
  Gaoler of Her Majesty's gaol 54, 158
  land, investment in 49–50, 53
  marriage 35, 53
  military service 34–6, 55
  popularity 53, 54–5
  resignation from police 54
Sneyd, Margaret (née Hyland) 53, 54, 158
Sneyd, Miriam (née Wakefield) 53
Sneyd, William Hartley 53
Social Darwinism 148, 165
social norms and behaviours, regulation of 7–8, 91–2, 95, 169
  female criminality 103–7, 118
  prostitution and medical examinations see also *Act for Prevention of Contagious Diseases* (1868) 113–14
sodomy 131
soliciting 112
solitary confinement 11, 148, 152
Sophia 22
sources 2, 11–12
South Brisbane ferry *34*
South, Eliza Ann *see* Lloyd, Eliza Ann
Southern, Thomas 41
Sparkes, Constable 31
special constables 96

Spring Gardens 14, 15
Stanley, Francis Drummond Greville (colonial architect) 132
Stenhouse, Edward 124–5
Stewart, Charles 98–9
Stewart and Hemmant's drapery store 64–5
strikes 125, 126, 164
  CIB 167
Sullivan, Constable 118
Supreme Court Constitution Amendment Act 130
swearing *see also* obscene/ offensive language 91
Swords, Stephen *see also* Bluestone Rum Case 47–8
Sydney police
  formation of 1–2

Talbot 58
Tamar 36
Therry, Justice 130, 131
Thompson, Catherine *see* Murphy, Catherine
Thompson, James 68
Thompson, WH *see* Sketland, WH
Thomson, Dr James Bruce 148, 157
Toongabbie 3
Toowoomba 96
  circuit court 130
Toowoomba Gaol 105, 106, 158, 160–1
Townsville 132
trade unions 8, 126
trading hours, enforcement of 92, 94
traffic control 100, 116
training 9, 38, 81, 170
  CIB 77–8
  Police Depot 81, 83–7
transportation 16–19, 169
  discontinuance, calls for 41
  impact of 8
  reconviction, rates of 18–19
Transportation Act for Removal to England Under Conditional Pardons of Colonial Offenders (1824) 19
treason 132
Tredennick, Constable James 31, 45–6, 50–1
Tyrell, Mary Anne 21

Tyrell, William 21
Tyrrell, Caroline Ellen 83
Tyrrell, Constable Thomas 2, 9, 81–2, 100–1, 169, 171
- awards 99–100
- background 80
- illness 100
- marriage 83
- police beat work 95, 98–9, 100
- retirement 100
- training 83, 86

Tyrrell, Fanny 83
Tyrrell, John Thomas 83
Tyrrell, Maria (née Molloy) 83
Tyrrell, Robert Alexander 83
Tyrrell, William 83

unemployment 95–6, 134, 153, 169
uniforms 88–9
- destruction of police 97–8, 104, 109
Urquhart, Inspector Frederick C 137–8, *138*, 139
utilitarianism 10, 133, 142, 168, 169

vagrancy 32, 94, 95, 125, 147, 156, 164
- women 103, 105, 106, 111, 117, 157, 164
Vagrancy Act 1824 (UK) 147
Vagrancy Act (1852) 112
Venilia 83
Victoria Army Barracks 83–5
Volunteer Fire Brigade 63, 64
Volunteer Force 56
volunteer paramilitary groups 5–6

Wade, William 110
Waintling, Henry 45
Wakefield, Miriam *see* Sneyd, Miriam

Warwick 40, 96
- district court 130
Water Police Force 5
weapons 88, 89
Western Monarch 119
white collar crime 124–8
White, Inspector John *138*
Whyte, Chief Constable William 4, 22
Wickham, Police Magistrate John Clements 21–2, 38, 49
- duties 39
Wide Bay 38, 73–5
Wilbred, Jane 44
William/Williams, Constable 27, 28
wireless communication 11
WM Sutton's Bush Commercial Hotel 27–8
women 169
- disorderly conduct 10, 102–3, 104, 107–8
- drunkenness 107, 164
- Female Factory (Queen Street) 157–8
- female prisons 157–61, *159*
- hard labour 104–5, 106, 162
- ideal woman 103, 118
- larrikins, as 111
- notoriety, power of 111
- obscene/offensive language 10, 103, 106, 107–8, 109, 164
- prostitution 112–14, 169
- riotous conduct 103, 104, 105, 107
- State Prison for Women 161, 162
- vagrancy 103, 105, 106, 111, 117, 157, 164
- violence against 108–11
Woolloongabba 41
Wyer, Detective 124

www.ingramcontent.com/pod-product-compliance
Ingram Content Group UK Ltd.
Pitfield, Milton Keynes, MK11 3LW, UK
UKHW021313180426
11947UKWH00015B/1210